To Meli
Best Wish

CRISS-CROSSING TO
FREEDOM

❋

The ups and downs of a life between the country and the town

FRAN ADAMS

Mereo Books

2nd Floor, 6-8 Dyer Street, Cirencester, Gloucestershire, GL7 2PF
An imprint of Memoirs Books. www.mereobooks.com
and www.memoirsbooks.co.uk

CRISS-CROSSING TO FREEDOM
ISBN: 978-1-86151-653-4

First published in Great Britain in 2022
by Mereo Books, an imprint of Memoirs Books.

Copyright ©2022

The address for Memoirs Books can be
found at www.mereobooks.com

Mereo Books Ltd. Reg. No. 12157152

Typeset in 12/19pt Plantin
by Wiltshire Associates.
Printed and bound in Great Britain

Remembering Lionel – a fighter to the end

Contents

—◆◆◆—

BOTTESFORDIAN

GRANTHAMIAN

CHELTONIAN I

MELTONIAN

CHELTONIAN II

STROUDIE

BOTTESFORDIAN

CHAPTER 1

Beanbelly

'Fraany Froo', aged 10 months

The Vale of Belvoir ('Beever') in Leicestershire is part of the vast floodplain of the River Trent in the East Midlands, and in this vale lies Bottesford, the village where I was born. Bottesford is in a northern tip of the county of Leicestershire, pinched between Nottinghamshire and Lincolnshire, and although the postal address is 'Bottesford Notts,' I am not defined as a Nottingham 'Bogger' nor a Lincolnshire 'Yellowbelly' but as a Leicestershire 'Beanbelly' and a Bottesfordian to boot.

I arrived at five minutes to 1 am on 12th September

1944. If it hadn't been for British Double Summer Time during the war, when clocks were put forward two hours instead of one, I would have been born at five minutes to midnight on the 11th, which was my mother's birthday. I was the third and youngest child born to Winifred and Reginald Carrington, a sister for Richard Lambley, who was four and a half, and for Helen Rosemary, aged seventeen months. My parents named me Frances Susan after my paternal grandparents, George Francis and Grace Susan, and because of my father's Huntingdonshire dialect I was always called 'Fraan', or even 'Fraany Froo'. I was a plump baby, with a fat round face, dimpled cheeks and a mop of black hair, not unlike Oliver Hardy (of Laurel and Hardy fame) I think, when I look at old photos.

My place of birth was 'The Laurels', Belvoir Avenue, the first house along a rough and rutted lane on the village outskirts, with about ten houses on our side. Opposite us lived old Mr and Mrs Parr, their spinster daughter Joan and later, their grandson Steven, whose mother had died. Their garden extended right up to Ducker's farm, where a wooden gate blocked off the top of our lane. (Since those days, this farm has been replaced by a large school, 'Priory Belvoir Academy' but as it is not accessed from the avenue that at least has not changed.) When we were old enough, Helen and I were often sent to Ducker's farm with a large jug, to fetch extra milk. Ann and Mary Ducker, both teenagers then, always invited us into their sparse kitchen for a chat.

The Laurels had once been a mill, but being double

gabled and pebble-dashed, it didn't resemble any mill that I knew. There were three bedrooms, and later a bathroom on the half-landing. Before this, we were bathed in a little tin bath in front of the fire.

According to my relatives, I spent hours in my pram, not being taken beyond the garden until I was 10 months old. This could be true, because we had a succession of relatives living with us, on and off, in those first few years. There was always someone to look after me if my mother needed to go out. She well remembered the first occasion she took me on the double-decker bus to Grantham. I screamed all the way and could not be pacified. Those big red double-decker buses were to play a major part in our early lives.

Our long garden was private, surrounded by high hedges of both laurel and privet, with a gas lamp standing outside the bottom corner. This was where Belvoir Avenue joined Belvoir Road, and Belvoir Road led to Belvoir Castle, the magical castle of our childhood, to which we always gravitated for bike rides and picnics. The castle stood proudly on a ridge overlooking the vale.

Our front door faced the lane, with a small wooden gate a few paces away, almost hidden by laurel bushes. Richard's bedroom was on this side, overlooking the Parrs' extensive vegetable garden and above it, a lot of sky. I remember Mum saying ominously, "Red sky in the morning, shepherd's warning," as we surveyed the vast expanse of red clouds from Richard's bedroom window one morning.

The bay-windowed front room was below this. We rarely

used it; it always felt so cold and never got the sun, or sometimes our relatives were lodged in there. But when I was three and all the relatives had moved on, I inadvertently locked myself in there. Mum had to fetch Mr Parr to rescue me. His large shape appeared at the window, topped with his battered trilby hat and he carried a long knife, which made me shiver. Fortunately, this was not to punish me but to open the window. He pushed the knife between the upper and lower window frames and wiggled it about until he'd forced the catch open. Then, raising the bottom window, he climbed in, grunting and puffing because of his age and portliness. I trembled as I watched him breaking in. It seemed possible to me that anyone could get into our house. Mum was so relieved when he let me out that I wasn't reprimanded at all.

The front room furniture was sparse – there was a utility-style settee and armchair, both covered in fake brown leather, with wide flat arms that sloped backwards. This made them perfect for sliding down, until I ripped one with my sandal buckle (so subsequent sliding had to be done furtively). There were two dining chairs, a large radiogram (which I don't remember ever being used) and a bookshelf in an alcove behind the armchair. From this shelf Helen and I sometimes sought out a medical book for mothers. The pictures in it fascinated us.

We shared the bedroom above the kitchen at the back. Until I was five, I slept on my father's old brown canvas camping bed from the forces. It had criss-cross folding wood and metal legs that stuck out at the top edges. It was so easy to bruise your knees if you knocked against them. From my bed I could see right into the branches of our neighbour's enormous tree and watch the antics of the birds, darting in and out, chirping and twittering or squawking and squabbling in the dark depths. A large hen-run surrounded this tree, and the constant 'cluck-clucking' from the hens below was like a soothing rhythm section to the bird song above.

The dining room faced southeast, with a bay window overlooking the garden. My father worked on this every time he came home, but that wasn't often. There was a herbaceous border under the window with a square lawn in front, screened from the remainder of the garden by trelliswork. This was covered with red and yellow roses, like little dog roses. A path behind the trelliswork led from another gate, crossed the garden and continued up past the kitchen door to the coal shed.

The rest of the garden was a long vegetable plot. As time went by, Dad did away with the vegetables, levelled out the ground and made a big lawn for us to play on, or to give himself less work to do, perhaps!

From an early age I helped Dad in the garden. He'd get me to remove the middle bud from the multi-flowered heads of his prize chrysanthemums (coloured dark red and bronze) that grew in front of the dining room window. He didn't get prizes but took great pride in them. Then at five, I was given a little plot of my own near the front door. Looking back, it wasn't much use to anyone else as the hedge shaded it, but I remember growing cornflowers and delphiniums there.

The path up the kitchen side was wide, bordered by a high brick wall. We had a rabbit hutch at the bottom end, and there was a pump outside the kitchen door. Where we adjoined our neighbours, several bricks had fallen from the top. By standing on these our short, bespectacled neighbour, Mrs Edwards, could chat to Mum over the gap. I often wondered if she'd dismantled the wall herself, for she detained Mum for an eternity, it seemed. The Edwards' red-bricked house had once been stables.

I was fond of the Edwards. From a young age, Helen and I would play with their great niece, Prudence Teagle, who had the fairest of long blonde hair, the palest of white skin and pale blue eyes. Prue was the pretty daughter of the Edwards's divorced niece, who spent her holidays here. We'd spend hours in their garden, making dens on the lawn with the wooden clotheshorse and blankets, or finding magical 'fairy-circles' of toadstools in the grass near the shed. On rainy days indoors, we made cardboard theatres and paper puppets, while 'Music While You Work' blared out on the valve radio and silverfish ran free in the back of the dark, damp crockery cupboard. Aunty and Uncle Edwards, as we called them, loved having Prue, whose father lived in South Africa.

My most vivid childhood memory is of when Richard came through the back door holding his wrist out in front of him with the bone sticking up. He'd fallen off his tricycle. I remember peeping over the kitchen table on tiptoes and seeing the stricken look on his face and the tears rolling down his cheeks. I vaguely remember Helen and me spending the night at the Carters' house up the lane, which must have been then. We'd climbed the dark stairs to bed by candlelight, with the flickering light casting frightful shadows on the wall.

Old Mr Carter kept a pig in a little brick pigsty. All their vegetable peelings were collected in a metal bucket in the kitchen, for pig-feed. Mr Carter was hard of hearing, always calling me 'Varnish' because he couldn't say 'Fraan'. Everyone talked loudly to him. We'd sit on the settee, watching him making a rag-rug. Using strips of material cut from his old shirts, he'd push them through some sacking material with a pointed piece of wood. His son-in-law Eric would sit opposite us, knitting – the only male I ever saw knitting, apart, that is, from my brother. (Mum taught the three of us to knit one cold night, huddled round the fire with our feet in the hearth. I was five then).

Mrs Carter, with her beaming round red face, would keep popping in from 'out the back' to repeat things loudly for her husband's benefit. She'd perhaps be lighting a fire under the boiler, to boil the sheets and towels. Margaret, their married daughter, was forever mothering us. She had no children of her own.

Before we were five, Mum took us for a walk every afternoon, always nicely dressed. On wet days she'd put leather spats over my leggings and shoes, buttoning them up the side with a special buttonhook. They'd been handed down from Richard, then Helen. Unless it was 'siling' with rain, we'd take our constitutional – up the Belvoir Road, past the house with the big tree in the back garden, past the Howitts' house with huge greenhouses behind, called the 'Vineries', and on past the Lees' big house where Richard's friends, John and Robert, lived. Beyond was the Winterbeck, a little stream running under the road. On the way back we'd pick 'keck' for our rabbit.

These daily walks were, I think, a throwback to Mum's former employment, for when she left school, she became a nursery nurse to Rosemary and Pam Turnor, the young daughters of Major and Lady Enid Turnor of Little Ponton Hall, not far from Old Somerby where she was born. It was something she'd done daily with these girls. They thought highly of Mum, and she of them; hence Helen's second name is Rosemary. She'd relate how she had to mince up raw liver each day for the girls to eat. It was good for their health. The thought of it made us two feel sick; it was like eating the food we gave to Binki, our cat.

There'd been occasions when Mum and these girls met the princesses Elizabeth and Margaret in St. James's Park in London, while out with their nanny. She even stayed at Glamis Castle in Scotland with the Turnors, going on grand picnics by horse and carriage. I'm sure this gave Mum aspirations to raise her own family above the humble levels of her beginnings. Indeed our family was already 'climbing,' with our father working his way up through the ranks of the RAF.

My mother was tall and good looking, taking pride in her appearance. Her auburn hair was curled upwards from the bottom, in a U-shaped roll, which she titivated with a fat knitting needle, standing on tiptoes on the hearth to see in the mirror. Most women wore a hat, which added to their smartness.

Mum told everyone what lovely girls we were and how well we got on. But we'd often fall out like animals, pulling hair and scratching faces, becoming quite vicious. Our punishment was a sharp slap on the backs of the legs. Then we'd have to play downstairs where Mum could keep an ear out for us from the kitchen. In spite of these episodes, Mum still extolled our virtues.

CHAPTER 2

Bottesford

Bottesford – Richard, Fran and Helen in the vegetable garden

Bottesford was quite large, even in those days, spanning both sides of the A52 Nottingham to Grantham road. The village church of St Mary the Virgin is the tallest in Leicestershire. Inside, there are many tombs belonging to the Manners family, the Earls of Rutland, who resided at Belvoir Castle. One tomb is famous for its inscription blaming the death of Henry and Francis Manners to witchcraft. They were the sons of Francis Manners, the 6th Earl.

Apparently, Joan Flowers from Bottesford and her two daughters were employed as extra staff when James I was to visit the Castle. Other members of staff disliked them, believing they had stolen certain items and committed other misdemeanours. As a result, they were dismissed, and they felt very bitter about it. When, later, the Earl's two young sons became ill and died, rumours were rife that the Flowers women were responsible. They were arrested, found guilty of witchcraft and sentenced to death. The mother died before she reached prison, but the daughters were hanged in Lincoln Jail.

In the village centre, the main A52 road coming from Grantham in the east bends sharp left into Market Street. On the right, just before this bend, stands the old Market Cross in the village square, and at the back of this square, which is actually a triangle, stood Taylor's, our butcher's shop. The carcasses were hung on big hooks from the ceiling, behind the great wooden cutting table. If Mum wanted some beef, the butcher would choose a suitable carcass, heave it off the hook and hoist it onto the table, where he'd proceed to hack and saw at the relevant area. Then, holding his long knife aloft, he'd sharpen the blade with an elaborate flourish, using an equally long sharpener, before cutting out a nice piece of beef for our Sunday dinner. Mum also bought 'lights' to cook for the cat; a sort of offal. We didn't have tinned cat food then.

Across from the bend, on the opposite side of Market Street, stands 'The Bull'. Stan Laurel and Oliver Hardy stayed there when appearing in pantomime in Nottingham. The landlady was Stan Laurel's sister, and Laurel and Hardy evenings are occasionally held there.

A hundred yards further along Market Street, the A52 turns sharp right, becoming High Street, while Belvoir Road carries straight on. There is a Bottesford by-pass now, so A52 traffic no longer has to negotiate those two sharp bends.

Monty's shop stood on the left of High Street, just past this corner. On Fridays, Mum would treat us to 2 ounces of liquorice comfits each, in little pointed paper bags. Picking out the same-coloured comfit to suck on, we'd try to make it last until we got home. Although Monty's sold all sorts, I only recall sweets and ice creams. They had a café on one side, facing a wide yard, with a row of small, brick terraced houses opposite. Our cleaning lady Ethel lived in one of these.

Then came Ottley's grocery shop. Groceries were rationed until well after the war. Only certain amounts of food could be bought with your allotted coupons, torn from a small Ration Book. Mr Ottley, a kindly man, always had time for a bit of chitchat. Once I fell over going to his shop. He sat me down next to the counter, and bathed the grit and grime from my knee, telling me how brave I was.

A short way down Belvoir Road on the left stood the Village Hall in a large, hedge-bound field. Fetes, football matches and other events took place here. Just before this entrance, a new house was built for Mum's hairdresser, Mrs Pacey. When I was four, she cut off my long ringlets and shaved my neck – which I hated. My hair was straight from then on, while Helen's dark brown hair always remained wavy.

Between this communal field and the cricket field which came next, there was a narrow lane leading to Dr Rankin's surgery. I recall screaming as the doctor pricked my arm, while Mum held me tightly. Perhaps it was my smallpox inoculation; very necessary in those days.

A line of old trees grew along the edge of the cricket field, and through the gaps we could see if cricket was being played. The gnarled tree roots clung to the side of a ditch, with a brook bubbling through, waving green weeds in its current. The wide grass verge beside this was a stopping-off place for itinerants.

Two colourful gypsy caravans camped here each summer. Their arrival was exciting but scary also, because any day soon, the gypsies would come a-knocking. "Cross my palm with silver," they'd say, or "Buy some pegs won't you," or "Have some heather to bring you luck, my darling." For more money you could have your fortune told.

Two women in colourful clothes would appear at our door. Their dark eyes flashed in their brown faces, which frightened us, as we peered cautiously round Mum's skirt. She'd buy their pegs, (made from split willow stems, each curved at the open end and held tightly at the top with a strip of tin). She hoped to keep on the right side of these gypsies; after all, we didn't want a gypsy's curse put on us. Within a week they were gone.

Occasionally a steamroller arrived, with a little hut-on-wheels. This really was exciting; the road was about to be tarmacked. Mum would keep us well back from the dangers as the steaming hot tar was poured onto the road like sticky black porridge. The smell was good for us, she said, so we'd keep taking deep breaths.

Following behind trundled the huge steamroller, puffing and rattling. As it progressed over the newly poured tar, with its enormously wide front wheel, it left a beautifully flat surface, steaming like a hundred kettles. Mum warned us not to tread on it or we'd be stuck there forever. The driver was hidden by steam and black smoke belching from the chimney. We were familiar with steam trains, but it seemed odd to see a steaming, smoking vehicle on the highway.

On past the cricket pitch were several red-bricked council houses and beyond them open farmland. Opposite, on our side of the road, was a large unfenced field of rough grass, with three ponds hidden in the undergrowth. Next came four brick houses with long front gardens, the end one being the Parrs', on the corner of Belvoir Avenue.

Continuing beyond our avenue, we'd come to the entrance to 'The Vineries'. In summertime, Mum often sent Helen and me to buy tomatoes straight from the vine. Entering those huge greenhouses was like stepping into an exotic foreign land. The smell was heavenly – like nothing else we knew.

In summer, Mum sometimes took us to Easthorpe to visit a friend, Mrs Rawlings (Auntie Rawlings). The footpath passed in front of the village hall, through a kissing gate and continued until it intercepted Easthorpe Road, at the other end. Auntie Rawlings' house was not far from here. Helen and I felt tempted to eat the gooseberries and blackcurrants growing in abundance in her garden, but we didn't want to make the grown-ups cross, so we'd only gobble a handful or two when we were absolutely certain they couldn't see us.

Opposite Auntie Rawling's house was an orchard, where a local lad, Neville Spick, kept two ponies. On one occasion, when we were about nine and eight, Helen and I were invited to ride them. All I ever wanted was a pony. I managed two circuits, avoiding the trees; but poor Helen was pushed off her pony's backside by a low bough. She landed in a pile of nettles. Next time round the pony jumped over her, as she couldn't get up. I dismounted out of sympathy. Then Neville rode round the field standing on his horse's back. We thought he ought to be in a circus, but then, if you had your own pony and practised and practised, you could probably do the same yourself.

CHAPTER 3

The Family

Some of the Lambley family. Left to right May, Beat, Laura,
Win and Kath, with Jim centre

My mother's family, the Lambleys, came from Old Somerby,
a village about three miles east of Grantham, up the steep
Somerby Hill on the A52, which passed the entrance to
Spittlegate Aerodrome. At the top, the ground levelled
out onto a vast plateau, part of which was the airfield. At
the far end of this was Somerby crossroads. Old Somerby
was straight on, while the A52 turns left, for Boston and
Skegness.

Minnie and Walter Lambley had nine children in their two-up, two-down semi-detached stone cottage, which had been in the Lambley family since being built in 1845. They were a God-fearing couple; Granddad never swore, while Grandma was only ever heard to call someone a 'little sod' or a 'brazen hussy'. If the children spoke at mealtimes, Granddad rapped them on the knuckles with his stick. Any who laughed also received a rap. The Lambleys were a well-respected family.

Granddad farmed two rented fields up towards the crossroads. On their living-room wall was a faded framed photograph showing Granddad winning a 'horse and plough' competition. They were so proud of that. In later working life, he was a 'lengths-man,' working for the council; looking after the road as far as the crossroads; cutting verges with his long scythe, layering hedges and filling in potholes.

Most of the time I knew him, he was retired. On Saturday afternoons, when we usually visited, he and Grandma would be sitting in their armchairs on either side of their newly installed, fawn-tiled fireplace, waiting for the football results on the radio, or perhaps picking a horse to win the next race. If a small grandchild was visiting, Granddad would sit him or her on his knee to sing his special songs; one about "All the little birdies going tweet, tweet, tweet" and another really funny one, "Susanna's a Funicle Man", with lots of snorts, raspberries and whistles, which had us in all stitches, especially when we tried to sing it ourselves.

At twenty-four, Granddad had been kicked on his shin by a horse, resulting in a big lump, where an ulcer later developed. This became more troublesome with age, and his grown daughters took turns to visit, cleaning, creaming and re-bandaging this smelly wound. Granddad didn't believe in doctors and never sought medical advice. Then, in old age when he became ill, a district nurse was summoned. She looked at his ulcer, and put on medicated powder instead of cream. It soon healed. All those years of suffering could have been avoided.

Grandma had been in service until she married Granddad. She worked really hard, rising early to tend the fire, which heated the oven and the large kettle of water. She'd bake pasties for the children's lunches, and carry hot water upstairs for them to wash, even when they were of working age. She'd then embark on all her housework: cooking pig's cheeks, making calf's-foot jelly, and all the cost-cutting tasks to keep those children fed and happy. After slogging all day, she'd make clothes on her Singer by the light of a paraffin lamp. (I'm honoured to own her old Singer machine now).

There were six girls and three boys. Then they adopted a baby boy and made it ten. They were a good-looking family. We've heard tales of the girls being pursued around the village square by admiring suitors, with Granddad hot on their trail. There were thirty-seven of us grandchildren.

Auntie Laura, the eldest, married Uncle Walter (Le-Hair), who'd been in the Army pay corps in India. They had one of each – Barry and Pam. Pam married a Scotsman, having eight bridesmaids (seven cousins) and a (cousin) pageboy in a kilt. We girls were paired in opposing colours, two in rose pink and pale blue, followed by two in pale blue and rose pink. Then a pair in primrose yellow and turquoise, followed by two in turquoise and primrose yellow – all with halos of little roses in all four colours. I remember the eight of us playing outside the reception hall, trying to do high kicks – like Can-Can girls – but the dress skirts weren't wide enough, so we fell over as a consequence.

Barry was an accomplished pianist, spoke many languages and travelled extensively. He made friends with a Dutch lady named Cora, who occasionally stayed with the family. Barry sometimes brought her round to our house. She was rather ugly, but we cousins found her quite amusing. In mid-conversation, her head would suddenly droop as she fell asleep and began snoring. We'd snigger on the settee, nudging each other. To us, she was Cora the Snora. Her story, however, was quite sad. During the German occupation, she and her sisters stole potato peelings from the enemies' dustbins at night, just to stay alive. Auntie Laura later gave refuge to a Hungarian boy during the 1950s uprising, probably out of the sympathy she still felt for Cora and her family.

Auntie May and Uncle Ted (Leeson) also had nine children, but unlike Grandma, they had six sons and three daughters – Paula, Peta and Penny. Most had lovely singing voices like their mother, and indeed their grandmother before her, who was often heard warbling above the congregation in Old Somerby church.

Uncle Ted fought through North Africa, Italy and Germany, and when Belsen was relieved, he was, reputedly, filmed by Richard Dimbleby for the BBC burying bodies with a bulldozer. We didn't know then what traumas they'd been through.

Three of their sons formed various music bands in their youth. One of them, Trevor, still tours venues around the Midlands. He was a bass player in the Merseybeats for a while.

Their lovable second son, Edward, whom we called Charlie, had Down's Syndrome. He loved conducting music. For his 50th birthday treat, the family arranged for the Salvation Army to play at his party. Charlie was in his element, conducting the whole band.

Mum and two of her sisters met their future husbands at dances held at RAF Spittlegate. Kath married a South African, Jacobus Gustav Strauss, who was then a Beaufighter pilot. Freda married Frank LeSueur from Jersey, who became a pilot instructor in Canada. His cousin, Bob LeSueur, is recognised in Jersey for his bravery in hiding Russian prisoners from the Germans during the occupation.

Aunty Kath lived at Grandma's during the war. She had three girls, Vivienne, Elaine and Johanna (six months younger than me). Sadly, Uncle Joe, by then a Mosquito pilot, was killed on 11th February 1945, three weeks before Johanna was born. We were closest of all to this family. I didn't need special friends at junior school because I had Johanna.

Auntie Beat, one of Mum's older sisters, and Uncle Roy (Matthews) lived at the end of a row of old brick cottages on the Grantham side of the A52 at Bottesford. A huge walnut tree grew outside their back door, with a hen-run in the orchard behind. Uncle Roy, who'd been a fitter in the RAF, and was in Malta during the siege, had a galvanised garage built on adjacent land, with two petrol pumps on the forecourt. Later, Auntie Beat sold snacks from a caravan: tea and coffee, fizzy drinks in large screw-corked bottles, wafer ice creams, biscuit packs and chocolate bars. But it was our cousins that we came to see – Dena, who was Richard's age, and the new baby, Melanie Jane, whom we were able to enjoy from babyhood. There were two older brothers, Jimmy and Tony, whom we rarely saw.

Mum would push us to Auntie Beat's in our old pram, facing each other with our feet in the 'well' (the base that lifts out). It was a lovely bouncy ride; quicker than us walking. Mum was a speedy walker, notorious for being late. Relatives tell of her running to catch the bus, with one of us under each arm.

Uncle Jim, the eldest son, and Auntie Nellie moved house a lot – constantly flitting between Grantham and Old Somerby, but keeping their garage business going on Bridge End Road in Grantham, also on the A52. I'm told they once lived with us at Bottesford, but I can't remember that.

There were five children. First was Diana, with long wavy red hair and full lips, looking like Diana Dors, I thought, when she grew up. Next came Cynthia and Janine, similar in ages to us two, then Robert and Howard. They all had fairish hair. Only Diana had red hair like Uncle Jim.

The relatives I do remember living with us were Auntie Freda, the youngest daughter, and Uncle Frank and their two boys, Frankie and John. John was a plump baby but Frankie was lean and mean. (Conversely, in his early teens, when he'd become muscular and charming, many of us girl cousins would willingly have married him!) He was three weeks older than me and we liked playing with the same toys – of which Frankie had many. While he played in his pedal car, I'd fetch something else from his RAF trunk and bring it outside to sit on. He'd immediately want that and would fight me, so I'd get off and climb into his car. Then he'd want that again. Once he scratched my face quite badly.

Uncle Frank's mother and sister from Jersey, Auntie Wally and Auntie Baba, came to stay briefly. They'd escaped from Jersey on almost the last evacuation boat. They soon found live-in jobs in a Grantham hotel.

The LeSueurs moved to Ruislip in Middlesex, where Uncle Frank worked at Northolt Airfield. There they had three more children, Paul, Zoë and Philip, before emigrating to Long Island, New York in 1957. Uncle Frank became 2nd Engineer at Idlewilde Airport – later to become Kennedy. Now the family could come to England every summer for free. We were fascinated by their newly acquired accents, and to learn that everything in the USA was faster, taller, deeper – ad infinitum!

Before they'd emigrated, Uncle Frank had always organised activities for us at Old Somerby, when they came to stay. We'd have competitions with the bows and arrows that we'd made, or play cricket in the 'Well' field at the back of Granddad's big back yard, which we considered as part of their garden. The village well stood by a footpath on the left of this field, which led from the 'bottom end' village with its post office and 'Fox and Hounds' pub, to the school and church at the 'top end,' half a mile away – the village being split in two. Cricket matches were played here in summer.

Best ever though, was when Uncle Frank's friend, Jackie Barratt, brought his accordion to entertain us. I can't recall how many cousins were squashed into that room but, with the table and chairs removed to the kitchen, we sat crossed-legged in diagonal rows. Jackie Barratt was trapped in the corner, his head almost touching the kitchen-door latch as the grandfather clock ticked solemnly nearby.

He played a German song, "Ich kann spiele", where we pretended to play many different instruments. With so much enthusiasm and close proximity, we hit each other with flailing hands and elbows. But it was all taken in good heart.

Uncle Frank's favourite was an Australian sheep-shearing song – "Clip go the shears boys, clip, clip, clip…" (Recently, while singing Sea Shanties in 'The White Star' in Liverpool, this song came up with words relating to the sea)!

When the LeSueurs came over in 1958, we had grown

too old for that sort of thing. We'd shut ourselves in Grandma's kitchen, leaving the grown-ups chatting in the living room. Here Frankie taught dirty ditties to us few select girl cousins, who were thirsty for knowledge.

Fair-haired Walter (Uncle Son) married Mabel, from Yorkshire. They lived around Harrogate. He was a tall, happy-go-lucky uncle – a little like Tommy Cooper in mannerisms, but slimmer and good-looking. At Grandma's he'd tell us silly jokes, play cards and sneak us a little glass of port at Christmastime, kept secretly in the back of the sideboard cupboard. They had three children, Harvey – a little younger than me, and twins, Alex and Elizabeth. I remember once, while Uncle Son was bringing a van full of cousins back to Grantham from Old Somerby, Harvey fell out of the back door on a bend. Luckily, he wasn't badly injured – just a bang on the head and a cut above his eyebrow. Auntie Mabel was furious. She was nursing the twins at Auntie Kath's house.

Auntie Mabel made gabardine mackintoshes, like our school ones, while Uncle Son had a succession of grocery and sweet shops. He always seemed cheerful, perhaps because of the lucky escape he'd had in the war, or maybe to conceal the sorrow and guilt he felt from his actions. He and his mate had hijacked a German ambulance to reach the beach at Dunkirk. Once aboard a boat, the soldiers either side of him were shot dead. One was the mate he'd just escaped with. The family thought they'd lost him, until he turned up at Old Somerby, with his tin hat and rifle in hand.

Uncle Tom, the youngest son, joined the navy during the war. He was tall, like Uncle Son, with dark hair parted down the middle, looking very handsome in his sailor's uniform. He and Aunty Viv had a daughter Judy (a little younger than me) and a son, Tony, both with fair hair and recognisably 'Lambley' faces. After the war, Uncle Tom played in the local cricket team in the Well Field.

Youngest of all was Uncle Ralph, the adopted one. Granddad's sister was in the process of adopting him when her two daughters caught an infectious disease, so Grandma took in Ralph for a while, but became so attached to him that she kept him. Uncle Ralph married Auntie Joyce, a local girl, and their son Colin is my youngest cousin. Ralph worked in Uncle Jim's garage, which later became an Esso garage, while Auntie Kath did the accounts.

The facts about my uncles' war experiences were taken from "Jimmy's War," by James G. Matthews, my cousin.

When I was nine, Uncle Tom drove Judy, Tony Johanna and me to Filey, for a week's holiday in Auntie Mabel's mother's many-roomed house. It was a long journey, crossing the River Humber over a long bridge. Every evening we played cards around the large kitchen table, drinking copious amounts of lemonade. You'd think we were on the 'pop', the way we laughed at everything. We loved emulating our cousins' Yorkshire accents – "Give-oop 'Arvé." "Wo'fah?" "Dorwn' knaw," was a conversation I relayed repeatedly. Judy woke me one night (we were sleeping end to end). "Fraan I've wet the bed". "Oh, so have I," I realised. "What shall we do?" "Let's just lie on it and see if it dries," was my solution. But I think we stopped drinking so much lemonade after that.

There were no donkeys on Filey beach, but amazingly they had ponies instead. All I'd ever wanted was a pony and now was the chance to ride one. The trouble was, it cost threepence a time. I could only afford three rides.

During that summer, competitions were taking place in several seaside towns. One day it was in Filey. The first 10 people to find 'The Picture Post Girl' and say, "Are you the Picture Post Girl?" would receive 10 shillings. We walked around the streets of Filey, hoping, although not expecting, to see this person. Then a car came by with her in the back. I chased after it, while the others wondered why I was bothering. But at the top of the hill, it pulled up outside public toilets. I arrived as the girl opened the door, and panted, "Are you the Picture Post Girl?" So I won a pristine 10-shilling note. The others were delighted. What a good time we'd have. But, after giving them threepence each and buying ice creams, I kept the rest for pony rides. That's where I learnt to trot on a pony.

★ ★ ★

My father was born in Eaton Socon in a terrace of cottages set back from the main A1 London to Edinburgh road. In his childhood the family moved to nearby St. Neots, in Huntingdonshire. There were five boys and one girl: Harold, Fred, Percy, Reg, Ted and Ena. Uncle Harold died in the First World War in August 1916, aged nineteen years. He is buried on the Somme in France. For years my brother, sister and I didn't know he'd existed. Nobody told us. Perhaps the family found it too painful to talk about him, so it became a habit never to mention him. He'd enlisted in the Huntingdon Cyclist Battalion, having been a cycle-builder and cyclist beforehand.

Our visits to the Carrington family were infrequent, as we didn't own a car. I remember Uncle Ted and Auntie Bessie's wedding when I was four, but don't remember much more than handing them a wooden spoon tied with a blue ribbon. Later, we visited Auntie Ena and Uncle Geoff in St. Neots, playing with our cousins Ian, Dinah and Trevor, in their back yard. I recall several rabbit hutches and motorbikes there – their family transport being a motorbike and sidecar. Then we were taken upstairs to see our Grandma Carrington. Dressed in black and crippled with arthritis, she remained in her rocking chair in front of the fire. There were no hugs or kisses; we just looked at her from the doorway, as the stranger she was. Very sad. That's the only memory I have of her. Granddad Carrington had already died.

Then cousin Joy married Roy. She was Uncle Percy's daughter. After the wedding, they went to southern India to become missionaries. After the reception we went to Uncle Percy and Auntie Elsie's house, at a place called Doddington, where we walked down a lane to see the old brick works at the back of their house.

On our return, Auntie Elsie was on her knees at the dining table, praying. Everything seemed so solemn until Uncle Geoff, with a twinkle in his eye, began playing jolly tunes on his mouth organ. That livened things up for us children. We felt much easier. Then Harold, Joy's brother, took us outside to blow on his trombone, but neither Helen nor I could get a peep out of it, however hard we blew. Harold played in a jazz band in Holland for years, until he and his Dutch wife moved to America. I haven't seen him since that day.

Uncle Ted, with black kinky hair like my Dad, was short of stature. His wife, Bessie, was taller, big-boned, with sparse fair hair. She'd been brought up in an orphanage and had a Cockney accent and a happy, get-on-with-life nature. She was lovely but called me 'Fraaan', 'Fraaany' or even 'Fraaany Froo' when I should have been way past that nickname. Uncle Ted owned a little black Ford car – very squat and box-like, the sort you might see in an old black and white movie. It didn't go much faster than a horse. They came to Bottesford in it, after their daughter Susan was born. It must have taken them hours. After that we looked forward to their yearly visits, to catch up on our cousin. They always brought a pork pie and sausages from 'butcher' relatives in St Neots. Susan was the only Carrington cousin we ever had chance to get close to.

My Uncle Fred and Auntie May lived in March in Cambridgeshire and had one son called Brian.

After being a butcher's delivery boy in his youth, my father was promoted to the rank of Squadron Leader in his 40s, having joined the RAF at 18 years of age. He was mentioned in dispatches in January 1941, but we haven't found out how he gained this merit – something to do with Dunkirk, we believe. He didn't fly planes but was a transport officer and was stationed at many places in the British Isles. Before the war he was posted to Iraq, Khartoum and Malta. We had a photo on the wall showing Dad and his friends diving into a pool in Malta. Their swimming trunks had been painted onto the photo, as apparently they were all 'starkers'. Helen and I had an occasional titter over this photo, thinking how naughty it was, swimming naked. After the war Dad was in Germany, requisitioning vehicles left behind at the end of the war. Then he was posted to India (at the time of partition) – I have his train ticket from Delhi to Bombay.

Dad retired at fifty, and prior to this was posted to Sutton Coldfield, enabling him to come home each weekend. We found it hard to get used to him being around so frequently. We'd eat our meals in the dining room instead of the kitchen, with the table laid properly, like in the officers' mess. Friday nights were tense. Soon after arrival, he and Mum would be rowing, but by Sunday everything was 'hunky dory.' We'd walk to the bus stop to sadly wave him goodbye. I think this pattern of behaviour is called 'storming and norming!'

We'd go to the annual RAF Sports Day in Sutton Coldfield, staying with Squadron Leader McGonnigal's family. 'Carri,' as Dad's mates called him, would always win the 100 yards sprint for the 40-pluses, while I, with my similarly short legs, would win the children's race. It was a doddle, because the youngest ones started at the front and had much less distance to run. The prizes were great, and the winner had first choice. First time I chose a doll's tea set and another year, it was the table skittles I proudly chose.

Several RAF families used to visit us. Aunty Mona and Uncle Dinty and their sons Dinty and Denis called by at Bottesford, on their way to or from Scotland, always bringing us a treat. Then Squadron Leader Griffin and family – Sidney and Anne (Enn) and their children, 'Enn' and Sidney, visited us after returning from a posting in

Africa, with tales of snakes, spiders, bedbugs and even a servant who'd tried to murder them, and with loads of black and white photos. They gave me a postcard I liked, showing African mothers washing their *kidogo totos* (toddlers) in a river.

Naturally, Dad was proud of his achievements, wishing to provide us with more than a village school education. So, we were sent to a private school for the first few years, which was Miss Tate's (formally 'Witham School') at Barrowby, a village six miles from Bottesford and two from Grantham. This meant travelling on the double-decker bus every day.

CHAPTER 4

Early Trauma

Miss Tate's pupils – Fran third from right

When I first started at Miss Tate's school, it was held in one room of the Old Rectory in Barrowby, there being only 15 pupils. The playground had once catered for coaches and horses, judging by the stable-like buildings to one side. On the opposite side was a wood, where we frequently went for nature walks.

Our bus stop was opposite Miss Tate's house. We'd play games around her hall carpet until she was ready to walk with us to school. We pupils sat at little pea-green tables in

U-shaped chairs, placed in a semi-circle facing her desk. First thing, she'd call the register and we'd answer "Yes Miss Tate," except for Susan Hudson, who was too shy to say it. We'd wait and wait, but she rarely responded. Poor Susan died from polio some years later, after swimming in the lake near her home at Woolsthorpe-by-Belvoir.

Some of the pupils stick in my memory – there was Anne Fillingham, with her hair parted in the middle and held back at the sides by big slides, just like Florence Nightingale, I thought. Her parents owned the George Hotel in Grantham High Street, where Auntie Wally and Aunty Baba had found work and accommodation during the war. Once we were invited to Anne's birthday party, which was the biggest we'd ever been to; it was held in the ballroom with waiter service. It was the same room in which Helen and husband Carl held their wedding reception, years later.

We were friends with Elizabeth Catlin, a pretty girl with short dark hair, whose family held the secret recipe for 'Grantham Gingerbread' and whose oldie-world shop and café was further down the High Street.

A Nicholas Parsons, who lived on the other side of Barrowby Hill, may have been related to *the* Nicholas Parsons, who was born in Castlegate, Grantham. *His* father had allegedly delivered Margaret Roberts (Thatcher). Each day we walked through the woods, to see Nicholas safely across the main road. That's probably why we had so many walks in the woods.

Two lovely sisters, Caroline and Susan Ryan, lived in a large house in Barrowby. Their mother was French. Also from the village came Graham Spriggs, cheeky-faced and always wearing his cap askew. He reminded me of Uncle Ralph, who reminded me of Norman Wisdom!

Two brothers, Anthony and Christopher Clarke, came from Belton on the other side of Grantham, a village 'tied' to nearby Belton House. Fair-haired Anthony had a gentle nature but dark-haired Christopher was to be avoided, always doing something sly and nasty to me when nobody was looking – like 'Chinese burns' on my arm. He even put red ants on me as I sunbathed on the lawn one day. Rowena Thompson, the rector's daughter, also came from Belton.

Three days a week, school finished at midday; on the other two, we finished at 2.30pm, having to wait for the next bus. Barely two weeks from starting school, I got fed-up, waiting to be taken to the bus stop. Miss Tate was busy with Helen. So when I noticed a box of fat wax crayons next to a faded old desk in an alcove, I decided to make it look pretty. I randomly and densely scrawled over the whole desktop in lovely rainbow hues. Then it was time to catch the bus.

The following morning after register, Miss Tate asked who had crayoned over the desk. Nobody spoke. My face was bright red; my head thumping. Yesterday, I'd innocently improved the faded desk-lid; now this! When nobody owned up at the second time of asking, Miss Tate used her next tactic, asking each pupil individually if they were responsible. She knew who was to blame but went all round the class first, letting me suffer. Of course, I owned up when my turn came, but it was an awful experience for a little girl, not long having left her mother's apron strings.

After my first year at the Rectory, the school moved to Miss Tate's own house, in the middle of the village. She lived with her sister, another Miss Tate, who was secretary at the Girls' High School in Grantham.

Our schoolroom now was bigger and brighter, and in the large garden, we each had a little plot to tend. I loved gardening, except when Christopher Clarke was around. He'd often catch me alone out there.

One term a missionary came to talk to us about Chile. She showed us on a map where it was, on the other side of the world; telling us about the people who lived there. When Dad bought us a globe soon after, I was fascinated to see all the different countries in the world and spent hours drawing maps.

Miss Tate was an artist and there was much emphasis on drawing and painting. We used good quality paper. I still have two of my pictures; one of a tiger in a forest, camouflaged by his stripes and another of washing on the line, where the woman of the house looks like Anne Fillingham. I must have impressed Miss Tate, for I received a prize for drawing when I left. It was a book of butterflies.

★ ★ ★

I was almost eight when I joined Helen at St. Wulfram's Church of England School in Grantham – commonly known as the National School for Girls. We were sent to school in Grantham because my father planned to move there when he retired, a few years hence. It was now an eight-mile journey on the bus. For a couple of years, Dena came with us from Bottesford, while attending Kesteven and Grantham Girls' School. She taught us popular songs, like Max Bygrave's 'Gilly gilly ossenpfeffer katzenellenbogen by the sea.' Passengers must have been fed-up with our repeated renditions.

Helen and I alighted at St Peters Hill in the middle of town, which was on the busy A1 Great North Road – prior to the bypass. Isaac Newton's statue stands nearby, rising majestically above the flower gardens and low hedges that surround it. In days of yore, he'd been a pupil at Edward VI (the) Grammar School, or the 'King's School' as it is generally known. Standing behind his statue is the Guildhall, an impressive brick building with a clock on top.

Crossing these gardens, we'd walk northwards down Castlegate to our school. It was next to the magnificent St. Wulfram's Church with its slender spire – the third tallest church in England, mainly because of its very tall tower. On the far side were the original buildings of the King's School, where Isaac Newton had been educated. Our playground wall, on the near side, bordered the graveyard, which was lined with tall lime trees that dropped sticky sap onto our playground in summer.

At school now I was called Fransiss, and Helen was 'Ellun. From then, I adapted to being two sorts of persons, wanting to be accepted by both sides. I'd talk 'Grantham' to the majority, and Queen's English where appropriate. The local accent gradually predominated but I could rise to the occasion when necessary. Helen retained her nice accent.

During my first term at St. Wulfram's, when I was adjusting to being amongst so many pupils, I was moved up to the next class. I was ahead of my year, having had the privilege of Miss Tate's teaching. So just before Christmas, I was thrust into a new class of 47 children. Perhaps I was educationally ahead but emotionally, I was in pieces. I absolutely dreaded filing into the school hall for morning prayers. I'd always been shy, but now I felt so embarrassed and guilty for being in the wrong class that I couldn't cope at all. If I was on the end of a row, either next to the class above or next to the class I'd just left, I'd turn beacon red, my face and hands breaking into a boiling sweat. This transferred to my hymn book, making the paper transparent and sticking the pages together. I didn't dare look up, but the more I kept my head down, the more the drops dripped off my nose. From then on, this blushing became a continuous scourge, which undermined my confidence and affected much of my life.

Before I moved on to secondary school, there was an extra dilemma. At our respective schools, Johanna and I both took the Eleven Plus exam for the first time when I was ten and Johanna only nine. She passed. So she was going to the High School at that young age while I had to repeat my year in the top class, where the girls I'd left behind now joined me.

Johanna had learnt to ride a two-wheeler bike before me and to swim before I could. Now she'd be leaving me behind. However, once I'd learnt to swim, aged seven, I couldn't get enough of it. In summertime, I was allowed to go with her to the outdoor pool in Dysart Park, off Bridge End Road, catching a bus home about 7pm. That enthusiasm paid off. In my final year I, and three other girls, represented St Wulfram's in the County swimming sports, winning the free-style relay.

I passed the Eleven Plus the following year, but dreaded the humiliation of being in a class below Johanna. I was beside myself with secret anxieties. But just a week before the beginning of term, I jumped off the side of the high slide in Dysart Park – for a lark – slipping on the sloping side as I took off and crashing to the ground. Nothing was broken, but my wrist was badly sprained. So I began the new school with my arm in a sling, which gave me something else to think about, I believe.

CHAPTER 5

Through Miss Selby Days

Performing Brownies – Fran third from left, back row
(courtesy of Bottesford Community Heritage Project)

I was four when Helen and I began dancing lessons at Miss Selby's, who was a peripatetic teacher. The Grantham venues changed from time to time. For a while the classes were held in the ballroom of the Guildhall on St. Peter's Hill, but I mostly remember the Westgate Hall, which was behind the Saturday market stalls in the middle of Westgate – a fairly narrow street, running parallel to the High Street, with a square at either end. The inside always seemed dusty, but there were chairs down one side where the mums sat and chatted while watching their offspring.

The younger ones went first, so in the beginning, we'd be up very early on Saturdays to catch the Grantham bus. I recall one particular morning when Mum was desperately trying to dry our vests on the fireguard, in front of the electric fire. Our tortoiseshell cat was fascinated to see the dangling vest ribbons swinging in the heat. She began playing with them. Next thing, smoke was rising. The ribbons had caught fire. Mum, hearing our cries, was in the room like a shot; just in time to save the vests. But the ribbons were shrivelled up. It was a close shave.

Aunty Kath's girls also went to Miss Selby's. Vivienne was a graceful dancer, staying on until she was a tall fourteen-year-old. But neither Elaine and Johanna, nor Helen, remained there for so long.

The first exercise was to walk round the room in a line, making a series of arm movements, progressing from the count of two up to the count of six; each time adding a graceful movement with the arms. Miss Johnson accompanied us on piano. She'd later become our piano teacher. Then came skipping – complicated skipping. We became very adept. After that it was dancing; folk dances from different countries, adapted by Miss Selby's choreography. I loved a Russian folk dance, where we made big sweeping movements with a scarf, leaning over from right to left, while doing a slow polka. Once, there was the

Scottish sword dance where I, now fourteen, was out in front of the class. I wasn't at all shy when I could show off.

We'd practise a group dance, then it was time for ballroom dancing. One of each pair would take the male part, usually the more able of the two.

At the end of term we held a dancing display. Mum stayed up most of the previous night, making us each a new dress for these occasions. One term we did a group dance as waterfalls, having long silver strips hanging from the entire length of each arm. By 1958, we were learning to Rock n Roll to 'The Yellow Rose of Texas.' Of course, when I left, I could waltz, quickstep, tango, samba, rumba and cha cha cha – and all this as the male partner! What a waste.

It became a wonderful habit that Auntie Kath and the girls would bus back with us on Saturday afternoons, staying until Sunday teatime. This practice seemed to last for years but couldn't have been as frequent as I thought; perhaps just during the summer months.

Those weekends were fabulous. Johanna and I would skip off to play in the row of trees along the ditch, beside the cricket pitch. We re-invented Enid Blyton stories about Noddy and Big Ears, or Mr Pink-Whistle, which entailed jumping across the stream. We never fell in but once, when, while trying to catch a frog in my hands, I dropped my prize book of butterflies into the water. Thereafter, the pages were stuck together.

After Sunday lunch, Dad marched us up the Belvoir Road for a walk along the Grantham canal, which still looked navigable. He didn't really march us but was enthusiastically 'stepping out.' We always walked westwards from the bridge. On the eastern side was a hill from where, so we were told, Oliver Cromwell's men fired canon balls at Belvoir Castle. That was an earlier castle – there have been about three altogether!

Arriving home feeling tired there was time for a light tea before the Strauss's had to rush for their bus to Grantham. Dad left later for Sutton Coldfield.

Every spring, we bussed to Stathern Woods beyond Belvoir, to pick bluebells. Carrying our bundles carefully home on the bus, we'd place them in buckets of water all around the kitchen, where they stayed until they died; like harvesting without a cause.

From about the age of six, we'd cycle to see Belvoir Castle, although the nearer we got, the more hidden it became. In those days there were vast slopes of unfenced, mowed grassland surrounding the Belvoir estate, and plenty of ice cream vans. People arrived by car, bike or bus, to picnic and admire the view. It felt like a holiday destination. Huge trees grew on either side of the road along the edge. We loved swinging on the low boughs, and sometimes spotted a red squirrel above us, or hares in the fields that sloped down to the vale.

Often we cycled with Dena, and Pat and Elizabeth Goodwin, friends from the village. Pat was Dena's age and Elizabeth nearer to ours. We'd choose various detours on our return, perhaps going through the villages of

Redmile and Plungar to see the little 'nodding donkeys' extracting oil from the ground. These were on the flat of the vale. Occasionally we'd venture into the hilly areas, like Woolsthorpe-by-Belvoir and Knipton Lake. But our return was always a downhill swoop – over the hump of the canal bridge, down to the Winterbeck and along the final flat half-mile to home. I can't remember any punctures.

One Sunday in the depths of winter, ten of us took a trek in the snow. Wearing our wellies, we wandered towards Easthorpe across snowy fields, somehow ending up at the canal, which was frozen underneath the snow. The older girls tested the ice before we tentatively stepped aboard, our ears alert for creaks and cracks. Becoming more confident, we progressed without mishap, eventually arriving in high spirits at our canal bridge on Belvoir Road. We carefully climbed the bank and marched home downhill in single file. In front was Dena, the eldest, followed in order of age by Vivienne, Pat, Elaine, Helen, Cynthia, Elizabeth, me, Johanna and lastly Janine, the youngest. We crunched our way home, enthusiastically shouting a ditty we all knew well, which speeded our return: "I left my knickers in Wyndham Park, I went to fetch them in the dark; I left, I left, I left right left; I left my knickers in Wyndham Park, I went to fetch them in the dark; I left…"

Wyndham Park is in Grantham, not far from the King's School.

Then one grey, misty Sunday afternoon, after attending Sunday school in the village school, one of us suggested going for a walk. We were Dena, Pat, Elizabeth, Helen and myself. The Strauss girls didn't come to Bottesford so often in winter. We wouldn't normally go walking on a misty winter's afternoon like that, but when you're in a group, you go with the flow.

We set off northwards, over the bridge by the ford near the church, then walked across the wet and misty meadow behind it. Crossing the railway line, we continued in the direction of Normanton: across fields, over gates and through gaps in hedges, not following any path but just heading for the hill ahead of us. When we reached the top, the light was fading fast. How had we got there? Which direction had we come from? We couldn't remember. Then, luckily, Helen could just make out the church spire, in the misty gloom below. She told us emphatically that we must head towards it. The spire had saved the day.

But it wasn't at all straightforward. If we climbed a gate at one end of a field, we couldn't find any gaps at the bottom end. We stumbled in the gloom, looking for escape holes, getting scratched and mudded in the process, and really quite worried. But as a group we remained resolute. None of us was crying.

Eventually, and in pitch darkness, we arrived back in the centre of Bottesford where we split up. Dena set off up the Grantham Road, while Pat and Elizabeth went in the opposite direction along High Street. We carried straight on down Belvoir Road, anticipating the warm welcome we'd get when we arrived home, like Prodigal Sons.

But not so! Dad had already left for Sutton Coldfield. Mum was furious. We were cold, tired and hungry and would have loved a hot cup of cocoa and a hug. Instead, we had to set about scraping all the mud off our brown Clarke's lace-up shoes, over layers of newspaper laid on the floor, before washing, drying and polishing them. Mum seemed more concerned about our nice leather shoes than about us. We'd never ever felt so unloved. Then we were sent to bed. The mud on our coats would have to dry before we could brush that off. It was not a situation we ever risked repeating.

Because we didn't attend the village school, Helen and I weren't integrated with local children. The boys from the council houses threw stones at us as we walked home from the bus. If we were lucky, we could run past their houses and dash into Belvoir Avenue before they spotted us. But eventually they lost interest, or ran out of stones. However, a gang of boys once jeered at us over our garden gate, as we played with our cousins. I grabbed a stick, and chased them to the bottom of the avenue, waving it furiously. What cowards they were. I was only seven.

When I was eight, Helen and I began piano lessons with Mr Carter, who lived opposite Bottesford railway station, near Auntie Beat's. What a drama queen I became! If anyone came into the dining room or spoke while I was practising, I'd huff and tut and exclaim, "Now I'll have to start ALL over again." As a result, my beginnings were often played beautifully, but I never mastered the ends very well.

When Helen and I joined the Brownies, we at last got to

know some local girls, although we never became friends with them, except Elizabeth, whom we knew already. I'm sure the object of Brownies is to make us better citizens but, apart from chanting various vows, it seemed to be about earning badges by learning certain skills. To have a row of badges sewn down your sleeve was merit indeed. We soon gained our first badge, for darning socks. We could do that already. Because the sessions were lively, I didn't have much time to think about blushing.

At Christmastime the guides, brownies, cubs and scouts put on a concert. I remember us Brownies standing on the village hall stage, identical in our papier maché deer heads, complete with red noses and antlers, singing (of course) 'Rudolf the Red Nosed Reindeer.' Then, when I was eight, I was chosen for the *leading role* in a play, as Milly Molly Mandy. Helen played my mother. At one point Helen and I found ourselves repeating the previous line, but a little prompt from behind the curtain set us on course, and we didn't do a bad job. But I haven't a clue what the play was about.

In midsummer 1953, the village celebrated the Queen's Coronation with a carnival-like procession, which culminated at the village hall field. We Brownies were dressed as Elizabethans on the trailer of a lorry. I was a 'Beefeater,' in knickerbockers and leggings; bright red-faced and sweaty, with all the spectators gawping. We'd watched the Coronation beforehand, on a tiny television-in-a-box-with-doors-on, in a lady's bungalow near Auntie Beat's house, where we'd sat close together, to watch this black and white spectacle.

From around 1948, Auntie Kath and the girls spent their Christmases with us. One Christmas Eve Santa arrived rather early, so Johanna and I quickly feigned sleep. Santa looked suspiciously like our Uncle Tom in stature, but in spite of my suspicions, I firmly and stubbornly believed in Father Christmas until I was ten. On that occasion I stayed up until midnight, wrapping presents to myself, so that I'd have something to open in the morning. I was quite faint by the time I went to bed. Mum and Auntie Kath were still out in the kitchen making jam and lemon curd tarts.

We always looked forward to the arrival of brown-paper-wrapped parcels from St Neots, tied copiously with string and with red sealing wax sealing all the knots.

Apart from each having a pillowcase of presents at the bottom of our beds, there were extra ones on the Christmas tree. We had to sing a song or recite a poem before we could have these. And all must be completed before the Queens speech at 3pm, to which everyone listened intently, while the lighted candles glowed on the Christmas tree – a great fire risk; but that's what we did then.

CHAPTER 6

Skegness

Fran riding proudly through Skegness, 1956

'Skegness Is So Bracing' – that's what the posters said on the colourful hoardings in railway stations. They showed a jolly, fat fisherman prancing across a vast beach, with the sea in the distance. Indeed it *was* very bracing, there *were* miles of sand and indeed the sea w*as* in the distance. Skegness, in Lincolnshire, is on the long, exposed part of the east coast, north of the Wash, on the edge of the grey and uninviting-looking North Sea. But I loved it. It was the only bit of coastline I knew, and I spent my childhood summer holidays there.

Mum's connections with Skegness began before she married, for she became chief cashier when Marks and Spencer's first opened. She was presumably working there when she married Dad, who was then serving in Bagdad. Richard was born in Skegness; then they moved to Ardrossen in Scotland.

In Skegness, Mum had made friends with Ethel Johnson, from Derby Avenue off Drummond Road, south of the town. Later, Ethel and her husband offered Mum the use of their house for two weeks each year, so we'd move in – always at the end of August into September. Auntie Kath and the girls came, and often a few extras as well. These were wonderfully carefree holidays.

At first, Johanna and I received 7d each a day from Dad. The others got more, according to their age. From a shop in Drummond Road, we'd both buy a giant black and white striped cushion-shaped mint-rock humbug for 6d, leaving a penny for next day. Every morning we'd have a good gnaw and suck on it.

Those late summer fortnights always seemed so sunny – often with a heat wave. Our parents would settle in the soft, warm sand at the top of the beach, while we'd run back and forth to the sea. When the tide was right out, we'd be almost out of sight from them, crossing two dry riverbeds to reach the sea. Now 'dry riverbeds' is a misnomer; these were very muddy. We'd struggle, often up to our thighs, to get across.

But that was all we knew. However, the incoming tide could sneak in behind, cutting us off. We always got back in good time, except for one occasion. Luckily Dad was with us; that's probably why we'd lingered too long in the sea. He urged us to swim across these two ever-widening rivers before it was too late. Very scary! I don't think Dad realised how quickly the rivers rose and I'm sure he was proud of us. We were much more vigilant after that.

After a swim, we were often caught in a sandstorm. The wind roared across the beach, picking up sand and grit and hurling it at our wet legs. It was so painful, but we took it stoically, knowing that our towels and a picnic were waiting for us up at the top.

Derby Avenue petered out into a sandy track leading to the beach. From here we couldn't even see Skegness pier. We were as near to Gibraltar Point as Skeggy – there was just miles of flat beach.

The older we got, the more we went into Skeggy. The boating lake was our main attraction, costing 6d to hire a rowing boat (3d each). We could spend a whole morning or all afternoon, going up and down the lake, landing on the islands and pretending to be the Famous Five, and becoming expert rowers in the process.

We discovered how to catch crabs, with a shrimp tied to the end of a piece of string. We'd search the edge of the beach for an old tin can and share the cost of a bag of shrimps. Then, dangling the string into the boating lake, we'd soon have a crab clinging to the end. Before long, the tin would be full of crabs, all trying to get out, so we'd tip them back in and start again.

'Skeggy's iconic clock tower stood in the middle of the main parade near the seafront and further up the parade was the swimming pool. Rather than swimming there, Johanna and I sometimes entered the 'Bathing Beauty' contest. In our stretchy little 'fit all' 'cossies, we paraded round the perimeter, past all the seated onlookers surrounding the pool. Although we never won, I heard someone say, "Oh she's got a nice smile".

Beyond here was the Embassy, where we'd all partake in Old Time Dancing on a Friday night. Walking there in the dark, with the evening air chilling our legs, we'd admire the recently switched-on illuminations. Once we saw a gang of Teddy Boys in Edwardian-style long-coated jackets and 'drain-pipe' trousers. With black bootlace ties and bright pink, orange or lime green luminous socks showing above their thick crepe-soled 'Beetle Creepers' they couldn't be ignored. Their greased hair was combed into a fold at the back, known as a DA ('duck's arse'). How nasty they looked, carrying motorbike chains and knuckle-dusters. We were told to ignore them, but were fascinated.

We knew all the 'Old-Time' dances: Dashing White Sergeants, Gay Gordons, Military Two Step – the lot. We'd even help the 'oldies' out. Afterwards, still hot from dancing, we'd amble home in a daze, to fall into bed tired and contented.

Through an old friend of Mum's, we made acquaintance

with someone who ran a holiday home for deprived Nottingham children. She invited us to a talent contest at the Embassy; not really a contest but a chance for these children to go on stage. One little girl recited a poem which ended: "and that cheeky little sausage followed me," making us all laugh. Then Elaine went up to sing 'The Cradle Song.' She sang it beautifully, bringing tears to my eyes. I felt so proud to be her cousin.

Johanna and I found many amusements. The smart Wrates photographers were everywhere, dressed in striped blazers and straw boaters. They'd snap the holidaymakers as they promenaded around town, then hand them a ticket. The next day, these photos could be purchased at the pier office, if desired. We'd spend hours cavorting in front of these photographers, performing all activities imaginable. Once we tied our legs together, like in a three-legged race, having to stop short before we collided with the photographer. We collected countless tickets, then queued up the next day to see the first photo, which we'd reject. Returning to the end of the queue, we'd wait with our next ticket, thinking how cheeky we were. Such a laugh!

Butlins Amusement Park was further up the promenade, north of the Embassy. Most rides cost 6d. I found the Big Wheel quite frightening the first time, but the Big Dipper was the ultimate of scariness for me. I only ever went on that once.

Mum told me about the man who'd jumped over the rifle-range counter to chase her out of the amusement park, after she'd made a derogatory remark implying that it was impossible to win. That incident had frightened her. When I had a go and missed all the targets, the lady took the gun off me and said, "Yer've got the wrong eye shut, dook."

Johanna and I went twice to Seal Island, one of the large sandbanks in the Wash, about seven miles from Skeggy. It was amazing, seeing so many seals loafing on the sandbank, or popping up around the boat; some were sweet white babies. On our second trip, the wind blew up, making the sea choppy. So, sitting sideways on wooden seating around the perimeter, we clung on, being rocked and swayed, shaken and sprayed; wishing we'd brought a mackintosh. One lady kept muttering, "Win oy git 'ome, um gunna tek a coupla' aspirins an' git te bed".

In January 1953, I saw the Daily Express on the table at Bottesford and was aghast. There were photos of fields of caravans submerged in seawater near Skegness. In fact, the devastating storm had affected the east coast from Scotland to Kent, and also Holland in an equally terrible way.

Absolutely traumatised, I began having nightmares every night, but not about being engulfed in water. My nightmares were about a Dutch lady in a large bonnet, standing by the window, staring at me. I knew she was Dutch because her bonnet was like the one in our encyclopaedia. Why Dutch? Was it because the Lincolnshire fens area is called Little Holland? Mum left a night-light burning every night for ages. Eventually I got over it.

The following September, things had changed. Great

sand dunes had been constructed along the top of the beach, planted with coarse grass that cut your legs if you brushed against the blades. But our holidays continued as normal and we got used to the dunes.

When we returned home, Binki had died in the care of our cleaning lady. She'd been poisoned after falling into a vat of creosote. I was devastated.

The last holiday was just before my 12th birthday. I'd been odd jobbing, to earn enough money to go riding every other day at Skegness riding school. I took a stout pair of corduroy trousers to wear. On alternate days I trekked to the other side of Skeggy, sweltering in my warm trousers; too hot to run but trying to hurry. The older staff remembered my Mum riding there, which perhaps gave me a few perks. I was taught how to groom my horse before putting on the bridle and saddle, and tricks to tighten the girth around the pony's stomach. Then I was shown how to mount properly and hold the reins. We were off. My lifetime's dream was beginning.

Sedately, we paraded up Lumley Road towards the Clock Tower. I felt so proud. Past the clock, we carried straight on to reach the beach and began to trot. When we cantered, I was taught to sit low in the saddle. Then soon we were galloping towards Gibraltar Point on firm sand. The ultimate! I was keeping up. I was almost in heaven.

I'd walk back in a dream – a sweaty one, for the weather was hot. I wondered if Johanna would be around. I'd abandoned her in preference to horses; she might have abandoned me! But I enjoyed the riding school so much that I spent the second week working in the stables. It was a slog walking there, but I adored horses and felt privileged.

The weather flipped on the Saturday we returned, and it was my birthday. Mum gave me a present wrapped in tissue paper; a little brown and white 'china' pony! At last, I had a pony of my own – Bah Humbug.

As we left for the very last time, sloshing our way to the railway station in the pouring rain, I'd never felt so depressed. I'd reached a pinnacle but was now at the bottom of a trough!

★ ★ ★

However, Skeggy holidays continued, although further up the coast, towards Ingoldmells. Aunty Kath and my cousin Jimmy Matthews had bought a pair of Bluebird caravans between them, pitching them on a caravan park down Wall's Lane, directly opposite Skegness Butlins.

Now our fortnights were in a caravan. It was great fun, converting the seats into beds at night, lighting the gas mantles and using a bucket for a toilet after dark. We all had a good laugh over our inconveniences!

At 8 o'clock each morning, Butlins' 'jingle' rang out repeatedly across our field: "Get up, get out of bed; enjoy your holiday," so that you couldn't bear to stay in bed. But after a while it didn't bother us.

Skegness was three miles away now, a long way to walk,

so we went there less often. But we regularly walked to Winthorpe, a miners' holiday village between Butlins and Skeggy. Here we could roller-skate, swim in the pool, play on the penny-slot machines or buy fish and chips from the 'Linger Longer' fish bar. The sea was nearer, so we swam in it often. One day, Skeggy had the highest temperature in England. That day Johanna and I roasted our bodies like coffee beans.

Following in Auntie Kath's footsteps, Dad bought a caravan, putting it on the same site. With rounded bottom corners it looked a little old-fashioned, but the interior was beautifully fitted out in proper wood.

Holidays continued. We shared our caravan with different combinations of relatives. Sometimes Aunty Beat and Jane stayed; another time Janine came. Auntie Beat had a great sense of humour, and Jane and I also had a laugh because we both got constipated on holiday – "probably due to the water," some said. It was true that cups of tea tasted totally different made with Skegness water. While I took Andrews' Liver Salts Jane had castor oil, so it was a competition to see which was best!

Richard was too old to come on our caravan holidays. He hadn't been around much in our childhood. After Miss Tate's, he was sent to school in Nottingham (a seven-year-old cycling more than a mile on the main road, to catch a train to the big city of Nottingham)! Then he went to Stamford boarding school. In his holidays he'd want to catch up with his best friends, John and Robert Lee, who sometimes came with us to Skegness. But they'd be off doing their own thing.

Then in 1961, Mum and Dad took Helen and me for a caravan holiday in Dorset. So the mould was broken, and we hardly ever went to Skegness after that.

GRANTHAMIAN

CHAPTER 7

One Four Two

One Four Two Harrowby Road

The sombre November day in 1954 when we moved to Grantham was not a happy one for me. I'd caught the bus to school from Bottesford, but instead of returning there, I ran the mile to our new house on Harrowby Road. Although I was fairly familiar with Grantham, I really wasn't looking forward to life in that big dark house that was to be my new home. I expect Helen was feeling similar. She'd begun her secondary school education at Melton Mowbray grammar school for one term only, with all the expense of a new school uniform. After Christmas, she'd have to move to Kesteven and Grantham Girls' School (KGGS), in Grantham. Meanwhile, she continued travelling to Melton via a different bus route.

My father had just retired from the RAF and had opened a new sub-post office next to Uncle Jim's garage. Our lives would be completely altered. Not only would our father be at home every single day but we'd have to live in this dark spooky house.

Our red brick house had 'Southolme' carved in stone above the front door, but from the beginning we called it by its number, 'One Four Two'. This once prestigious house, with its wide south-facing frontage overlooking a large garden, with extensive views towards Great Ponton and the A1, had once belonged to none other than John and Robert Lee's grandfather. Joined on to the back of it, along Harrowby Road, was a row of bay-windowed terraced houses. Then, due to the builder's changing circumstances, most of the front garden was sold off, allowing for more terraced houses to be built in continuation down Harrowby Road, thus blocking the views that had once been enjoyed. The remaining narrow margin of front garden was now referred to as 'the side of the house', although still wide enough for a herbaceous-bordered path through to the back. The small road-facing garden remained the same, with two bushy broom trees in front of the large, stone mullioned, square bay window, which was topped with a fancy brick balustrade, forming a balcony. The front door, now at the side, also had a balcony above, as did the large square dining room window that came next. These were pretentious balconies, accessed by climbing out of the upstairs windows.

That first day I arrived 'home' to find the wide front door wide open. Stepping inside, I crossed a mosaic floor, laid out in squares and borders of small tiles coloured blue, pale yellow, black and white (a Victorian replication of a Roman floor). When I reached the grand mahogany staircase, I turned left down a very dark passage lined with mahogany panelling, going high up on both sides. Then, in the darkness, I bumped into a door. I pushed and pushed but it was so stiff. Then a helping hand opened it from the other side and my father was there to greet me.

I was now in the maid's quarter, which was paved in red tiles. On the left was the 'breakfast room,' where Dad pointed to a long cream-painted box up on the wall, with little glass windows along its length. This, he told me, indicated which room the maid was to go to. (There was a pull cord in each bedroom, which activated its own little window in this box, making the cover swing backwards and forwards). I imagined we'd have a lot of fun with that.

Further down the passage was the kitchen. Mum smiled up at me. She was boiling the kettle on the gas cooker, to make a pot of tea. She looked tired and strained. A cup of tea was just what they needed before setting about sorting the beds for the night. There was much to be done before bedtime.

Meanwhile I poked around to find out what else the

back-end of the house had to offer. Down a step was a lobby to the back door, which opened into the back yard. The large pantry was opposite the kitchen, with a white marble slab to keep food cool, and a 'safe' with a metal mesh door, to keep out the flies. The high shelves on one side would, by next year, be filled with big jars of bottled pears and other fruits from the garden. Back up the passage was the 'shoe room' – quite a novelty but from then on, Helen and I would be expected to clean our shoes every school day, in the meticulous fashion that Dad would show us. Using his metal 'shoe-last,' he'd be forever tacking new leather soles onto our shoes or metal segs onto the worn edges of the heels.

Outside the breakfast room door was another lobby, with a second door next to the 'stiff' one. Dad unlocked it and switched on the light. It was the cellar. I tentatively crept down the brick stairs, pressing my hands against the whitewashed walls for support and comfort. It was damp and musty down there and I soon scuttled back to the top. Was the inside of a burial chamber like this?

After a cup of tea and ginger biscuits, I went off to explore by myself. I ran to the top of the posh, red-carpeted staircase with its wide, polished mahogany banister, and looked back along the landing. Behind the stairs were three dark-wood cupboards reaching the ceiling, with huge drawers underneath. I stood on a chair to unlock the first long door and climbed inside. Wow! Spooky, but great for hide and seek!

Of the five bedrooms, four were large, with the next to last being single. It had probably been the maid's room; now it would be Richard's when he came home from boarding school. The landing seemed to take up a vast amount of space.

Looking up the landing from the front bedroom door, with the dark cupboards on my right, there was a square landing space to the left, over the front hall, with a door to bedroom two. The large window above the front door, now looked onto the gable-end of the house next door, but in spite of this, it was the lightest part of the landing. A rectangular roof light above the stairs afforded a little more light.

The wide landing ran alongside the polished, ornate mahogany rails, topped with the broad banister. At the top of the stairs there was enough space to put a big table, which we did, later. Now the landing kinked to the left before continuing towards the back, passing two more bedrooms on the left. On the right were the doors to two box rooms. It was dark and spooky along here.

On reaching the door to the last bedroom, the landing turned sharp right, skirting the second box room. There was a large frosted-glass window looking out over the gardens of the houses joined to the back of us, although I couldn't see through it. Then finally, the landing turned sharp left, past the bathroom door and straight into the toilet, where I *could* see the back gardens from the window but they weren't very interesting.

The back bedroom was large with two windows – one facing south, from which I could see distant lorries on the Great North Road. The other faced west, down our back garden. I peered out. Ours was the only garden that extended to Cecil Street; the other gardens of the terraced houses of Harrowby Road and Cecil Street met in the middle, being shorter and narrower than ours.

The bathroom had a large old-fashioned bath, with a lever that had to be dropped, instead of a conventional plug. After I'd fathomed out how to use it, I ran water into the bath, to make sure it didn't leak. By now Helen had arrived home, so I went back downstairs to say a quick hello.

Helen and I were becoming more distant from each other since she'd started at Melton Grammar School. She was always reading books and seemed grown up and rather aloof, while I remained the tomboy I'd always been. Sometimes I felt I didn't really like her, especially as I always had her hand-downs. Soon after we moved, she was bought a new bike while I, as usual, inherited her old one. Admittedly I'd recently dismantled my little bike in the back yard, to paint the frame blue, and was unable to re-assemble it.

Now it was dusk and I still hadn't seen the back garden, so I nipped out of the back door. The yard was large, paved with blue-black bricks and bordered by a brick wall. I counted seven lilac trees growing round the edge. Amazingly, the large bedroom at the back of the house overhung half the yard, with a mere pole propping up the corner! This overhang would allow Mum sheltered hanging space for her washing when it was raining.

A central flight of brick steps led down to the garden with a good-sized lawn and beyond it, a plot for soft fruit and vegetables. Two apple trees grew along trellises, on the right of the lawn, hiding the greenhouse from view. Then, further down on the right, the gable end of our neighbour's house in Cecil Street formed a massive, house-high garden wall, with several fruit trees growing in front of it.

A path on the left led down to a tall wooden gate. This accessed a narrow alleyway, leading to our garage on Cecil Street (which we didn't use) and our neighbours' back gardens. Beech trees, which needed frequent cutting back, grew along the inside of the wooden fence at the bottom of our garden. It was too dark to see much now, so I returned to the house for tea.

I can't recall seeing much furniture in the house – what we'd brought was lost in it. But upstairs, my little divan was placed next to Dad's bed in the front bedroom, while Helen's was placed adjacent to Mum's, in the big back bedroom. I was ten years old and didn't question why. It may have had something to do with Dad's snoring.

Those first few nights were fraught with fearful nightmares of ghosts charging at me – conventional ones that I'd seen in 'Dandy' and 'Beano' comics, but very real to me. It was comforting to hear Dad snoring in the bed beside me. In the mornings he'd often teach me snippets of German he remembered. Unbeknown to him, this helped me forget the traumas from the night before. "Mein hoot es hat drei ecken – drei ecken hat mein hoot" (my hat has three corners) is all I remember.

Mum and Dad were forever buying furniture from auctions, with the intention of taking in lodgers, which would help pay for the mortgage. This prestigious house cost them £3000. It was going to be hard work from now on. Soon it was furnished with some very good bargains.

Some Saturday mornings, I'd cycle down to see how Dad's new post-office was going. I might wander into the garage to say hello to Uncle Jim and Uncle Ralph, who could have done without my intrusion I'm sure, being either elbow-deep in black grease or serving petrol to a customer.

While Dad served *his* customers, I'd inspect the birthday cards on the rack, look at the adverts in the front window or wander through to the office at the back. This was the office of old Mr Johnson, from whom Dad rented his post-office space. Dad had allotted the first post-office savings book to me. It had 'Bridge End Road No 1' emblazoned in gold letters on the front. I was very proud of that. He put a big poster on the sidewall, warning people to report the 'Colorado Beetle' if they saw one.

On several occasions I took money to Lloyds Bank for Dad; a thrilling responsibility, showing he had great faith in me. I secreted the money in a safe pocket – usually £50, a great deal of money then. Feeling important, I'd jump on my little black bike and pedal up to the traffic lights on Bridge End Road. When the lights changed to green, I'd ride across London Road (A1) in front of all the big lorries held up by the lights. Soon they'd pass me as I headed towards town, dwarfing me with their huge sides, as I kept a straight course in the gutter, heading towards St Peters Hill. Once past the statue of Isaac Newton, I'd stick out my right arm, to cross in front of all that traffic and reach Lloyds Bank on the next corner. What a buzz it gave me, riding into town on a busy Saturday morning. After safely depositing the money into Dad's account, I'd ride back to tell him, "mission accomplished!"

I continued finding new things at home. In the big box room were objects from Dad's past: blue-covered RAF exercise books on various subjects, including agriculture, where his writing and diagrams were extremely neat. There were metal trunks brought back from different countries. In one there was a large, grey patterned snakeskin and a water-buffalo hide. Dad made our music case, school satchels, handbags and shopping bags, from the leather he had. I watched how it was done.

The cheetah skin, with its beautiful markings, was brought out and laid on the floor of the square landing, complete with claws, ears and holes where the eyes had been. It wasn't seen as wrong in those days to bring such souvenirs from abroad and treasure them.

One day I lifted up the heavy sash-window in the second bedroom, and climbed onto the balcony. But as I clambered out, the window slid down by itself. Now what was I to do? I kept leaning over to see how far it was to jump, feeling quite unsure and dithery. Then our neighbour, Mrs Curtis, called loudly over the wall to Mum, "Mrs Carrington, I think your daughter's trying to commit suicide!" With that, Mum came up to rescue me. She wasn't cross but she didn't like the neighbours knowing our business. Usually, we only saw Mrs Curtis on her back doorstep every morning, scraping her burnt toast.

On the left of our garden steps, almost hidden by forsythia, was a little shed, nearing a state of collapse. Johanna and I started a club in there – a gardening club. We made badges and bought a packet of seeds for sixpence. The fun, however, was the administration: the lists, the paperwork, the planning. But soon it became too cold and wet in there, so we started another club in the big box room. As the door was red on the inside, we called it 'the Red Door Club' and made badges for the 'RDC', beginning more plans and lists.

Apart from playing hopscotch on the path outside my house, or making an icy slide in winter outside her house, we'd sometimes hang out of her landing window on St Catherine's Road to sing hymns in loud quavering voices, just like Grandma. Passers-by seemed either astonished or embarrassed.

That first winter in Grantham was snowy, and Johanna took me to her school playground in nearby St Anne's Street, where an icy slide had been made down the sloping playground, illuminated by streetlights. It was super-daring to zoom down this glassy slide, taking turns with local boys and girls, none of whom I knew. Then on my third attempt, some boy stuck his foot out and tripped me up. Bang - I landed on my nose! Blood poured down my new navy-blue pure-wool coat that Mum had recently bought second-hand from Mrs Catlin. Johanna and her friend Christine Proffitt, who lived in Cecil Street, escorted me home through the back gate.

The following summer, Johanna and I went for a whole day's hike, taking a bottle of lemonade and jam sandwiches in our school satchels. Halfway up Somerby Hill, we stopped to play in the derelict terraced houses above the entrance to Spittlegate Aerodrome, before turning down Whalebone Lane at the top – where once had been an arch of two enormous whalebones, standing over the road.

Chatting in broad Grantham accents, we imitated conversations we'd heard: "Well ah sez to ower Petunia, ah sez; ah sez, well, ah sez; if yow don't 'oorry oop, ah sez, aah'll gu withowt yer, ah sez…" while we headed towards Little Ponton. Then we found the narrow lane leading to 'the secret valley,' which led up to the High Dyke, part of 'Ermine Street' the Roman road that motorcyclists loved to race along. Further on was a signpost to Boothby Pagnall, a village near Old Somerby. We didn't quite know where we intended to go, but we went full circle and ended up in Old Somerby, which we knew well.

As we cut through a farmyard, we saw a lovely haystack, hidden from view – an irresistible temptation. For the next half-hour we clambered up, to slide down again and again, dragging the hay as we went, ending up with itchy bites and scratches all over our legs and thighs. We left the poor haystack looking the worse for wear as we walked across the Well Field to say a quick hello to Grandma and Granddad before returning downhill to home. It had been a satisfying day.

The word "bored" didn't exist in our vocabulary. If we had nothing better to do, we'd take car numbers on our neatly drawn out, clip-boarded paper. Cars were few and far between then. Most men cycled to work. After the factory hooters had hooted at dinnertime, hordes of cyclists tore up Harrowby Road hill from Bridge End Road, like the Tour de France, past our house, racing towards Cherry Orchard (a huge council estate). Within the hour, they'd be tearing back to work again. Then, after the 5pm hooter, they'd all rush home for tea.

Grantham had some major factories: Aveling and Barfords, near the post office, where huge dumper trucks and diggers were made; Ruston and Hornsby on London Road, where caterpillar traction had been developed; Neal's Cranes on the opposite side of town, and also Marco's ammunition factory. The town had a large railway station on the opposite side of town. Sometimes we went there to take train numbers instead. The houses in the streets nearby were black with grime from train smoke. If we were nearby and knew that the 'Flying Scotsman' was due, we'd climb to the high embankment to cheer it on its way. That was thrilling. It came through often from London to Edinburgh.

Once a group of us ventured south along the embankment and spotted a wooden bogie abandoned on a railway siding.

We couldn't believe our luck. We'd probably seen them in old films because we instinctively knew how to propel it along the track, by pumping the wooden handle up and down. Eagerly we clambered down and crossed the main line to have a go; waiting impatiently for our turn. What a unique opportunity. However, when the track reached points onto the main line, we could go no further. Never mind. We'd had a rare and illicit privilege. I've never seen a bogie since.

Every week, Helen and I travelled by train to Bottesford, keeping up our piano lessons. Our piano was placed in a fireplace alcove in the dining room, which was left of the entrance hall. When cousin Barry bought a new piano and gave us his old one, we placed that on the other side of the fireplace, near the bay window. Mostly we played his. It had such a light touch. But being so dreadfully cold there in winter, we didn't practise half as much as we should have done.

Mum and Dad bought a large, beautifully polished second-hand dining table, which extended halfway down the dining room. Occasionally we ate our Sunday dinner in there, depending on who was visiting us, making a roaring fire in the red-tiled fireplace in winter. However, the best thing was playing table tennis on that table. Mum had once been Ladies' Table Tennis Champion in Grantham but I don't remember her ever having time for a game with us, although lots of friends and cousins did.

Johanna and I once found two large portrait photos

of Mr Thompson on the sideboard in the dining room. (He was the wealthy old man who owned the post-office building and probably the garage next door.) Johanna disliked him. At every opportunity he'd call at their house to wash-up for her mum. We propped a photo on the floor against a cupboard, removed African wooden knives from hooks on the wall and threw them with a vengeance at Mr Thompson's face.

Mum had never taken me to the dentist until we moved to Grantham. In her childhood, the family cleaned their teeth with soot, scraped from the back of the fireplace with their toothbrushes. My first visit seemed horrific – I needed nine fillings straight away. Then my eye-teeth protruded high up on my gums, so a plate was needed to re-align them – after three teeth had first been removed to make more space. So understandably, I disliked dentists.

Another new experience, but much nicer, was visiting the library, which was round the corner from the town hall, at the top of the bus station. In the children's section I discovered the 'Twins' books. The first one I chose was 'The Eskimo Twins'. I was hooked! I think I went through most of this series, learning about people from all over the world, from all those places I'd been drawing maps of, from the little globe Dad had given us.

I was always drawing horses and had a large frieze I'd painted hung on the classroom wall, depicting horses going down to a stream in a Dartmoor-like landscape. Then, the following year, an inter-school art exhibition was held for the Grantham area. Two of my paintings were chosen for display in the Public Library – one of gypsies around a campfire, where one was dancing with a tambourine, and another of two gypsy horses standing end to end under a tree.

I was absorbed with gypsies at that time, having decided to become one, when I grew up - a proper Romany gypsy. I'd had a flash of panic one day at Bottesford, wondering how I could face the big wide world as a constantly blushing adult. It seemed an insurmountable problem. I'd need to escape from this world I was in. It was bad enough going into prayers at school; so was sitting round the dinner table, trapped. I just couldn't cope, trapped, face to face with other people. If I were a gypsy living outdoors, I'd be free. It had even become an issue to walk down a long straight road like Harrowby Road, seeing someone coming towards me. It might be someone I knew or perhaps a policeman, who'd be very suspicious of my red face. Sometimes I'd work myself into such a state that I'd turn and walk back the other way. If I ran, or rode my bike, I'd be ok. At junior school, I always ran to school but as a teenager, this seemed unseemly, unless I could feign being late.

Funnily enough, I could be quite cheeky, even brazen at times, but blushing was what embarrassed me. I was pre-primed to blush whenever I had time to think I might. Then everyone would be staring at me. O me miserum! But I suffered my bad moments and then forgot about them when something else occupied my mind.

CHAPTER 8

The Lodgers

⊰─◆─✣─◆─⊱

"They're not lodgers, they're paying guests," my mother
would insist, as if it wasn't nice to be taking in lodgers. I
couldn't see what she was so worried about, but the first
occupants were definitely not paying guests. They didn't
eat meals with us. They were a young couple with a baby,
desperate for somewhere to live and happy, it seemed, to
be ensconced in the front room. With its large, square bay
window, high ceiling with an ornate ceiling rose, and a large
fireplace, it wasn't ideal, and must have been difficult to
keep warm in those early months of 1955. There wasn't
much privacy either, having no net curtains at the windows.
But the broom hedges would have thwarted the prying
eyes of passing neighbours. Life couldn't have been easy
for them. I presume they fetched all their water from the
bathroom, even for the baby's bath.

Sometimes I was invited to help bath the baby, which
quite fascinated me, for I wasn't all that familiar with the
anatomy of little boys. As soon as he was lowered into the

water, he would pee up towards the ceiling, which made his Mum and me laugh.

Mum and I kept discovering nappy droppings on the tiled floor, in the darkness behind the stiff door. Perhaps just the effort of opening this door caused the mother to lose grip of the nappy as she carried it to the dustbin. Why she didn't empty it into the toilet upstairs we didn't know. Mum tut-tutted, but said nothing to the mother. Anyway, they weren't with us for long and we never saw them again.

The next lodger was Miss Goodier. She was the Art teacher from my school, pleasant, but pale, thin and delicate looking. She took the second bedroom adjacent to the square landing and ate breakfasts and evening meals with us – so she must have been a paying guest. It was less embarrassing for me to have a third party at the dining table; a bit of distraction. I can't remember how long she stayed; perhaps to the end of the school year in 1955.

Miss Goodier did basketwork, and with our permission, often soaked cane in the bath overnight. But our enduring memory is of her seemingly permanent hay fever. Every morning her red eyes would be streaming as she sneeze, sneeze, sneezed all through breakfast. Her nose was red-raw. It was quite off-putting.

By now I'd devised a habit to avoid helping with washing-up after tea. I'd excuse myself and slip upstairs to the toilet, where I'd sit singing my heart out for a good half hour. I was always singing since we'd moved here. Maybe the high ceilings enhanced my voice. At Bottesford, Mum sang all the time – 'Speed Bonny Boat like a Bird on the Wing, Over the Sea to Skye' (one of the first songs I learnt from her), or Kathleen Ferrier's 'What is Life to Me Without Thee' and 'Blow Ye Winds Southerly.' One I really loved was Ruby Murray's 'Softly, Softly Turn the Key and Open up My Heart'. Now Mum seemed too busy to sing.

I'd practise the songs I'd heard practised by the senior girls at school; the girls who didn't make it to the grammar school or the Girls' Central School, so were kept on until they left, at fourteen. But Mrs John, the Welsh music teacher, had great faith in them and devoted much time to teaching them songs. These I practised on the toilet after tea. The hardest was a carol; 'A Virgin most Pure as the Prophets do Tell'. Miss Goodier, hearing me from her bedroom, told Mum I had a lovely singing voice, which chuffed me no end, although I only had the guts to sing to myself.

Helen and I had just moved into the third bedroom opposite the box rooms when I caught Hong Kong 'flu. She probably moved out again because I was very poorly, spending a couple of weeks in bed, alternately sweating and freezing as the fever took hold. The doctor called frequently. As I improved, I sat in bed making things from a bag of Dad's leather off-cuts in many colours and types, including pale patterned pieces of snakeskin and bits of chestnut-brown crocodile skin. These I cut into thin strips, weaving or plaiting them into different patterns. Aunty Kath would come up and put her head round the door for a chat. She mostly called by for a cup of tea on her way home from the garage. My legs were quite wobbly when I first got up. It took a while to feel strong again. As an experiment, Mum and Dad got me taking a cod-liver-oil capsule every day, to see if it staved off further infections.

In the early months in that bedroom, I'd have terrifying nightmares of ghosts – rushing round the landing corners from the toilet and straight through my bedroom door with an audible "WHOOSH" – one after another in flapping white sheets, with big black holes where their eyes should be. I was petrified.

It became obvious that the income from paying guests wasn't enough to help with the mortgage, so Mum began teaching at the Boys' National School, at the back of our school. What a hard life was in store for her!

I'd be the first to arrive home now. The back-door key was hidden under the doormat in the covered yard. As soon as I got in I raided the food cupboard. First I'd help myself to eight ginger biscuits, then mix teaspoonfuls of Horlicks and Ovaltine together in a cup, mixed with a little water, which I'd eat with the teaspoon. This secret treat only lasted while I was at the National school. When Mum got home I'd be all refreshed, ready to run to Bush's shop on Dudley Road for anything she needed. (Dudley Road was parallel to Harrowby Road and Cecil Street). Mr Bush greeted everyone with "Ellow Dook" in a Grantham accent that my American cousins still love to emulate. We had an account where every purchase was written in a little notebook, which he'd tot up at the end of the week – every shilling, penny and halfpenny, no matter how many customers were in the queue. I'd stand awkwardly, red-faced and sweaty at the head of the queue.

No bread ever tasted more delicious than Bush's. Mr Bush and his equally affable, blond-haired son David, would get up at the crack of dawn to bake bread, together with doughnuts, cakes and buns, which were laid out in the window, where wasps and flies enjoyed them as well. Helen and I found the crusts of the loaves irresistible, eating much of them before we got home.

The quickest way to Bush's was through the back gate, along Cecil Street and down Granville Street, passing Finch's corner shop at the end of Cecil Street. We only bought Silvikrin shampoo sachets, hair rollers and the like from there. The aisles were crammed together and the vegetables were always rather 'tired'.

Granville Street ran downhill from Harrowby Road to Dudley Road. On the bottom corner stood the Lord Harrowby pub. Bush's shop was opposite this, on Dudley Road, where the back gardens sloped down to the River Witham. From the front of our house, heading down towards Bridge End Road, there was first St Anne's Street, then Stuart Street and lastly Bridge Street, near the bottom. They joined Harrowby Road to Dudley Road in a grid-like layout. Heading the other way, first was Granville Street, then St. Catherine's Road a quarter of a mile further on. This ran down across the river and up into town to St Peter's Hill traffic lights. Auntie Kath and the girls lived near the top corner with Harrowby Road – the corner where cousin Harvey had fallen from the back of the van.

Our next paying guest arrived after Miss Goodier's departure. She was Miss Brabazon, originally from Dublin, and Auntie Maureen to me. She was tallish, square and bony, with yellowy-brown-hair and a long gaunt 'Irish' face with flared nostrils. She worked in the offices at Neal's Cranes, on the other side of Grantham, walking there and back at speed, looking at the pavement with her face parallel to the ground. Mum cooked egg and bacon breakfasts for her and Dad each morning, but Miss Brabazon liked a round of buttered bread with hers, to put her bacon in for dinner.

Mum would dash off to school when she'd washed up, arriving home in the afternoon looking weary and having to start all over again. In wintertime she'd first clean out Miss Brabazon's grate, bringing down the ashes and the coalscuttle, to be filled in the coal shed in the yard. She'd carry this heavy scuttle back upstairs, but didn't light the fire. Next the breakfast room fire needed doing. I often helped, making firelighters from folded newspapers. Sometimes I'd fill the coalscuttle or chop wood on the block in the coal shed, to help things along. The coal occupied only a third of the long wooden shed in the outer yard, which had a heavy sliding door.

To speed things up, Mum would stick the shovel at the front of the grate, laying a sheet of the Daily Express across it. As the flames took hold, the Daily Express would get drawn in on either side of the shovel. The trick was to cause a vacuum without the paper catching fire.

In wintertime Mum, still wearing her camel coat, would begin preparing vegetables for dinner (or tea, as we called it in those days – dinner being around midday and lunch being elevenses in the morning). We mostly ate greens and potatoes with a chop, perhaps lamb or pork, or sometimes steak and kidney pie with Mum's crusty pastry on top. We had to provide decent food for our paying guests, so we reaped the benefits ourselves. There was always a pudding of some sort: baked rice pudding or apple Charlotte etc. Apple pie and custard was the favourite for Sundays. Mum made gorgeous pastry.

After tea, we relaxed around the fire in the breakfast room, listening to the radio, which was much more entertaining then. I remember 'Our Day and Age' on a Monday night, where true mysteries were solved. It was gripping – even for me. Mum had her school books to mark but not to the extent that teachers do today, with all the Ofsted stuff.

Soon after Miss Brabazon was established, Dennis joined us. He was perhaps in his late 40s, taller and thinner than Dad but with similar hair – black and kinky – and more of it. His complexion was swarthy, but he was always smart in a suit and tie. He worked for the Post Office, having a van to travel from phone box to phone box. He had the front bedroom, although his evenings were spent with us. Mum and Dad now shared the back bedroom.

While Mum was preparing tea and before Dad arrived home, and Helen was perhaps upstairs doing homework,

Dennis and I sat by the fire in the breakfast room. He'd test me on 'Word Power' from the quiz in his 'Reader's Digest' magazine, or any other topics of interest. I'd sit on a little stool in front of the fire while he took the winged armchair at the side of the hearth. He kept a tin of snuff in his pocket and showed me how to sniff it from the back of my hand. In winter, we'd spend many convivial pre-tea evenings, learning new words with a sniff of snuff. After tea, he'd probably bag the same winged armchair as we listened to the radio until bedtime.

Helen and I occupied our evenings in various activities: knitting, sewing or making wool rugs with pre-cut, short lengths of thick wool that we knotted through a meshed base, using a special hooked, wooden handled tool (a craze of the time). We never sat empty-handed. That was the perk of radio; your hands and eyes were free! Knitting wool came in skeins and one of us would hold the skein on both forearms, while the other wound it into balls.

Mum couldn't cope with all the housework. When there was no Miss Selby's, Helen and I were asked to dust and vacuum on Saturday mornings. Mum later confided that Helen wasn't as thorough as me, so from aged ten, it became my permanent job to clean the house on Saturday mornings. Meanwhile Helen biked down to the Co-op on Bridge End Road (opposite Dad's Post Office) and brought back the main week's shopping in the large pig-skin shopping bag Dad had made, trapping it in the V of the bike frame to push uphill to home.

There was so much cleaning to do – the breakfast room, the lounge, the hall and passages, the stairs and landing, and Mum's bedroom. In the lounge we had a large, high-backed mahogany sideboard with a big mirror. The shelf below was adorned with carved ivory animals in a long trailing double line, looking like they were heading for a waterhole; souvenirs from Africa. It took ages to take them off to dust and re-arrange.

But Mum's bedroom was by far the dustiest. She wore a 'Playtex' rubber roll-on corset, which she powdered to get on, so the dressing table was thick with dust every week. I'd take dusters full of dust downstairs to shake in the yard, being very thorough, which is what Mum appreciated about my cleaning. Each year I scrubbed and sealed the mosaic floor. It looked good with the sheen of sealant on it. We didn't want to scrub it too often.

Miss Brabazon lived with us for years. On Saturdays she visited her sister and family at Cherry Orchard, the vast post-war area of council houses. But her sister, Kay, lived in a road of brand-new private houses there. When Miss Brabazon first arrived, her sister's family, Kay, husband Bill, daughters Patsy and Jean and the new baby, Billy, lived in a basement of a town house, which was dark and oppressive. They'd just returned from Africa and needed to get onto the housing ladder. Soon they got moved to Alma Park, a run down, out-of-town ex-Army base, where difficult families were housed in concrete houses – not the sort of place for the likes of the Clarke family. However, most of the troublesome tenants had been rehoused, so Bill and Kay stuck with it until they could buy a place of their own. I'd cycle to Alma Park on Saturday afternoons, with Auntie Maureen riding Helen's bike, which she was allowed to borrow.

It was like an adventure playground there; so much bumpy ground to cycle over, so many humps and hollows, that we had a fabulous time. Patsy, Jean and I only came in when tea was ready. After tea, Auntie Maureen and I cycled home. I got on so well with them all. Patsy, a little younger than me, had a square fresh face and brownish hair, while Jean, the younger one, had a long freckle-covered face that seemed at odds with her deep blue eyes and black hair, cut short with a straight fringe. (The Woodland Trust is now based at the former Alma Park.)

After they'd moved to Cherry Orchard, we'd entertain everyone with our singing. Taking turns, we'd stand on a dining-room chair as if on stage. I felt uninhibited there. In good weather we'd climb the trees at the bottom of their dead-end road. These girls were amazing; not only as bright as buttons but fearless when it came to tree climbing. I thought I was brave, but I couldn't climb to the heights that they did. My legs turned to jelly. I'd felt so proud that I could run halfway up our lilac tree in seconds, but these trees were in a different league altogether.

On Sundays Auntie Maureen went to Mass at 11am, then to the Catholic Club. Mum kept her Sunday lunch warm until she arrived home around 3pm. Our family joked that she went to confession first, then to the pub.

Dad was an early riser and was always first in the bathroom, followed by Auntie Maureen, then Dennis. Meanwhile Mum washed at the basin in her bedroom, then hurried downstairs to start cooking. Helen washed there next. Me, I didn't wash much in those early days, although nobody seemed aware of the fact.

Sometimes I'd be in the bathroom while Dad shaved. He showed me how to splash my face with cold water then hot, then cold again. It was good for the complexion, he said. Dad and I both had rosy complexions. On Saturdays I had a bath, so I was always nice and clean for the start of each week.

For Helen and me, our home didn't quite seem to belong to us with lodgers there although, for me, it eased my embarrassment at mealtimes. Auntie Maureen always rushed down to breakfast. She'd devour it quickly, then dash off with her bacon sandwich in hand. Helen tried to finish her cereals before Dennis arrived. I stayed on – I was fascinated. He'd arrive without urgency, bringing those now familiar smells: Brylcreem on his black shiny hair, aftershave on his swarthy chin and Colgate toothpaste. Mum brought in his cooked breakfast, and the combination of smells was nauseating. Then he'd shake HP sauce over everything. That was the pits!

With his cup of tea on the right and Daily Express propped against the sauce bottle on the left, he would avidly read the paper, his hand permanently on the cup handle and his face facing the opposite way. Picking up the cup, he'd bring it across to the front, then, turning his head at the last minute, take a huge noisy slurp of tea, followed by a loud "HAA" as he exhaled and turned back to read the paper with hardly a glitch. Meanwhile the cup seemed to return to the saucer by itself. Every sip was like this, every day. I learned it off by heart to show my cousins. Dennis left us when I was about fifteen. Maybe he got promoted.

Auntie Maureen moved out when I was seventeen. We had one more lodger after her – a French student teacher from the High School on a one-year exchange. She was Josette from Montpellier and at nineteen, not much older than Helen. They got on really well, especially as Helen was taking French A level.

A while before this Mum changed schools, to teach at Gonerby Hill Foot primary school, north of Grantham on the A1. Now she had to catch a bus from the bus station. Helen and I took on more daily duties. Mine were to wash up the breakfast pots and to make the fire in the breakfast room, after school. I can't remember what Helen's tasks were.

I was in the First Eleven hockey team by now and often practised after school. One winter's evening I arrived home at dusk to find Helen and Josette sitting shivering on either side of the fireplace in the breakfast room, waiting for me to clean out the grate and light the fire. Admittedly, it *was* my allotted job, but I felt *just* like Cinderella.

However, it was Mum who bore the brunt of the hard work. Sundays weren't a day off for her. We'd usually have a fried breakfast on Sundays. (Actually, it was often Dad who cooked it on that day – showing us exactly how it should be done!) While Mum cooked Sunday lunch, Helen and I made things for teatime; Helen making a lovely trifle and often a chocolate cake, while I made flapjack (Mum's 'wartime' version without golden syrup). Mum made pastry for an apple tart with enough left over for jam and lemon curd tarts for tea.

When I think back to all we ate on Sundays, I feel quite appalled. After our cooked breakfast and lovely roast dinner, followed by apple pie and custard, there'd be a huge tea in the front room (after we'd acquired a television in 1957). It was wheeled into the lounge on the three-tier trolley that Dad had made. There'd be bread and butter with ham and sometimes pork pie and salad. Then trifle and cream followed by flapjack and homemade chocolate cake as well. If we had room, there were jam and lemon curd tarts to finish off with. Where did we put it all?

I have a feeling that once we got stuck in front of the telly on Sunday nights, Helen and I stayed there until bedtime, not helping Mum at all. After washing up she'd iron both our school uniforms ready for Monday. She wouldn't delegate. It didn't matter that I'd ironed ten sheets the day before, she still wouldn't allow us to iron our uniforms – a self-made slave!

Dad still wore his blue RAF shirts; the earlier ones had detachable collars, which were always soaking in a bowl of starch near the kitchen sink. Mum hated doing them.

When those had worn out, he wore RAF shirts with collars attached. Mum, Helen or I were forever turning the collars and cuffs on the sewing machine to prolong their life.

I have to say though, that when it came to school holidays, I felt really sorry for Mum. Instead of having the rest she so deserved, Dad would decide to prune the fruit trees or discover some other urgent job waiting to be done at home, so Mum spent the best part of her holidays running the post-office. Poor Mum!

CHAPTER 9

Sainte Frances

Choukee in front of the shed

Following in the footsteps of Saint Francis, I was truly an animal lover. But my love was mostly misguided, and I regret that I caused more harm than good, in most cases.

During our first springtime in Grantham, I found two featherless baby birds lying beneath the pear tree – fallen from a nest. Their bulging eyes were closed, but they were alive. I had to end their lives to save them from suffering. I knew that people sometimes drowned kittens and decided I must do the same with these poor creatures. So, holding them one in each hand by their scraggy little necks, I submersed them in the water-butt for ages, standing on tiptoes to reach the water. When I lifted them out, they opened their beaks and gasped. How could they have lasted so long? I hated repeating the process. I should be doing them a kindness! I held them underwater for longer this time. Still they gasped when I lifted them out. I was fraught and flabbergasted by now. So finally, I submerged them for an eternity. I felt so cruel. This time they really were dead and I gave them a little burial under the tree.

I was in the top class at St Wulfram's now – for the second time! On the classroom shelf, four tiny black frogs jumped onto the rim of our aquarium – the net result of the frogspawn put in earlier. The teacher asked who had a pond at home. I put up my hand. However, we didn't exactly have a pond as there was no water in it yet, but I could soon remedy that. Dad had let me have the long rockery at the bottom of the garden. In it was a concrete hollow for a pond, about the size of a washing-up bowl.

During the last lesson that day, these four little frogs were hopping about under my desk lid. I kept checking on them. Then I carefully walked home, balancing them on my atlas. It was so tricky. Once home, I filled my 'pond' with water from the water butt, setting the frogs free around the edge. In the morning all the water had gone; so had the frogs!

The following springtime I found a baby blackbird scuttling on the ground among the fruit trees. I had to take responsibility for it, for there were no parents to be seen. I didn't quite know what to feed it on – maybe bread and milk. I went into the pantry and pulled a piece of bread off the loaf, soaked it in a saucer of milk then went outside to catch my little bird again. I knew that parent birds put food down the throats of their babies, so I stuffed some of this sloppy bread down my little orphan's throat. I didn't know how much it would need, so just gave it two throatfuls. After school that day, I caught my baby bird and fed it in the same manner as before. Next morning it was easier to catch. I thought it must like the food it was getting. I continued this routine for a few days, with the bird becoming used to me. It seemed to be getting fatter.

I thought I should teach it to fly. I had a good idea. I'd place it on top of the mop and thrust it into the air. When I pulled the mop away, it would have to fly down. I did it gently, the first few times. It didn't exactly fly, but came flapping down with a gentle bump. It needed plenty of practice.

On the third morning of flying practice, I knelt on the lawn and my little blackbird hopped eagerly towards me, across the grass. Looking trustingly into my eyes, it jumped onto my outstretched hand, fluttered in the air, then fell back – dead. Would I ever learn?

The next winter I discovered a black cat in the front garden, hiding under the holly bush, which was tucked between the bay window and the fence to next-door. It had five tiny black kittens. The next morning all the kittens were dead. Mum told me the cat had probably killed them because I'd disturbed them.

We began putting food in the coal shed for the poor mother cat and I named her 'Choukee'. She was a beautifully sleek cat with a little white dot on her chest. In springtime she gave birth to five more black kittens. They were adorable and of course we couldn't prevent them from entering the house. One Sunday, after Helen and I had laid the table for dinner, I found all five kittens prancing about on the table – clambering up the tablecloth and pulling cutlery onto the floor. It was a riot. I wish I could have filmed it. Anyway, nothing was broken and we eventually found homes for these kittens. Choukee was now an established house cat.

There were times when she followed me to school, which was along Harrowby Road, across the top of St Catherine's Road and the same distance again, in an almost straight line along Sandon Road. I won't say I didn't encourage her. I thought it was wonderful that my cat wanted to come to school with me, and I didn't feel self-conscious walking to school with her following me.

One day after school, she was nowhere to be seen. I went home without her, hoping she'd be ok. Then about 8pm, Miss Hurst and Miss Field turned up at our front door, one carrying Choukee. She'd made her way into Harrowby House, part of the original school before it was modernised, where these two teachers lived.

The very last time she followed me, she was heavily pregnant. She slept on a girl's blazer in the cloakroom all day, before I led her home. Her kittens arrived the next day. How fortunate that they hadn't arrived earlier! I didn't encourage her after that. She was neutered and became a lovely pet for years.

After we'd had an attempted break-in, Dad acquired a dog. We named him Bruce. I don't know his provenance, but he was about a year and a half; black, boisterous and barky and not well liked by the neighbours. I thought he was gorgeous. He was very agile, a cross between an Alsatian and a Labrador, and we were told he could jump a six-foot wall, although he never jumped over Mrs. Curtis's wall, which wasn't that high.

Dad took him for early morning walks; down the hill to Bridge End Road, left towards the bottom of Somerby Hill then left again, up Cold Harbour Lane. (The bottom part of Cold Harbour Lane was fenced off then, enclosing a wood, which hid St. Vincent's Hall. This was an ex-RAF property, where the 'Dambuster' raid had been plotted).

Cold Harbour lane led to Hall's Hill, or the 'hills and hollows' as we called them; a place full of bomb craters, where the German pilots had missed their targets. It was popular for walkers, dog-lovers and lovers; tobogganists too, when we had snow. Grantham lies in a big basin, with hills on all sides: north to Gonerby, east to Somerby, south to Great Ponton and west to Barrowby. From the top you could see it all, with the spire of St Wulfram's church rising above.

Soon *I* was taking Bruce for his early walks. I didn't mind, although I was frightened of being caught on top in a thunderstorm, so when low, ominously dark clouds hung around, I'd race home down the other side of the hill.

Neighbours began complaining about Bruce. If he got out, he'd jump up at them in his exuberant, welcoming fashion. I can now see how scary this could be. So he was chained up in the yard by day, until one of us arrived home. I hated this curtailment. One day, I arrived home to find him missing. Mum said he'd gone to be an Army dog. I was gutted – I hadn't even said goodbye. But I accepted that he'd have a better life in the army and was proud to think that his physical abilities would be used for the good of the country. Years later, I found out that he'd been put to sleep. I felt so hurt and betrayed.

At sixteen I committed my most heinous crime to animals. I was walking home for dinner when I saw a beautiful young cat on the garden wall of Harrowby House. I went to pick it up to give it a cuddle, but it declined my attention. I tried again and caught it in my arms. But it wasn't having any of that. It struggled from my arms and ran across the road, straight into a double-decker bus. In absolute horror, I watched it go round the wheel of the bus – in pieces. I was inconsolable. In school that afternoon, my classmates couldn't comprehend what was wrong with me. They'd never seen me cry. I sobbed and sobbed. How could I have caused such a terrible thing to happen?

CHAPTER 10

K.G.G.S.

My carved cat

Many Lambley cousins went to Kesteven and Grantham Girls' School. First it was Pam; some years later it was Dena, the next year Vivienne, and two years after, Elaine, Helen and Cynthia. The following year, in 1955, it was Johanna, me in 1956, then Janine, followed by Judy and lastly Peta.

A generation earlier, our mother and four of her sisters had attended the school, plus Auntie Joyce, who was in the same class as Margaret Thatcher, or Roberts, as she was then. Auntie Kath didn't pass the 11-plus exam, but to me, she seemed the brightest of the bunch; she was forever holding us in deep and meaningful discussions and always tackling difficult crossword puzzles. Did she feel she must continuously prove her intelligence? In her teens, she'd had peritonitis and almost died. Had Granddad believed in doctors, she might not have suffered so. Luckily, she pulled through.

Once I'd got into the rhythm of my new school, I didn't worry that Johanna was a year ahead of me. I rarely saw her or any of my cousins during the course of the day. On the few occasions when I passed Cynthia in a corridor, I'd greet her with "Hyacinth", which she must have found irritating. I was in the 'A' stream, like most of my cousins and applied myself well, getting good results. However, early in my second year, I'd met the boy I wanted to marry – Jim, the boy who'd tripped me up on that icy slide when I was ten. I spent my waking hours drooling about him, making up poems and sentimental sonnets. I even bet half-a-crown with a prefect who'd taken over the class that I'd marry him.

However, I still worked enthusiastically in my favourite subjects. Patsy Smith and I were like lightning at mental arithmetic, shooting up our hands and almost jumping out of our seats to be first – *then*! I also loved geography, and history was ok, especially when Miss Prew asked me to make a chalk drawing of Tattershall Castle on black paper (we'd recently visited it), which was hung on the classroom wall. But most of all I loved art, gymnastics and games. I had the choice to be in either the hockey or the netball team. I chose hockey; a good choice with my stocky legs. I always hoped they'd grow longer in my teens, but they never did.

Morning prayers continued to be agonising. I thought I'd be bound to blush, and when we filed out, everyone would see my red sweaty face – so I did blush. It was mortifying.

Surprisingly, I auditioned to be in the choir. Could I have stood facing the whole school, to sing in the choir, as Elaine did? I don't know. It might have done me the world of good, had I been accepted, but I wasn't. Maybe I was too nervous, or perhaps 'Our Blest Redeemer' was not the best hymn to choose for my audition. Or was I just not good enough?

However, for every event going, I'd be up for it. The first one was a gym display in our newly opened school hall, with drop-down, pull-out modern equipment lining the walls, or suspended from the ceiling, plus the old school 'horse' for vaulting over. We'd show the parents how well it worked and how proficient we were. Those of us taking part were often excused from lessons – and how our muscles ached from so much practising!

Christine Proffitt had now become my best friend. We'd vie for first place in art exams, and we shared a penchant for writing poetry and loved gym and athletics. But while I was built like a Welsh pony, Christine was like a gazelle. I was good at short races and relays, but could never match Christine in the hurdles. We'd practise and practise for sports day. Christine could make the statutory three paces between the hurdles, while I had to take five, so I could never enter that event. Surprisingly, I did well in long jump – one of my favourite events.

With our new school extensions completed – new cloakrooms, toilets, showers and a school hall with a stage, plus a three-storey classroom extension constructed mainly of glass, (the architectural mode of the time) – the school instigated a dancing festival and a music festival, to take place in alternate years. The music festival came first. Our class sang 'Waltzing Matilda' amongst other songs, and Christine and I secretly sang it in broad Australian accents, which had us in fits of laughter. When Roger Trafford came to perform extracts from Dickens, we found him hilarious. Christine and I sat on a front row bench, secretly sharing a tube of Rowntrees' fruit gums, and got into a teenage laughing mode that we could not suppress. Our sides ached so much in the end.

In the dance festival the following year, Christine and I were the main participants in our class. Our dance depicted the Hungarian uprising against Russia. I was the only class member able to do a semblance of Cossack dancing, so I was chosen to go onstage first. Christine came next. We represented the Russians, while some young first formers acted as Hungarian children, ravaged by the Russian invasion. Wearing billowing white shirts tucked into black tracksuit bottoms, with wide colourful cummerbunds around our waists and black shiny Wellington boots, we looked quite the part. It was a dramatic dance, set to Brahm's Hungarian Dance No.5. I came prancing diagonally across the stage in four big leaps, to squat and 'Cossack' (ha!) then gesture for the next person to come on. Christine leapt across next and did her bit, followed by two more 'Cossackers'. After a little routine the music changed to a sombre, oppressive mode. Now our class made nasty repelling motions towards the poor little 'Hungarian' children, trapped in the corner behind netting and dressed in rags. They were crying, holding up their arms for protection. That dance is inscribed in my memory.

Then it was the music festival again. Apart from our class singing three lovely songs, there were other musical events. I played a piano duet with Josephine Bailey, who lived further up Harrowby Road. We won. It so happened that in the audience was Mary Ducker – formerly from Ducker's farm at the top of Belvoir Avenue – who was now a pianist. She took Mum aside and advised her that if I kept up with my music, I could get into the Royal Academy of Music in London, no problem. But I didn't keep up my practising. Anyway, music wouldn't have been my first choice for a career. I didn't actually want a career – I wanted to get married and have babies. That would replace the need to run off with the gypsies.

In the 4th form, I had an emergency dental appointment, having had toothache all night. Jim met me and we walked arm in arm to my dentist in town. I was in school uniform, although not wearing my hat (it was a silly-looking beret that stuck up at the front). I was seen and reported on. The next day I was in dire trouble, summoned to see the formidable headmistress, Miss Gillies. She was Scottish, with a flat white face, a hard expression and little eyes. Her greying hair was held back in some sort of loose bun. She'd been Margaret Thatcher's headmistress as well, so she must have been nearing retirement.

I quaked in my shoes as she severely reprimanded me for not wearing my hat outdoors (an unforgivable school crime), and laid into me with her bitter tongue. Even worse, I was seen hanging onto a boy's arm while in school uniform. Outrageous! Then, surprisingly, she softened. "Is that the boy I heard wind of some years ago?" she asked. "Well perhaps it's not a bad thing that you've stayed together. But my advice is that you get to the top of your profession before you get married." She repeated that advice three times. That was it, and I took her advice, in the end.

Christine and I had made close friends with Pat Bowser, who lived right at the bottom of Dudley Road in Witham Place, which was considered to be a slum, then. Dudley Road ended in a narrow bridge that crossed the river into Witham Place, where the 'soon to be condemned' houses ran the short distance to Bridge End Road. It was always full of mothers shouting across to each other, children's skipping ropes across the street and toddlers scuttling about on their potties. You had to walk round them all.

Pat lived with her mild-mannered father and a houseful of cats. They were everywhere – all over the furniture and on the table. The house stank of them. But despite the deprivations of her home life, Pat was in the 'A' stream with us, keeping up a fairly smart appearance. She was a loyal friend.

In our fifth year, we three girls sunbathed in Pat's back yard to revise for our GCE's, in between reading the juicy bits in 'Lady Chatterley's Lover,' of which Pat had a copy. How could such a 'mild' book have seemed so titillating then?

In the summer it was swimming, swimming, swimming, or occasionally tennis on the school courts or in Dysart Park. I preferred hitting a ball against a wall, which I often did at school. I tried this at home, standing on the large front doorstep to hit the ball against our neighbour's gable-end wall, until Mrs Curtis came out yelling at me. I didn't know her mother lived in that downstairs room. I felt very sorry – not just for her mother but for myself!

I often rode my bike round and round the yard, incessantly singing every pop song in creation. Mum occasionally looked up through the kitchen window, probably wishing her life was as carefree as mine. Bill Curtiss, next door, was probably mightily sick of me.

When I was sixteen, we had a craft competition at school. I'd become quite interested in carving, having recently made a sculpture from gypsum, of a couple embracing on a bench (probably inspired by Rodin's 'The Kiss' but not so erotic). It now took pride of place in the school library. Following that, I planned to make a carving from an old table leg Dad had given me. The night before, I made the desired shape in plasticine; a stylised model of a cat.

Using a sharp vegetable knife, I began carving. I was well pleased with my finished cat, except that its ears were shorter than intended. Dad told me how to French polish it, then left me to it, while he and Mum went to some RAFA do at Spittlegate. When they returned after midnight, I was still polishing away. The sanding had taken ages, but the French-polishing took even longer. By 3 am I was satisfied with it and went to bed.

Well, my wooden cat, winning first prize, was put on show in a new glass cabinet in the school entrance hall. But as I didn't see any other entries to this competition, perhaps there was no merit to it after all! Earlier that year we'd had a painting competition, which Christine had won and I'd come second. Mine was titled 'Hope' – the silhouette of a young couple sitting on the edge of a cliff, looking towards the sunset, with rocky cliffs of pink and dark blue, in 'Cubism' style. Of course, the carved couple on the bench and the couple looking towards the sunset were representations of Jim and me.

In the 5th form I was in the First Eleven, and there'd be a match most Saturday mornings in winter, half of them being away matches to surrounding towns. Although I was always sick on car journeys, I never had a problem on the old buses taking us to matches. I'd be too occupied with the singing and camaraderie.

That same winter, I was in a team of school swimmers, picked for special training in the pool at RAF Cranwell.

These journeys seemed quite long on those dark winter nights, with the windows steamed up and no happy singing going on.

During the summer I swam with Johanna every day after school unless it was raining. Uncle Ralph had given me a large inflatable tyre to take to the baths. We performed such antics with it. At 4d to go swimming, there was 2d left from our 6d allowance, which we spent in the sweet shop by the park gates, buying a stick of liquorice to stick in a little bag of kali.

At my last swimming sports day, I entered the underwater swimming competition. While everyone cheered the competitors, I sat quietly behind the diving board, taking in deep breaths. This event took place after the final race and by then, I was well prepared. I dived in and almost reached the far end of the pool – 50 yards away. I knew I'd never make a pearl diver, but I'd far outswum the other contestants.

I moved into Lower 6th, after my GCEs, still not knowing what to do with my life and hoping perhaps that Jim and I might get married, which would save me from following a career. But Jim never mentioned marriage. I had seven 'O' levels and opted to study maths, geography and art at 'A' level. However, this combination of subjects wouldn't fit into the curriculum, so I was only able to do pure maths, which I hated. So I dropped maths altogether, and studied for two more 'O' levels.

Daily, I'd pass a group of small children from a nearby children's home on their way to St Anne's school. One little boy, Graham, looked a sorry sight with his runny nose and inadequate winter clothing. I began knitting hats, and mittens for him and the others, considering that I'd quite like to work in a children's home when I left school. So, keeping this in mind, I continued my studies.

CHAPTER 11

Teen Years

Fran aged 13

Weekends were family time. In our first few years in Grantham, Johanna and I often went to the Granada cinema on a Saturday afternoon, whatever films were on – anything from a cowboy film to a 'Carry On'. Back then, we had three films: the supporting film, followed by Pathé Pictorial, which was a documentary, then the main film. We certainly got our money's worth then. Nowadays you have to endure the gut-rumbling volume of noise, plus half an hour of flashing, epileptic-inducing adverts that drive you mad, even before your one and only film begins.

In those early days, Mum, Dad, Helen and I would catch a bus to Old Somerby on Saturday evenings, where Mum, Dad and other relatives who wished to join in played Solo (a card game) with Grandma and Granddad. Sometimes we'd have a sandwich or a piece of homemade cake before playing began. Grandma always cut her loaf horizontally *after* she'd buttered it, unlike most people who slice downwards then butter it. We'd have cheese sandwiches, while Grandma preferred calf's-foot jelly. I didn't even want to try that.

Meanwhile, Helen and I would sit knitting on the settee, or the armchair tucked into the fireplace alcove. For a break, we'd scan Jimmy's books on the shelves above. Cousin Jimmy was studying law and living with our grandparents at that time. His books included some on cases of murder and incest, and these were very informative. The card players had no idea what was avidly absorbing us. Usually though, with the droning voices in the room, I'd eventually fall asleep, to be rudely awakened to get my coat on, ready to dash for the bus. It could be very bleak, standing at the bus stop in all weathers, listening for the distant rumble of the bus as it came over the hill from Boothby Pagnall.

Before we had TV, we'd catch an evening bus to Somerby in the week, to watch 'Quatermass' on Uncle Jim and Auntie Nellie's TV. They were living in School Lane, which connects the 'bottom end' of the village to the 'top end.'

Now, at the bus stop, we'd be shivering from fear rather than cold, after watching all those scary scenes.

At thirteen I made my first garment on the sewing machine, a straight winter skirt with a pleat at the back. Mum had given me her old flared skirt of tweed 'dog-tooth' check in fawn and tan, with enough material to cut out the pattern. I lined the skirt with a slippery satin. It was a great success and I began to look more grown-up.

In spite of Dad running the post office and having an RAF pension, Mum teaching, and then two lodgers bringing in revenue, we never seemed to have much spare money. From the market, I'd buy jeans for 10 shillings and shoes for £1, out of my pocket money of 10 shillings a week, with minor increases through the years. Helen and I made our summer dresses with cloth off the market at half a crown a yard (25p now). I'd buy long cardigans (Marks and Spencer seconds) going cheap on another stall, which I liked wearing over a white T-shirt with my rolled-up jeans. With Mum occasionally buying second-hand clothes from Mrs Catlin, previously worn by Elizabeth, I was provided with enough to get by, but not necessarily of my choosing.

Circular skirts were fashionable during the early 'Rock and Roll craze; they twirled out when you spun round to show off frilly knickers. We began making frugal dirndl skirts; simple tubes with two rows of elastic in the waist, and a border or two of bric-brac braiding above the hem, making them look 'folky'. Then gored skirts came back into fashion (just like the one of Mum's that I'd cut up

– but shorter) where several flared panels were machined together. They didn't even need a waistband, just a zip up the side.

Vivienne was really helpful. She showed me how to tackle difficult patterns with facings. Soon I became quite confident; so much so that I made two dresses for a friend of my mother, after she'd recommended me. This was a bad deal. The material was slippery and had to be run through the machine with layers of tissue paper on top, to make sure it stitched properly. A right pain – and so time consuming. I didn't benefit from the money I earned.

Mum continued going to Mrs Pacey's after we'd moved to Grantham. Now she was offering to take me for a more grown-up hairstyle. I'd worn my hair in a ponytail since going to High School. Now it was cut to shoulder length and curled. But three days later, when the waves had gone straight, I didn't like it at all. I returned from school on the third day and sat before Mum's triple-mirrored dressing table to cut my hair to a different style. Dena was a trainee hairdresser and I'd watched how she'd cut Jane's hair.

I began around 4.30pm. Mum came looking for me after 9pm – it seemed I hadn't been missed until then! By now I had an urchin cut – very short indeed; in fact very similar to the way Jane's hair had been cut. The next day, at Miss Selby's, all the mothers said how it suited me, so I've cut my own hair ever since, apart from on half a dozen special occasions. Part of the reason was that I found it too embarrassing to sit at the hairdresser's with my blushing face reflected in the brightly lit mirrors for all to see. Another reason was, of course, that it was cheaper.

At home, Helen and I regularly listened to Radio Luxembourg, to the quarter of an hour slot with 'Elvis versus Cliff Richard,' which we never missed. We were now finding common threads of interest. Mum and Dad had bought the three of us a 'Dansette' record player, but as Richard was hardly ever home, it was just Helen and I who played it. The first record I bought was a 78rpm, 'To Know Him is to Love Him' by the 'Teddy Bears', although my favourite singer became Brooke Benton. But I loved most recordings from the late 50s and early 60s. Helen had a penchant for Johnny Mathis and Cliff Richard.

I was thirteen when Helen asked if I'd like to go with her to see Emile Ford at the Granada. We thought it was a fantastic performance and afterwards we went round the back of the cinema to catch him leaving, hoping for his autograph. A single policeman stood in front of the door to his dressing room, barring the way to us excited, jostling teenage girls. Helen wasn't prepared to argue with a policeman, but I was. Together with a tall girl, who happened to be Josephine Bailey, we shoved and pleaded, eventually pushing behind him and rushing through the door. Up the flight of concrete stairs we raced, only to find his dressing room empty. Emile Ford and the Checkmates had left by the front entrance. The policeman must have known.

Helen got me interested in choosing pin-ups to put on the wall by my bed. Each week she bought the 'Picture-Goer' magazine, often ordering photos from it. I can't remember all of the five I chose, but my favourite was Richard Todd. There was also Tab Hunter and 'Sabu' the elephant boy. In later years, Richard Todd came to live at Great Ponton.

We needed to earn money in the holidays, for the extras we wanted – not just clothes but also records to play on the Dansette. Miss Brabazon knew an Irish man from her church, Bill Green, who organised gangs of women for work on the land. We got in touch, and so it was that we began our first paid job. Together with Helen, her schoolfriend Jane Chesney and Christine Proffitt, we caught a bus on St. Catherine's Road at 8am, opposite the day nursery, where working mums left their children for the day. What an eye-opener! We stepped aboard to find it filled with smoking, cackling women, wearing scarves on their heads like Hilda Ogden of 'Coronation Street.' They seemed so coarse – swearing and coughing.

In the smelly old bus we travelled to a farm at Donnington, in the fens. We were going cauliflower packing. Everyone worked in pairs, packing only the most perfectly white cauliflowers into wooden crates, first cutting off the outer leaves and throwing them onto a conveyor belt. As Christine and I were only fourteen, and not considered capable of packing cauliflowers properly, we were put on the end of the conveyor belt, gathering up discarded leaves and cauliflowers to throw into a huge bin. Luckily we were young and supple enough, for it was a strenuous task, leaning low over the conveyor belt, scooping up armfuls of smelly leaves all day. One day, looking forward to our break, I asked the passing foreman, "Have you got the time Charlie?" "Yis dook, if you've got the inclination," was his provocative answer.

The following year I went potato picking, alone. Back then we had to fill hundredweight hessian sacks, tie the tops with strong metal ties, then hoist them off the scales and drag them a few yards down the field to stack them. We'd stand astride the newly turned row of potatoes, and with bent backs, throw them into baskets between our legs. When full, we'd empty them onto a riddle and shake them. The little 'pig potatoes' fell through, so they didn't go into the sacks. The lady picking in front of me kept helping me to finish my stretch. I couldn't keep up. She was Dot Short, whose two daughters had been at the National School with me. Patsy, her eldest, always walked on tiptoe as she couldn't put her heels to the ground. In spite of this she was always smiling – like her Mum.

At sixteen, I went bulb picking; tulip bulbs grown in a vast field. One day a small plane sprayed the adjacent field with an insecticide called Messistox. The wind blew it all over our field. Goodness knows what it did to our lungs.

The tractor driver, Jackie, a good-looking lad with blue eyes and jet-black hair, was, apparently, the youngest of twenty-two children. His father had had eleven children with his first wife, who subsequently died, and eleven more with his second wife. On the two days that Jackie was off sick, I volunteered to drive the tractor. I'd watched what he did. I'd been bulb picking in my bare feet (a trendy thing to do in those 'hippy' days), so I drove the tractor likewise. I kept the plough in a nice straight line until it reached the end of the row, by which time the tractor would be almost on the edge of the dyke. Then, making a sharp turn by pressing a pedal behind the large wheel, I'd continue back down the next row. I shudder now, thinking how near I was to the deep dyke; turning the tractor on the edge of the ditch, with no roll bars to protect me, had it rolled over.

Dad was about to re-carpet the landing that summer. Near the top of the stairs was a long low cupboard stuffed with books. This was placed diagonally across our bedroom as a temporary measure until the new carpet was fitted.

I felt uneasy, getting into bed that night. Helen was away, but I felt a presence in the room as I stared into the darkness. Suddenly one of the cupboard doors popped open and I froze, shutting my eyes tightly, scared stiff. I agonised for ages, then reasoned that the books might have been pressing against the door. The little ball catch could have popped open under pressure. So, believing this to be the case, I relaxed.

Then minutes later, the door clicked shut again. Now I was truly frightened, lying tense with fear for ages. Eventually I told myself to 'get a grip' and get some sleep – I couldn't stay in this stiff mode all night. As I turned over to settle down, a deep, gruff, yet kindly voice by my pillow, said "goodnight," and I automatically replied "goodnight," then went rigid. I lay awake for the rest of the night, stiff as a dead body, petrified. I was dying for a wee but didn't dare get out of bed until daylight. It was the worst night ever.

The last occasion I worked on the land was my ninth. Charlie had told us that the first ten years on the land are the worst (I didn't quite reach that milestone). We were to be picked up at Cherry Orchard. Patsy Short and her younger sister Dawn would be going and said I could leave my bike at their house.

I was early, so they asked me in. I was so shocked to see how little they had in their living room: a bare table, a chair and a pram. The walls had been whitewashed and the children's clothes were in neat piles on the shelves, either side of the fireplace. Their pale little brother took his pile and dressed himself, then Patsy sent him to the shops for cornflakes and milk for his breakfast. I knew their mother Dot had recently had another baby, but didn't know her whereabouts. I felt guilty, seeing how little they had compared to us.

The following Sunday, we were invited to a fête at Little Ponton Hall. Helen was at college by now, so it was just my parents and myself. I hurriedly shortened a dress that had been Helen's; tiny flowers on a white background, like a 'Laura Ashley' fabric. With red bric-brac braiding around the square neckline and hem, it looked really pretty.

After the fete, we enjoyed playing croquet with the Turnors in the early evening sunshine. But as we drove home, my thoughts turned to the Short family, and all the other women who worked in gangs for most of the year.

When they got home, they'd have cooking, cleaning and mending to do. When I got home, I'd collapse on the settee, exhausted, waiting for Mum to cook the tea – and I only worked for a few weeks each summer. I'd met some tough women who worked their socks off to provide for their children. I had a great respect for them now.

At eighteen, Christine and I rented a stall on the market, to make some money before Christmas. Unfortunately, we couldn't rent one until Christmas Eve, which fell on a Saturday.

Christine had painted large oil paintings while I'd made craft items. After producing twenty scraperboard pictures of plants, Dad showed me how to frame them in his workshop, using sharp tools and fine tacks. (He was always enthusiastic. It was he who put up the Christmas decorations and he who wrote the cards.) Meanwhile I knitted hat and mitten combinations, made tubular leather pencil cases with zips, shoulder bags with appliqué patterns and fancy cushion covers. From the autumn leaves I'd pressed, I made large framed, pressed leaf pictures on stained hardboard, having learnt this technique using jelly-varnish.

On the day, we arrived early to set up our stall – and oh, the interest shown by so many people. "If only you'd been here a few weeks ago," they said. "We've bought all our presents now." And that was the tone throughout the day. By evening time Christine had sold only one painting and I about £13 worth of my stuff. All that effort!

When I brought my leftovers home, relatives and

neighbours snapped them up like vultures. It was gutting. I learned that 'craft' items don't make the money they deserve.

CHAPTER 12

The Chosen One

Jim.

Following my flowering into womanhood two days after my thirteenth birthday, my hormones changed me from tomboy to mad about boys in a matter of weeks. This 'surprise' happened on a Saturday morning, and I carried on as near to normal, cycling to market for Mum for some Lincolnshire sausages.

But after finishing our sausage dinner, my secret could be kept no longer. I found Mum alone in the kitchen and confessed what was happening, like a naughty child.

"Oh" she said, "I thought it wouldn't be long. You've been complaining about backache for the last few weeks." *Thanks, I thought, you might have warned me.*

After my transformation, I seemed fixated on boys. I made a list of all the lads in the neighbourhood, looking for that tall, dark and handsome one who is supposed to be every girl's idol, but only coming across one who fitted the bill. He seemed rather aloof and serious. Anyway, I wrote him a note to ask if he'd like to go out with me, then chickened out and didn't send it. I'd listed a few other local lads who were not tall dark and handsome but not bad, either. Amongst them was John Reynolds, the boy next door (joined onto the side of us); not bad looking but seeming more interested in scouting than girls. There was also Jim Adams from back along Harrowby Road, near the corner with Granville Street, and his mate Johnny Lyons from Bridge End Road.

On Mischievous Night, November 4th, Janine and I decided to go out 'mischief-making.' (Janine now lived nearby on Harrowby Road, after the family had moved back to Grantham). We were acting like rebellious teenagers, even though Janine wasn't a teenager, yet. It would be a laugh.

So, in the darkness of Cecil Street, we tied two front door handles together with string, knocked on both doors then ran and hid. Well, neither door was answered – nobody heard our knocking. So further up the street we repeated our trick, banging a little louder this time. Then off we ran, up St Anne's Street and onto Harrowby Road, laughing as we imagined two irate householders trying to open their doors. We continued round the block, and as we came down Granville Street, Jim and Johnny, two of the boys on my list, were walking up the road. They smiled as they passed; Johnny's smile was a wide, leery grin. We walked round the block again, passing them in almost the same place. What a coincidence! This time we said hello. Wow! This was really something! We repeated our round-the-block walk, wondering where we'd pass next. This time it was outside the chip shop in Cecil Street. Both pairs of us grinned and chuckled, as if it was another unexpected coincidence. But time was getting on now, so we headed home.

That Jim wasn't bad looking, I mused, even though he wasn't like the image I'd had in mind – he was blond and blue-eyed, with slightly slanting eyes, in a Scandinavian sort of way. Then I heard that Johnny actually wanted to go out with me, while Jim confessed, many moons later, that he'd always wanted to go out with Elaine – he loved her dark looks.

In the next few weeks, I kept bumping into Jim, for he only lived thirteen doors away. I'd round the corner into draughty Granville Street, to find him flying his balsa-wood aeroplanes in the middle of the road, or I'd bump into him as he came out of Bush's shop. Fate was making our paths cross and we'd exchange a few shy words. I was getting quite keen on him now, in fact, I was becoming besotted.

By the way, his first name was not really Jim, but a less

common name that I felt embarrassed to say. We were too shy to call each other by name anyway; so, he called me 'Dook' (a perfectly natural name to call someone in Grantham), while I called him 'Dooky'.

He gave me a Parker pen that Christmas of 1957 (his mother's suggestion). I still cherish it. However, when my parents became aware of our friendship, they forbade me to see him. I was only thirteen anyway. But Dad didn't like Jim. He was the boy who'd carved his initials in huge letters on our garage door in Cecil Street. Besides that, Jim's father was a factory worker while my father was a Squadron Leader. *My* father wasn't going to allow *his* daughter to go out with the likes of the Adamses. The battle had begun! But, for me, Jim was the one.

At the slightest opportunity, I'd call at his house on the way back from Bush's shop, in the dark before my father returned from work. I was only allowed out at night on Thursdays, when Helen and I had our piano lessons with Miss Johnson.

Jim left school the following summer, just before his fifteenth birthday, and began a brick-laying apprenticeship with Eatch's (a building firm whose yard was near Uncle Jim's garage). In the winter he finished work before dark and, if I could coincide with going to Bush's at the appropriate time, we could meet up in Cecil Street on his way home. I won't forget one wet night when I was fourteen, when he came round the corner from St Anne's Street wearing his black beret at a jaunty angle, like a Frenchman, and with his clothes covered in white dust. We disappeared down a dark passage in Cecil Street – where many front doors are down a joint passageway. After a passionate 'snog' in the darkness, we parted reluctantly, looking forward to our next secret 'rendezvous'. I arrived home wet through and nonchalantly hung my mackintosh on the hook outside the breakfast-room door.

The next morning my secret was out. My navy mac had dried with white handprints all over the breast area – not only proof that I was still seeing Jim, but what I was getting up to. Dad, who was steaming like a wild animal, longed to thrash some sense into me. Fortunately, he had to get to work and Mum to school, so nothing could be done right then.

Before Dad arrived home that evening, I'd locked myself in the dining room. No pleading from Mum would make me unlock the door. In the end they went to bed, while I spent a cold night on the carpet. I didn't come out until Dad had left for work next morning. I felt wretched at school all day.

When I arrived home in the afternoon, Mum was waiting there to march me down to the Welfare Office, "to get you put into a home," she said. Luckily, the office was closed, so we just came back and carried on as normal.

I needed to be more careful. Sometimes Jim and I met secretly in the dark alleyway that accessed garages at the backs of houses. One day, some spy informed my father and that evening he raced upstairs to my bedroom like a rampant bull, beating me over and over with a thick bamboo pole. When we played hockey at school next day, I blatantly showed off the blue-black stripes across the fronts of my thighs, which had risen into big lumps. Nowadays my father would have been reported, but nothing was said, and my thighs remained corrugated for years and years. But that didn't stop me. I became more determined.

While Mum marked her schoolbooks after tea, Dad usually fell asleep, doing his dockets in front of the telly. I'd casually leave the front room and hurry down to open the middle door quietly before rushing to the back door. Then I'd race down the garden in the dark, scraping the back gate open as quickly as possible, before charging along Cecil Street and up to Jim's house, where I'd arrive all breathless. His mum, Lottie, was always pleasant but his dad, Cliff, was gruff and hardly spoke. If nobody needed to wash in the kitchen sink, Jim and I could spend a little time in the kitchen together. He had lots of interests as well as flying planes. He collected birds' eggs, rare stamps and matchbox covers and also liked looking at insects through a microscope.

Life continued in the same vein. Every time I got found out, I'd put some distance between myself and Dad; running down the hall, racing upstairs two at a time and along the landing, to lock myself in the toilet until things had calmed down. Dad never caught me and one time he stopped at the bottom of the stairs, clutching his chest. Once, in the kitchen, he tried to hit me on the head with the poker, in a frenzied temper, but Mum and Miss Brabazon got between us, preventing him from finishing me off, perhaps. What an episode that was.

After these events, Dad would bring me a little treat next dinner-time, like a peace offering; often a packet of dried dates. He didn't say anything; just handed me the gift. I'd often reciprocate by digging up dandelion roots from the lawn with a kitchen knife. We knew that we didn't hate each other. In fact, I loved my father and there were plenty of good times as well.

It was Mum who made me feel bad. She was full of suspicion, looking for early signs of pregnancy, absolutely convinced that I was up to something, when in fact I was not. I didn't have a key, so I had to ring the bell whenever I came home from anywhere. Mum let me in, surveying me with sly suspicion and making me feel dreadful.

I was fifteen when it came to the point where I thought "She thinks I'm up to no good, so I may as well be" (I'd planned to save myself until I was married). But on a chosen day, Jim and I climbed through a broken fence into St Vincents wood (the Dam Buster's wood) looking for somewhere dry and secluded to lie down. I was wearing a beige reversible mac that Auntie Freda had given me, when she'd last come over from America. Now I'd reversed it and was wearing a coat covered with large orange poppies. However, the bottom line was that we didn't succeed, and I came back through the fence *almost* as pure as when I'd gone in.

I had the bright idea that if we joined the local youth club, we'd be able to see more of each other. The club met on Sunday nights in St Anne's church hall, further down Harrowby Road, opposite the top of St Anne's Street. It was necessary to be confirmed first so, in preparation, we attended classes in St Anne's church. The church was opposite the top of Granville Street; brick-built with a black pitched-roof and an Anglo-Saxon bell on top. This rang with a monotonous tone that was only acceptable because it was ancient.

Then Jim discovered he needed first to be christened. He thought of changing his name, but didn't in the end. After the confirmation we joined the youth club, where Jim soon felt he didn't fit in; the others seemed rather posh to him. However, we weren't really interested in the club. Most Sunday evenings were spent outside in the dark, passionately embracing. Records were constantly being played upstairs. We heard 'True Love' by Grace Kelly and Bing Crosby so frequently that we called it 'Our Tune'.

One day I called at Jim's house to be met by two policemen who questioned me. Did I know where Jim had gone? He was missing. Well, I knew something bad had happened at his house – to the extent that he'd thrown the television out of the dining room window and had broken the railings down the stairs – after his father had shouted "You hate your mother, don't you? Well, she's not your mother, your mother's DEAD." Jim had been in a terrible state of shock when I'd last seen him. I knew he was planning to cycle off to look for his real father, although I didn't know he'd already left and didn't have a clue where he'd gone.

When Jim's Dad finally left for work, his Mum sat me down to tell me the family saga.

Lottie's mother, Lizzie Miller, had been in service to a wealthy Lincolnshire farmer when she was a girl. He'd made her pregnant. She'd kept her baby – a daughter named Ada. Then later she'd married and had more children, one of whom was Lottie.

Ada grew up and married Jim Graham, a cartoonist on a Glasgow newspaper. They set up home in the village of Worstead in Norfolk, having four children – Jim, Victor, Winifred and Enid. Winifred died at eighteen from leukaemia.

Enid, a pretty blonde blue-eyed girl, married Clifford Gore when she was eighteen. A year later, in 1943, she gave birth to a baby boy, and as was quite common in those days, she was confined to bed for three weeks. It was then that she died from thrombosis. Her husband was in army prison in France for stealing army blankets, so couldn't come home. But when he did, Ada and Jim wouldn't let him see his son. They didn't like him and wanted to keep baby Jim for themselves.

Meanwhile, Lottie (who was a generation younger than her sister Ada) married Cliff Adams, from Swansea. Cliff had run away to London at fifteen, to avoid going down the mines. There he'd trained to be a turner, before coming to work in Grantham. Cliff liked his beer, drinking many pints per night to sate his thirst after a hard day's work, which left Lottie short of money, often having to ask Mr Bush for credit to tide her over. Cliff sometimes thrashed her with his leather belt when he returned from the pub, but that didn't make him a disrespected member of the community. He was in fact the local Treasurer of the 'Buffs' - the Royal Antediluvian Order of Buffaloes, a benevolent society, similar to the Masons. On special occasions he wore a wonderful purple cloak with his grand chain of office hanging round his neck.

Lottie had been a ballroom dancer before her marriage, winning cups with her dancing partner. She continued dancing for a while after her marriage, before her son David was born. But sadly, David died from meningitis at ten months old. It was around this time that Enid died.

Meanwhile, the grandparents in Norfolk were struggling to cope with baby Jim. It didn't help matters that Jim Graham suffered from shell-shock. They sent a telegram to Lottie and Cliff Adams, begging them to fetch little Jim, knowing their son David had recently died.

Lottie and Cliff caught a train to Norfolk to fetch the baby. He was in a dirty state, and suffering from gastroenteritis. Furthermore, he wouldn't stop crying. But after a while he was well, although he didn't sleep at night.

Then a telegram arrived from Worstead, pleading for the baby to be brought back – they missed him so much. This was very distressing for Lottie, she told me, for she cared more for baby Jim than she had done for David, her son.

However, two weeks later they received a telegram begging them to fetch him back again.

This pattern of going back and forth from Worstead to Grantham and Grantham to Worstead went on for two and a half years, until Clifford Gore's sister came down from Wigan, demanding that either one couple or the other must adopt the baby. And so, Jim became an Adams. Poor distraught Ada, having lost two daughters and then her grandson, drowned herself in the water butt. Meanwhile, Lottie gave birth to another son, Richard, and the two boys grew up as brothers.

When Jim was four, Cliff took him to visit his relatives in Norfolk. From her front-room window, Lottie saw them returning up the road, and noticed that Jim's head kept twitching. He'd acquired a nervous tic, probably due to revisiting the place of his early trauma. This lasted for years. A psychiatrist would place him in a room full of coal then observe him through one-way glass!

After almost a week, Jim returned. He'd cycled to Norfolk to seek out his real father, not knowing that he came from Wigan. He told me how cold and hungry he'd been, and how he'd collapsed on a grass verge one rainy night, too tired to carry on.

Jim had packed up his apprenticeship, having lost the nerve to climb the scaffolding. He just couldn't cope and was now unemployed, living at home. This didn't help matters. His hard-working father cycled home every dinnertime, making time to check the hens on his allotment, before cycling back to work. The allotments, behind the houses opposite us on Harrowby Road, covered a vast area, extending from behind the church hall to behind the church, and stretching back to Hall's Hill. Cliff had two large plots and grew so much that Lottie could barely cope. She salted large sweet-jars of runner beans and pickled onions and bottled whatever she could. There were always piles of fresh produce on the kitchen floor. The arrival of freezers several years later became her saving grace.

The cemetery abutted the allotments behind the church, and was equally vast, with a long low wall running along the front of it, along Harrowby Road. There were grand wrought iron gates at the far end, while in front of this wall grew a row of horse chestnut trees on a wide roadside grass verge. It was a pleasant aspect for the people living opposite.

In spite of my father's objections, I'd vowed to stick by Jim, to try to bring happiness into his troubled life. My constant pre-occupation with him helped to deflect my obsessive thoughts of blushing. With Jim, I could cope.

Jim had never been into our house. Now, out of spite, his father forbade me to enter their house. But where could we go? At sixteen, I was very occasionally allowed out at night with Christine, since Auntie Kath had told my father how unreasonable he was being. But Mum's suspicious scrutiny was even more intense. We'd lost interest in the youth club, as we'd never integrated. Now, when we had the chance, we might clamber over the cemetery wall in the dark, to share a little passion amongst the gravestones. It wasn't very romantic and I often wondered if dead folk were turning in their graves, or their spirits frowning on us from above.

We would go for walks up Hall's Hill, with Jim often taking his Observer book of beetles and sometimes his guitar, which he was learning to play. Once, a whole herd of curious cows surrounded us in a field, huffing warm air down the backs of our necks as Jim serenaded me!

The following winter, with nowhere else available, we'd go to the pub; not the Lord Harrowby at the bottom of Granville Street, which Jim's father frequented, but the Royal Oak, down Stuart Street, the next street down from St Anne's Street. We'd scrape together enough money for one drink each, which we made last all night.

In those early days, we'd happily play crib with the chaps in the saloon. I don't remember any rowdiness. Most men were past middle age, tired from a day's work and just there for the quiet company.

Then things started going wrong in the Royal Oak. Sometimes Pat, the landlady, had a black eye. On one occasion, her partner had pushed her down the stairs. How she kept going I don't know. The telly would suddenly go off as we sat watching, in the scruffy little lounge. Then while Pat searched for a shilling, the lights would go out, then the gas fire. In the dark she'd be scrabbling for coins for all three meters, to get everything up and running again. Fewer and fewer patrons came to the pub now, until it reached the point where Pat would send us to the Lord Harrowby with money and a basket, to buy bottles for her pub. It closed soon after.

One evening Jim rang our front door bell. I don't know why. My father answered and they almost came to blows when Jim pulled Dad's tie out. But surprisingly, they had a long conversation on the front doorstep. As a consequence, my father persuaded Jim to join the Army. Soon he was doing six weeks of intensive training in Hampshire, which he quite enjoyed. He became extremely fit. When he qualified to be in the REME I wore a little REME badge on my school tie. I remember at school, some visiting male official asking me what all my stripes, stars and badges represented on my tie, and having to explain the badge.

Jim began to dislike army life – the unfairness, the bullying and the downright disrespectful way that the less able soldiers were treated and spoken to. Also, he didn't like being regimented. He was too much of an individual. So he paid the price and bought himself out. However, being in such a fine state of fitness, he joined the local amateur wrestling club in Grantham. He almost qualified for the British quarterfinals, developing a marvellous physique, of which he was so proud.

Charlie Holmes, a well-muscled weightlifter Jim knew from those days, was a window cleaner. One hot summer's day, after he'd cleaned our windows, I paid him at the front door. I was seventeen, and wearing a pair of short shorts. Some time later, on my way to Bush's shop, I passed Charlie's ladder on Granville Street. "Just a minute" he called and came running down the ladder. "I've been thinking – how

would you like to enter the Miss Midlands competition?"
How chuffed I felt as I walked down the street. Did I look
that good?

When I told Jim that evening, he laughed out loud.
"It's not a beauty contest," he said, "it's a weight-lifting
competition." I can't tell you how deflated I felt! Charlie
died soon after. He fell from his ladder – only a few rungs
up, but he was found to have a thin skull.

The Labour Exchange arranged for Jim to go on a
six-month mechanics' course at a Government Training
Centre in Sheffield. He bought a motorbike and off he
went, spending the week in digs. That first weekend was
spent mainly with Jim revising the workings of carburettors.
We sat on a bench in Dysart Park where he explained all
the diagrams of carburettors in detail. The following week
it was tappets and pistons. At the end of six months, he was
pretty clued-up with the workings of combustible engines,
as was I! He'd passed his driving test in Sheffield and bought
a small black 100E Ford.

With his newly acquired skills, Jim began working in
a garage, but he felt awkward with the young mechanics
there, on day release to college each week, so he found
a job with the Automobile Association. He'd seen AA
men on motorbike and sidecar combinations, helping
holidaymakers whose car radiators had boiled over. It
seemed a good number. But he was put straight onto night
patrol on the A1, south of Grantham. On his third night,
he had to rewire the rear lights of a lorry trailer, in pitch

darkness and pouring rain. Jim felt he was being 'used' and gave in his notice the following morning. He was really disillusioned now. He'd tried the Army; he'd tried mechanics. Next, he got a job as a vegetable cook up at Spittlegate, which was now a WRAF camp.

By now, Jim had progressed so well with his guitar playing that he was invited to play rhythm guitar in the Concords, a local pop group. Groups like this were popping up all over the place. Brian 'Liquorice' Locking, from the Shadows, had cut his teeth in a skiffle group at the Lord Harrowby in Granville Street. He lived opposite the cemetery on Harrowby Road. Cousin Trevor knew all these up-and-coming musicians.

Now Jim spent Saturday nights playing in surrounding venues. I never got to see the Concords perform as they travelled in a van that was choc-a-bloc with lads and equipment; no room for girlfriends. But I witnessed his practising and harmonies and knew all the songs.

Jim had several cars as time went by, the most memorable being a Wolseley 680 (once used by the police), with a long bonnet and split windscreen. It was so spacious, like driving a barge, and had been cheap because it only did eight miles to the gallon around town. We'd be forever taking empty lemonade bottles back to scrape together enough money for a gallon of petrol. Finally, Jim exchanged it for a motorbike and sidecar, an old M20, ex-army bike with stiff suspension. We had great fun with that. For my 21st birthday treat, Jim took me to motorbike and sidecar racing at Cadwell

Park. It was so exciting, seeing the bikers hanging over the sidecars as they hared round bends, barely an inch off the ground. With the lovely sandwiches that Jim had made and the pineapple tarts and cakes that were my contribution, we had a great day out.

In my late teens I began going to Communion early on Sunday mornings – I was praying that I could marry Jim and make him happy. The sparse congregation consisted mainly of middle-aged to elderly 'spinsters of this parish.' I had great belief in God then. Only He could help me!

One day we went to see my Grandma. She enjoyed chatting to Jim, especially when she realised she'd known Lizzie Miller in her youth. They'd lived in adjacent villages. I have a nagging suspicion that Grandma, who'd also been in service until she married, might have suffered a similar fate to Lizzie Miller; because, many years later, I was told she'd been eight months pregnant when she married Granddad. Had he rescued her?

Jim's Great Grandma, Lizzie, now came to live at Harrowby Road with them, as she was becoming frail. It seems odd that while she was Jim's great-grandmother, she was his brother Richard's grandma!

Meanwhile, the situation between Jim and his father got worse, with frequent rows. His mum, who was going through a difficult menopause, confided in me, saying she felt like a sponge, having to come between both sides of their arguments. I loved her to bits, as did Jim. She was a saint.

Now the Labour Exchange offered Jim a place on a woodworking course; another Government Training scheme, this time in Leicester. They were trying to help him, because of his difficulties at home. But Jim didn't leave home; he travelled daily to Leicester by motorbike. He'd hated his digs in Sheffield, so he didn't want a repeat.

He found he was very adept at woodwork, but now needed a job. The rows at home became so bad that in the early summer of 1967 his parents took out a court order, banning him from the house. The Labour Exchange offered him a job in Plymouth, at a firm called Pirelli's. Jim, supposing this to be a mechanic's job, because of the famous car tyres of that name, arrived in Plymouth under a great misapprehension. His new employment was as a grill chef with an Italian family. He'd been found accommodation; now all he needed to do was learn this new job.

In the meantime, I was at college in Nottingham, almost at the end of my final year. My plan was to join him in Plymouth, when I finished.

CHAPTER 13

Student Nurse Carrington

───◆◦✣◦◆───

Being in the 'A' stream at school meant most likely becoming a prefect in the Upper Sixth. Prefects had to take over a class if a teacher was called away. No way could I do that – to face a whole class of girls with my beacon-bright, perspiring face. Panic was welling inside me. I would have to leave and become a nursery nurse.

Mum said, "You can't throw away all those 'O' levels (I now had 9) to become a nursery nurse; why don't you take up proper nursing?" Elaine was training at Addenbrooks hospital in Cambridge. Mum had visions of me going to some big teaching hospital. That would get me away from Jim.

I didn't want to be a nurse, neither did I want to upset Mum – so, compromising, I secretly enrolled at Grantham Hospital. Not what Mum was hoping for, but what could she do? Therefore, without enthusiasm, I began training to be a State Registered Nurse in September 1962.

The first six weeks were in the Preliminary Training School (PTS). Of the dozen new recruits, half were West Indians. Of the two Sister Tutors, one was a man with an oscillating eye that looked up to the sky. He was very nice and taught the theory side of nursing. I didn't take to the female tutor at all.

Most evenings I'd either cycle home or go to see Jim, returning before lock-up time at 10.30pm. I hated my room because of cockroaches. In this oldest part of the hospital, I'd be crunching on them as I walked down the semi-lit corridors at night. They swarmed from a hole in the kitchen wall to cross the corridor into the maternity wing. On reaching the landing, I'd unlock my door and throw it wide-open, switch on the light, then stand aside. The cockroaches rushed out, away from the brightness, and I'd shove them towards the West Indians' door with my shoe, assuming they'd cope with them better than I could.

I dreaded switching off the light. The cockroaches might crawl up the legs of the bed to join me in the bedclothes. You see, I'd read about a girl in Sheffield, who'd had a bouffant hairstyle like Dusty Springfield (kept in place for several weeks without combing). A cockroach got into her hair and ate through her skull, which killed her. We didn't know about 'fake news' then, so I don't know if this was true or not. It frightened me nevertheless. Then one morning I discovered two huge cockroaches hiding in the toe of one shoe.

During an 'invalid cookery' lesson, I asked the head cook who was teaching us if he knew that cockroaches were swarming out of the kitchen every night. He replied "Dook, if yow knowzuva kitchen as ode as this un that en't gottenney, yow coom un tell mi." So, he was obviously aware of the problem!

We pre-student nurses were allotted to one ward or another for part of the day, performing basic duties. I was on Medical Ward. I'd far rather have been on an Orthopaedic Ward; you could see what patients' problems were. However, I fulfilled my duties, cleaning the mouths of patients who weren't eating much, using bicarbonate of soda and water mixed in a saucer. Using cotton buds dipped in my mixture, I carefully removed the gunge that formed in their mouths. When a sweet old lady died, I had awful nightmares of her body being consumed by worms. I'd never encountered death and wondered if I was cut out to become a nurse.

We marvelled at the contents of preserved things in jars that lined the schoolroom shelves, including a 22foot tapeworm, an inside-out stomach lined with undissolved aspirins and a cancerous breast. They made me shudder.

One day, when the tutor was called away, we began larking about. Nurse Haydon had picked up a large spider and was coming towards me, glaring with 'voodoo-like' eyes. In mock terror, I ran away. As I glanced round to see how close she was, I slipped on the polished floor, falling flat on my stomach, and leaving my left leg round the other way. Getting up off the floor was excruciating. What had I done to my poor knee?

We went on educational visits which involved much standing about. One was to a dairy and another to some waterworks. I stood around, changing from one foot to the other to ease the pain in my knee. It was hard to concentrate. I tried to keep it low key and didn't want a fuss. But the cook noticed how much it bothered me, and knowing that the orthopaedic surgeon, Mr Jackson, was holding a clinic that afternoon, he arranged for me to see him.

It turned out that my cartilage was torn and I'd need an operation, but the attendant Sister cheerfully assured me I'd be home in no time at all, right as rain. Footballers were soon playing football again, after this operation. Before my departure, I gathered my belongings and asked the West Indians if they'd look after my china pony and dog from the mantelpiece, and my double Everly Brothers LP that my brother had given me. That night I was whisked by ambulance to Harlow Wood, an orthopaedic hospital between 'The Dukeries' and Mansfield, an ex-army barracks in woods in the middle of nowhere.

My bed was halfway down a long ward, with 16 beds on each side. During the night, some old lady shouted a bloodcurdling "Murder!" while another screamed in a dream. It was awful.

I was to have a 'manipulation' the next day, to see if it would negate the need for an operation. But the manipulation didn't work. My cartilage was split right round and had shot across the joint. I spent another sleepless night in pain. Mr Jackson would operate on Monday.

That weekend I had no visitors. It was a long way to come and everyone thought I'd be home in a jiffy after this minor operation. I acquainted myself with my neighbours. On my right was a pretty young French woman, Lillian. She'd begun to grow a beard. Beyond her was Brenda, sixteen, from Derby. Both were having reformative operations, to remedy the damage caused by polio. There were two permanent patients opposite me, Joan and Mary, both suffering from multiple sclerosis and overweight. Mary was forever eating 'Chipples', the smell of which I came to despise.

The lovely Ward Sister was young Sister Bebb. She remembered Aunty Laura having her bunions done, and Aunty Beat, who just missed out on the new technology of hip replacements, having a steel plate fitted. Afterwards, she could only sit on the edge of a dining chair with her leg down at an angle; unable to enjoy a comfy chair. She'd hurt her hip doing gymnastics at school.

The following Monday my meniscectomy was performed. When I came round, I found a lovely bouquet of flowers on my locker – a present from Grantham Hospital. That was kind. (I later received a small sum of money for compensation for my accident at work!)

Mr Jackson made his rounds the following Thursday, with his entourage of trainee doctors and nurses. He asked me to lift up my leg. (Since my operation any movement had been excruciating). So, feeling impatient, he lifted my leg high and let go. I screamed as the leg crashed back onto the bed. It was agonising.

After that episode I developed a fluctuating temperature, going from high to below normal several times a day. Although I couldn't see my charts, I was secretly taking my temperature, the thermometer being behind me on the wall. I was encouraged to drink plenty of orange juice from the jug on my locker and could have a bedpan at any time. But the nurses seldom pulled the curtains; there wasn't much privacy.

Nights were purgatory. I couldn't sleep a wink, hearing the man stoking the boiler every night and seeing his shadowy figure at the bottom of my bed. An old lady would scream, while others shouted out "Nurse!"

One night, Leah, the victim of a serious road accident, was brought in. A lorry had slammed into her 'Initial Towel' van as she'd made a right turn. She shook continuously; white as a sheet. It was unnerving being just a few beds away, with constant nursing around her. Luckily, she survived. She was mother to three small children.

When Sister Bebb brought round the morning post, I'd feign sleep. I couldn't even be bothered to talk to her. I was washed out. Soon I was being tested for all sorts of illnesses – TB, polio etc. They kept taking blood, but nothing was diagnosed, except that my knee capsule was full of blood. It needed aspirating. For this, I was wheeled to some lesser theatre, along the ramps and walkways of this sprawling hospital, with awnings to keep off the rain. After a local anaesthetic, the young Indian doctor proceeded. I winced as he thrust the huge needle deep behind my knee. This alarmed him. Hadn't the 'local' taken? I explained that I was watching a reflection of the procedure on the shiny lampshade above my head! It was a reflex reaction. He was visibly relieved.

So far, I'd only seen Mum and Dad for just half an hour. The husband of Mum's fellow teacher was a pastor. They were praying for me in his church. Blimey!

Halfway through my third week, I attempted to walk on crutches. I felt it would be a long haul. Meanwhile the lovely Occupational Therapist got me making a black and white stuffed cat. It turned out really well, so I began another. It was good to be distracted and busy. Lillian and Brenda both wanted to make one, as did a few others nearby. Our area became like a pre-Christmas toy factory and I finished them all off – stuffing legs, sewing on eyes and putting in whiskers.

I didn't need a bedpan now – I was 'painfully' mobile. I encountered Joan in the toilets, sitting in her wheelchair, washing her hands. "Pet," she said, "would you pull my pants up for me." Then "Thanks Pet; I'll do the same for you one day!"

I'd been on penicillin for some time, and now I was obviously allergic to it. Angry red circles covered my palms, knees and elbows; like intensely itchy nettle-stings. I hadn't slept for three weeks and didn't feel hungry either.

In the third week, Jim cycled to see me; I was impressed. He'd brought me a big bar of whole-nut chocolate, but I gave it back to him for his long journey home, making my inmates chuckle. Then Pat Bowser visited me. What a star. She'd caught numerous buses to reach this Godforsaken hospital, and stayed for the whole of visiting time.

During my final days, I was taken into the swimming pool for exercises. What an awkward lump I'd become after all that swimming ability! My athletic days would be a thing of the past.

After a month, I could go home. Mum, Dad and Auntie Beat fetched me, arriving at 8 o'clock at night. I was tired. Another hour and I'd have been settling down for the night. I was scared to be going home, traumatised and already institutionalised. My hands hurt and itched incessantly. I could hardly be bothered to talk as I hunkered into the corner of the back seat in the dark, constantly scratching my hands.

I felt like a lodger, sleeping in my own bed. When I saw my reflection in the mirror next morning I was flabbergasted. I'd lost 2 stones and those big thighs were gone, in fact my left thigh looked wasted – I could get hold of the bone.

Now came a month of physiotherapy at Grantham Hospital. I made the daily two-mile trek, slowly limping all the way; past the High School, then on past the Boys' Central School, just as the boys were coming out en masse, which was excruciatingly embarrassing. The only alternative was to cycle there – which was a real challenge. I could barely bend my knee.

However, the challenge was well worth it; not only did it

save much embarrassment but it aided my mobility in the process. At first, my progress was more of a balancing act. Standing on the pedals, I could push down and back only a couple of inches; then after a few days, a bit further. Finally, I could sit on the seat to do this.

The physiotherapy itself was rather 'heavy', to say the least. One of the two physiotherapists (both well-built Scotsmen) would lay his whole weight across my buttocks as I lay face down, while the other grasped my ankle, pulling and twisting my leg. It seemed most unconventional to me – but what did I know? My personal triumph was when I turned the pedals in a complete circle.

Just days before Christmas, I resumed work. My PTS group had moved on, and I would be starting with a new group in the New Year. When my belongings were returned, my china pony's leg was broken and both LPs were cracked across the middle. Nurse Sinclair, who handed them back, wasn't unduly concerned; I felt really hurt. Was this done deliberately perhaps, out of jealousy of my comfy status, or had there really been three accidents? I'd thought they were my friends.

I was put on Private Ward, another old part of the building, and was surprised to find there a second-year student I knew, a pretty Jamaican. She had sepsis from a back street abortion and was really poorly. I recall only one other patient, a man with shingles all over his head who was forever wandering about.

My new PTS began in January. Alarmingly, I wasn't

allowed to attend any lectures or classes that I'd already done. This disconnected me from my group and made me feel isolated.

Then it was back to Medical Ward with increased duties. Four heart attack patients shared one bay – all recently retired from the railways. Returning from an afternoon off, I'd be greeted with, "Oh here's our little ray of sunshine. Can I have a bedpan please nurse?" They'd been hanging on, because I always obliged. Whenever I stood taking their temperature and pulses for a whole minute, I'd blush. They were all looking at me. Anyway, I found the wards much too hot.

In February I developed shingles – just a small rectangle under my left breast. I was given a fortnight off work. Everyone said how painful shingles was; I must keep warm at home. But mine didn't bother me much, and I spent several cold snowy days in someone's shed on the allotments while Jim adjusted tappets on his motorbike, improving the performance of the engine. It was pretty cold, but at least we had time together.

After that I was put on the Children's Ward, more my sort of ward. The junior nurses carefully cleaned the wards, taking extra care in cleaning the wheels of beds and lockers, where germs most likely lingered. Thinking of contract cleaning today, where a wet mop might be swished under each bed, missing the slippers and the wheels, I'm not surprised by mass outbreaks of diseases.

Stupidly, I'd complained to Matron that I wasn't

practising what I'd been taught in PTS. The next thing I knew, I was injecting the bottoms of three tiny babies, mentally dividing their buttocks into four quadrants, to inject in the correct place. There were two three-year-old girls on the ward for ages – Christine, who was learning to walk and talk after having measles, and Pamela, with a muscle-wasting disease of the upper body. Her little face looked so old.

A young gipsy boy was brought in, screaming and squirming – absolutely traumatised and vomiting mouthfuls of phlegm. He had an ulcer on his back; a hole, which needed stuffing with medicated ribbon-gauze. I was given the task to bath him beforehand. What a performance that was. He was like a wild animal and tried his hardest to escape.

I was not happy with my life, eating in my room at night and just managing to have breakfasts in the refectory. I didn't seem to belong to either PTS group now, having spent so little time with the second group. I felt like a lost soul.

In this low state of resilience, I caught Asian flu, which was doing the rounds. At home, the doctor visited me regularly. I then made a big decision; I sent a letter to Nottingham Technical College, asking if I could complete my A level Art there. An affirmative letter came from the Art College further down the road. When I returned to work, I handed in a month's notice. The subtle punishment was night duty on the Maternity Ward.

Sharing a room with a nurse I didn't know and with the sun seeping through the red curtains, it was difficult to sleep in daytime. The twelve-hour night-shifts were tedious, if no births were taking place. The Sister read newspapers by a glowing coal fire while I stood in a cubby-hole, cutting lint into small squares, with my knee constantly aching. I was privileged, however, to help with seven births (if holding a leg is considered helping!) With newspapers covering the floor, and placentas wrapped in newspaper like fish and chips, it was quite basic.

I did my morning rounds, swabbing the tender parts of recently delivered women. On my trolley were two large metal jugs of warm water, one containing blue Rockall and the other pink carbolic. Sometimes a mother complained it was too hot, while others found it too cool. I tried to get it just right. It was more embarrassing if I knew the mother – like the new secretary from KGGS!

When the morning staff came on duty, they'd flip the continuously crying babies onto their stomachs, which usually shut them up. This practice has since being blamed for cot deaths.

So my unsuccessful nursing career came to an end after nine months. This had been the darkest part of my life. I attended an interview at the Fine Art department and was accepted. They preferred students who weren't straight out of school, they said.

That summer I spring-cleaned the house from top to bottom, compensating for my failure to stick to the nursing career. I had no savings. My pay had been £12 per month plus laundry and board.

CHAPTER 14

Art Student

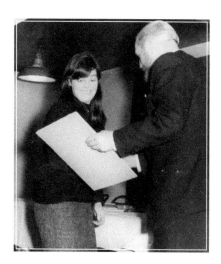

Fran receiving intermediate certificate at Nottingham College of Art.

The very first morning of college, I missed the train to Nottingham. I ran the mile back home in a panic, not sure what to do. But Dad came to the rescue, driving me to the edge of town where, to my surprise, he thumbed me a lift. It was a beautiful early September day in 1963 and I was wearing a long cardigan over a short shift dress. However, Nottingham was clothed in thick fog when I arrived. It was freezing. From where I was dropped off, near Trent Bridge, I had no clue how to reach the College of Art on Waverly

Street. However, two bus journeys later, plus much help from passers-by, I arrived on time. Dad always said, "You'll never get lost as long as you have a tongue in your head."

I was in my element, partaking in all manner of art forms; nevertheless, I couldn't shake off my continuing problem of blushing. Although I journeyed on the train with Johanna, who worked in Boot's laboratories, my panic rose as the train began to fill. A group of ex-Brownies from Bottesford regularly sat on a long facing seat nearby. I wasn't sure if they recognised me but I knew them. As they laughed and joked throughout the journey, I'd sit red-faced and miserable, looking out of the window, while still trying to hold a conversation with Johanna. She must have felt embarrassed just sitting next to me.

At lunch times, in bad weather, I'd eat my sandwiches, seated on the cloakroom floor with a few others. It was here that I became friends with Jan Wright from my class, who couldn't face eating in the refectory either.

Soon I'd completed my first term. It was Christmas and I was penniless; desperate to earn some money. What I did do moved me to write this poem.

Turkey Plucking

First term at college, last day of term;
Christmas! Absolutely broke.
Must get a job but where, when?
It's ok in summer, there's work on the land;
But winter's no joke.

I call on the Ganger to see what's about.
"Not much now; bit late.
Sadie's gang might take you on;
It's turkey plucking.
Lorry leaves at eight."

Mustn't miss it, mustn't be late.
Running - gasping in bitter cold air.
Lorry's still waiting, I climb aboard.
Women with fags; kids with dummies.
They don't care.

I care. I go half-heartedly.
It's the money; I just need the cash.
Put up with it girl; try anything once.
The turkeys will be dead.
Just give it a bash.

The barn is bare except for bales of straw.
"Choose yer bale – that's yer seat."
I hear turkeys next door – **live** turkeys.
What? They haven't killed them yet;
This Christmas meat!

"Ge te the counta. Fetch wun."
I go with trepidation.
They catch mine and force it in a funnel;
Then break its neck and lob it in my arms.
A dire sensation!

"De the wings fust. Plook it whal it's warm."
It lurches on my lap.
Is it dead? Are you sure it's dead?
What am I doing here? Why did I come?
I think I'm in a trap.

"Yer won't plook it when it's cald."
I try. I persevere.
Tough feathers. Sore hands. Sore heart.
Keep going girl - nearly there.
Oh what am I doing here?

"Tek it te the counta. Git anutha."
"Sorry miss, not good enough."
I bring it back and try to strip it better.
They're on their third – this is my first.
Mine's cold now and tough.

Cold feet. Cold hands. Cold noses.
Feathers everywhere.
Dummies lost – dummies found.
Cigarettes smouldering in wasted feathers.
Does anybody care?

Back to the killing counter once again,
Holding my nerves steady.
Keep going girl – you need the cash.
There are presents to buy and cards to send.
Oh, will I have it ready?

For four whole days I force myself,
Plucking breasts and legs and wings.
Come Christmas lunch my stomach churns.
"Sorry; can't eat that poor turkey Dad.
I'll just have pineapple rings."

And I was turkey plucking on the Belvoir Estate.

The following spring, my brother married Bettina in St Anne's church. She was a beautiful half-Indian girl he'd met while working for London Cementation. She'd come to Liverpool at thirteen with her two younger sisters and two brothers. Both their grandmothers had been Indian, while her grandfathers had been British officers. The whole family came down to meet us, bringing all the ingredients for a proper chicken curry. They were a warm and loving family and we jelled instantly.

It was a pretty wedding with five bridesmaids: two sisters from both sides, plus Bettina's best friend Betty, all dressed in long turquoise satin dresses, with stiff headbands of the same material. It snowed as we came out of church, but soon the sun reappeared. I saw Jim's Mum, and others, watching from their front-room windows.

Richard had been living on a small boat on the Grand Union canal, becoming friends with Roland 'Skid' Crow, who converted working barges into 'live-aboards' at Aylesbury Boat Basin. Richard went into partnership with Skid, but three weeks later Skid died from a heart attack, leaving Richard in charge.

Richard and Bettina moved into a flat in the Manor House, Princes Risborough (owned by Lord Carrington!) Their daughter Caroline was born on their first wedding anniversary.

The company could have been a success if customers had paid on time, but they didn't and it was eventually wound up. Luckily, Richard got a job back with Cementation, this time in Doncaster. While living there they decided to emigrate to Canada.

★ ★ ★

I wasn't sure which direction to take, after my year in Fine Art. Then I remembered how I'd loved drawing plans of the houses I fancied living in and how they might look inside. So it seemed an obvious choice. I'd take up Interior Design.

Mr Uttley, in charge of the department, was a large kindly man, with a smiley round face, twinkling blue eyes and a neat little moustache and beard. You couldn't help but warm to him. In fact, all the tutors were very personable and treated us as equals. There was a lovely atmosphere.

We shared a large well-lit room, with all three years. The third-year students at the top end, faced downwards. We had large solid desks for our drawing boards, with plenty of cupboard space underneath. There were eight in this first year. I was the only girl, relishing the privilege. I'd been amongst girls for far too long.

Notable in my year was stocky Costas Michaelides, a

Greek-Cypriot, a lovable hothead who once tried to open a stiff upper window with a brick, breaking the glass of course. We were a good mix. Nawzad, an Arab in the second year, was still struggling to look after himself. We had a laugh when he turned his washing pink in the laundrette, with some 'leaky' red pants.

In the third year there were just three students. Plump and smiley Mary Spencer had shoulder-length blonde hair and looked like a farm-girl but had recently won a kitchen design competition, giving her the opportunity to design Benny Hill's kitchen! In the middle was well-spoken Roger Lezmore-Neale, married with a baby and sporting a small moustache. Then on the end was Roger Carrington, tall and slim, with untidy dark hair, who delighted us with his renditions of 'Alfred and the Lion' in the appropriate northern accent. We greatly respected these three. As a whole we were full of exchanges and ideas. With my hair now long, I could hide behind it whenever I felt embarrassed, feigning concentration on my work. It was quite an asset.

Interior Design was an in-depth course, including: history of architecture, colour theory, building construction, technical drawing, the qualities of textiles, and many ancillary subjects. Representatives came from various industries to instruct us. There was Mr Con, a rotund Vietnamese, who taught building construction; all three years together. I recall the day he didn't turn up. We took turns to fill the huge blackboard with words containing 'con' with accompanying illustrations. It was hilarious.

In an evening class, we were instructed on a vast range of fabrics and their properties. Also as a whole group, we undertook plant-drawing and furniture design where we attempted to make the piece we'd designed, using super-sharp saws and chisels to practice our dovetail joints etc. It was a very varied and interesting course.

Mr Uttley took us on excursions in his large van. In my second year we visited Haddon Hall in Derbyshire, then Hardwick Hall in the afternoon, making copious sketches of interesting features. Haddon Hall, one of my favourite stately homes, belongs to the Manners family from Belvoir Castle.

One winter, Mr Uttley had us all swimming in the local Victorian baths. The following summer he took us to Coventry Cathedral, then to the Tibor Reich factory in Stratford-upon-Avon, to see the famous carpets and textiles being made. There was never a dull moment.

Johanna had married at nineteen and gone to live in Australia. I missed her and wouldn't see her again for years. I began crocheting squares on my train journeys now – using all the oddments I'd accumulated; making three squares going, and three coming back; enough for two blankets. Now, at twenty-one, I was eligible to vote. Mum and Dad were staunch Conservatives. Imagine my surprise as I stepped outside the railway station one night after my evening lecture, to be met by a 'Conservative' driver, waiting to take me to St Anne's school to vote. I wasn't interested in politics then; it was rather embarrassing. Anyway, I voted

Labour, then accepted a lift home. Ha!

My first and possibly most in-depth project was to design a swimming-pool complex for Nottingham. We had to explore the current provisions in Nottingham before deciding on our plans. My design, with its retractable glass roof, seating around pillars, tropical plants and medicated streams that must be walked through to reach the pool, went down very well. The main pool was of Olympic proportions. There were saunas and Turkish baths, and an underground restaurant, where swimmers could be observed through a glass wall. It was quite avant-garde and *almost* landed me a good job later on.

Our Intermediate exams were very important. For 'architecture' I chose the history of windows, finding all examples around Grantham. For 'colour and design' I chose examples of 'bad practice' and used antiques in modern settings for my 'interior' project; something that I was keen on.

Christine Proffitt, who'd passed her driving test, drove me several times to Stoke Rochford Hall in her father's Jag. I took measurements and drawings of the magnificent Victorian baroque fireplace, for my 'measured drawing' project. Christine and Jim's brother Richard did their teachers' training in this fabulous building, south of Grantham, which had originally belonged to a member of the Turnor family.

In order to receive a major grant award for my final year, the board of adjudicators insisted I must live in Nottingham, to attend ALL evening classes. As a temporary measure, Jan's family allowed me to lodge with them until I found somewhere to live. Jan was away now but I got on well with her sister Kath. Their house was about a mile from our college on Waverley Street past the Arboretum to the top of the hill, across a busy main road, then down across Forest Fields, where the famous Goose Fair takes place each year.

As I paused to cross the main road, three car drivers stopped in quick succession, thinking I was prostituting. What a shock! It wasn't as if I was dressed provocatively. I'd have to be careful; I was not in Grantham now.

It felt cosy and safe living with the Wright family – too much so perhaps, because I wasn't making any effort to find somewhere to live. I accompanied them each week to meet their relatives in a pub. They were a lovely warm family. But after Christmas, they implied that it was time I found my own accommodation. I heard of a room for rent in a nearby back street and went to have a look. A West Indian man led me across a dark room, up a tiny back staircase to a bedroom, with barely room to get in and shut the door. I quickly declined.

The next place on offer was in Robin Hood Chase, a flat on the middle floor of an otherwise empty house. In Victorian times, Robin Hood Chase had been prestigious; it was surrounded by iron railings and accessed through high wrought iron gates. The mature trees in the middle partly hid the houses around the edge. It looked very appealing, and I accepted. There was so much space.

It was the night of the Wright family get-together, and I excitedly told the relatives of my newly found flat. Their faces dropped. "Don't take it," one of them warned me, "even the policemen walk round there in pairs. They found a dead prostitute there in the telephone box not long ago." I cancelled it next morning and began looking anew.

I'd just bought the caravan from Dad for £75 – having already paid £25. But as Dad never gave me his contribution to my grant, he didn't ask for the rest. On his advice, I put adverts in the 'Sheffield Star' newspaper, hoping to bring some income. Mr Uttley, knowing I was flat hunting, suggested moving the caravan to a site at Trent Bridge, instead of paying for a flat. Good idea in principal but highly inconvenient in practice! Anyway, living on the other side of Nottingham didn't appeal to me.

Soon I found a first-floor flat on Waverley Street, opposite the Arboretum, with two rooms and a kitchen for £3 per week. The larger room had a fireplace, and a door to the kitchen behind, from where a side door opened onto the landing. The other room was narrower, with a door opening directly onto the landing, opposite the shared toilet; shared with God knows whom. It wasn't very savoury, but I could cope.

I soon had enough furniture from relatives - a single bed and bedding, a chest of drawers, a rug and a pair of curtains. The kitchen table with matching chairs were horribly heavy, made from tubular metal. They easily tipped over. But all was freely given and I was grateful. Cousin Trevor brought me with my belongings to Nottingham in his van.

The bedroom window was so tall that no curtains fitted it. I came up with an ingenious idea; I made chains from paper clips, to hang from each curtain hook. As I was opposite the Arboretum the two-foot gap was no problem at all.

Having a caravan 'to let' made me an entrepreneur, so I rented out my spare room. Carol answered my advert and moved her stuff in – a metal bunk bed and not much else. She was a bright, intelligent social worker; unlike her greasy, long-haired milkman boyfriend, Vernon, who frequently stayed over. Often, on cold evenings, they'd come through the adjoining door to sit on my bed in front of the coal fire. It wasn't my intention to share my room, but what could I do – leave them shivering next door? It was difficult to get any artwork done.

Every Monday I brought a carrier bag of food with me from Grantham: a box of Weetabix, milk, half a dozen eggs, potatoes and anything else to help me through the week. On Mondays I'd buy a pig's hock (ankle) from the butcher's, to boil in a saucepan. This would last for a few meals during the week. I'd buy a cooking apple and a packet of crisps each dinnertime, and managed on only 10 shillings per week (50p). I was getting thinner.

Once, while the three of us were eating our tea, Vernon said to Carol, "Eh y'eh yock yet?" which is pure Nottingham talk for "Have you eaten your hock yet?"

I'd bought two pairs of warm winter trousers from Mum's

club book, both in a subtle check pattern and slightly flared. Then I found a three-quarter-length, slightly flared grey coat, which I dyed purple. The result was a pleasing muted mauve. Together with the floppy cream-coloured berry I'd knitted, which I wore at an angle, I felt more 'with it,' influenced, no doubt, by Mary Quant, which gave me a modicum of confidence. Now I felt slightly braver as I walked down the road to college each morning. Every single morning that February in 1967 was cold and frosty with a clear blue sky.

One day Carol rescued a small mottled kitten from a telephone box that we adopted and called it Twiggy. We kept her indoors with a litter tray in the kitchen. I looked after her during the week, while Carol cared for her at weekends. One evening I found her trapped under a kitchen chair, which must have tipped over with the weight of a coat on the back. She was in a sorry state with blood coming from her nose. That dark, rainy night, I took her to the PDSA by bus. She fully recovered, and we didn't hang anything on those chairs after that.

The man living above us was a pimp with a wooden leg. We'd hear him coming down to the toilet – step-stomp, step-stomp, step-stomp. He rarely went out, as he kept himself by soliciting two girls from my college. There were frequent, muffled comings and goings on the stairs in the evenings. On the rare occasions I passed either girl on the staircase, we ignored each other.

By late spring Jim was out of work again. He'd turn up at the flat in the week, then drive me home on Fridays. It wasn't really convenient having Jim there – an extra mouth to feed and no time to concentrate on my college work – but this was the first time we'd been together properly. We fitted a bolt to the middle door, as we didn't want Carol and Vernon walking through to my room. Anyway, I was fed up with them wandering in and out, although it seemed a bit mean and cowardly, doing it without saying a word. Jim spent his time aimlessly playing with Twiggy. He was depressed, with no real aim in life.

This only lasted a few weeks, for it was around this time that Jim was chucked out of home and went down to Plymouth to start his new job. I arranged to join him, as soon as I finished college in July.

The check pattern on my trousers was wearing off – it was only printed on the surface. So I returned them to the club with a complaint, ordering a set of saucepans and a frying pan in their place.

Now it was my finals. The main project was to design a theatre foyer, which was completely out of my area of interest. Furthermore, I didn't realise until it was too late that we could spend the whole month on this main project, by which time I'd taken on a morning job in a laundry, being almost penniless. It was a two-mile run each way. The rest of the day and evening I spent sitting on the bed, with my drawing board balanced on my knees or on the chest of drawers. Sometimes I'd work on the kitchen table, where the light was better, but I was frequently interrupted by Carol and Vernon, who took an interest in my progress.

Finally, my college course was completed. I handed over the rent book to Carol, and Trevor came to take me, together with my belongings and Twiggy, back to Grantham. Mum and Dad were going to look after her. There waiting for me was £16 from caravan rentals; enough to book a coach seat from Nottingham to Plymouth for two days hence, with plenty of cash left over. My new life with Jim was about to begin except, that very day, he'd given in his notice at work. He'd had enough of being a grill chef. Within a week, he'd be jobless again.

Undaunted, I packed my holdall and took the train to Nottingham for the coach trip. Jim met me at Plymouth coach station, more depressed than enthusiastic. We caught a bus to his digs on the outskirts of town, where his kindly landlady allowed me to stay for free. I had a little bedroom to myself.

I don't remember how I filled my time. I just know that Plymouth traffic seemed to speed round the new one-way system, which was like a great racetrack; and when I had a bath, I couldn't get rid of the soap. The water was so soft.

The following Saturday, we set off to hitchhike back to Grantham. That seemed our only option. We wandered around Plymouth for ages before walking through the suburbs to find a road which led in the right direction. It was late in the day by the time we hitched a lift to Bristol, where we were dropped off near a flyover, after midnight.

The smell of fried onions whetted our appetites and we found 'Smokey Joes' underneath the flyover. We stood amongst tramps and the like to consume our hotdogs, then looked for a bench to lie down. But every time we settled on one, a policeman would approach us, so we'd move on. We were worn out. As the sun rose, we picked ourselves up and started all over again. We were lucky enough to get a lift in the right direction, without having to trek to the outskirts of Bristol. We weren't in the mood for walking miles.

Later, as the lorry came down a long, tree-lined promenade in the middle of Cheltenham, with grand Regency buildings set well back to both left and right, our tired dispirited souls were uplifted. It all looked so beautiful on that sunny day.

As we progressed up a long steep hill, on the other side of town, Jim noticed a Youth Hostel sign and made an instant decision to stop. The driver obligingly pulled up for us to alight. For a while, enlightened, we gazed in awe at the vast panorama from the height of the hill. It was breathtaking. We were smitten. Tomorrow we'd go back down to have a better look at Cheltenham.

Therefore, after doing our YHA chores the following morning, we bussed into the town to explore. It was then that we made up our minds to live there. We'd fetch our few belongings from Grantham and begin a life together in this beautiful town.

Two days later found us returning from Grantham to Cheltenham on a 'Black and White' coach. I'd hardly slept the night before, wondering how on earth I'd carry everything to the bus station: extra clothes in my holdall, three saucepans and frying pan and my unwieldy portfolio of college work. Amazingly, Dad, who was no longer standing in my way, drove me to the bus station. Jim was waiting for me, having spent two nights at Auntie Beat's.

At last we were there. Jim carried my portfolio by its strong leather strap to the top of the Promenade, where we plonked ourselves thankfully on a bench to scan the local newspaper we'd just bought. Opposite us was a grand building called Kielers', an antique furniture establishment on four floors. I fancied I'd try to get an interior design job there when the time was right. Meanwhile, we needed accommodation.

Barely half a mile away was a bed-sit advertised at £3 per week. We trudged uphill through the impressive Montpellier area to find Elmfield, on Overton Road; a grand Regency house with a huge elm tree at the side. We rang the bell. A grossly overweight lady came to the door, limping with a bad hip. She was Mrs Davidson, the landlady. Puffing and gasping, she led us up to a room on the first floor; and there in that room, with its double bed, a wardrobe with drawers under, two armchairs, a table with a Belling cooker on top and a washbasin in the corner, plus the electric slot meter, on which Mrs Davidson would frequently alter the tariff, we had a place to call home.

The very next day Jim took on a driving job with the prestigious Cavendish House store on the Promenade while, within the week, I secured a job with William's Cycles, selling prams and toys in the other half of their shop. We were sorted!

Mum with Rosemary and Pam Turnor and their dolls at Little Ponton Hall

Helen and me with our dolls, with Mum

Mum, Dad, Helen and me with Binkie, Bottesford 1952

Dad in Africa

Dad winning the officers' race

Sir Isaac Newton

Family group on garden steps – back row L-R Fran, Miss Brabazon, Richard, Mum, Dad. Middle row L-R Johanna seated, Helen, Auntie Kath, Vivienne, Patsy Clarke, Janine seated. Centre front Elaine, with Jean Clarke with the fringe.

St Wulfram's winning swimming team.
L-R Linda Parker, Fran, Diana Horn, Christine Millhouse

Pam's wedding. L-R Paula, Cynthia, Fran, Elaine, Wilson & Pam, Helen, Johanna,
Anne (not a cousin) and Jane, with Robert Leeson centre.

Cousins in winter – L-R Helen, Johanna, Dena, Cynthia, Elaine and Fran

Celebrating Grandma and Granddad's 50th wedding anniversary. L-R: Alex Lambley
(twin), Robert Leeson, Tony and Judy Lambley, Jane Matthews, Paula and Peta
Leeson, Eileen and Susan (friends from the village), Fran, and Elizabeth Lambley.

Cousins in Skegness – front row L-R Janine, Johanna, Jane, Cynthia, Helen.
Behind: Dad, Fran, Auntie Kath and Mum.

Grandma and Grandad celebrating their 50th wedding anniversary
at Old Somerby School, 1956.

Chris and Maggs

Fran (15) with Janine on Wall's Lane, Ingoldmells

Jim with his mother Lottie and her niece, Linda.

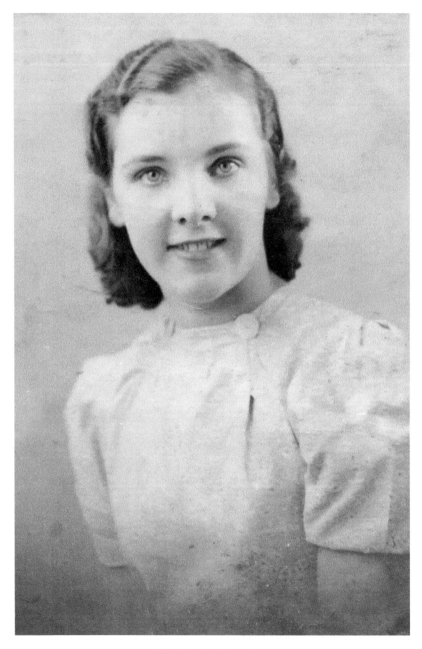

Enid, Jim's birth mother

Jim, Fran and Helen seeing Mum off to Canada for the first time, 1970.

FRAN ADAMS of Rodborough Popmobility Group presents a cheque for £214.75 to Elizabeth Sargent for Woodchester display mosaic. The money was raised by sponsored exercises.

Presenting a charity cheque – from the Stroud News & Journal, 1987

Cheerleaders – first group

Cheerleaders – later group

Mum, 81, and Uncle Tom, 68, after the attempted robbery
(courtesy of the Grantham Journal)

Richard and Bettina

Freedom

CHELTONIAN I

CHAPTER 15

A Day to Remember

Our wedding

At the very last moment, my mother's words ran through my head - "I hope you know what you're doing." And I hesitated before saying "I DO".

Jim had arrived back at our bed-sit in the early hours of the morning, having been on a night out with his new mates, the Cavendish House delivery drivers. He was surprised to find me still up, sitting on the end of the bed finishing my wedding dress. He said he hadn't particularly enjoyed his night out. He wasn't much of a drinker. But his mates had wanted to give him a stag night, so he'd gone along to please them. Anyway, in no time at all he was fast asleep, while I'd lain awake worrying if I'd be up in time to finish everything off.

By 9.30 that morning, Jim was all dressed up in his dark suit and tie, ready to go. He waited impatiently as I struggled to iron the fiddly seams of my lace overcoat, hand-stitched and made from curtain material. At 10.30am he was due to meet one of the drivers, Keith, who had volunteered to be a witness. And I wasn't ready to leave; in fact, I wasn't even dressed.

The original plan, enthusiastically plotted by the drivers, had been to drive a parade of Cavendish House lorries up the Promenade in Cheltenham and round to the Registry Office in Royal Crescent, which lay just around the corner, behind the bus station. The bride and groom would be seated in the leading lorry. However, Mr Trainer, the Transport Manager, had got wind of this plan and put a stop to it. So all the other drivers, except Keith, were obliged to work until midday that day – Saturday 9th September 1967. We were all disappointed. We'd been looking forward to that dash of eccentricity. However, it couldn't have been a more beautiful, sunny September day – outside!

By 10 am Jim became so impatient that he slammed out of the door in a huff – forgetting to take our two packed holdalls, which were sitting on the floor near the door. Realising I didn't have time to be so fussy, I switched off the iron and hurriedly put on my wedding attire: an A-line cream-coloured crimplene dress, cut just above the knee, with long bell-shaped sleeves. Over the top I carefully teased the flimsy white lace coat. It wasn't flowery but made up of simple horizontal lacework curtain material. I had sewn a border of frilly lace around the edges – along the bottom, up the fronts and round the neck. There was more around the edges of the sleeves, and all these lacy borders were just short of the edges of the dress. Then as an extra, I'd sown on seven pearl buttons and crocheted seven loops in white thread to fasten the bodice of the coat – seven being my lucky number. It was all cheap material, although I thought it looked quite good. But there was no time to admire myself in the wardrobe mirror, nor even time to comb my hair properly. I grabbed a holdall in each hand, slammed the door shut and ran for it.

Luckily, I didn't pass anyone on the wide staircase or in the hallway, but then, most of the residents didn't come out of their rooms very often. However, I'd have been mortified if the landlady had caught me in my wedding dress, running out of the front door. We'd pretended to be married when we'd taken on the bed-sit, several weeks ago. This was a posh Regency house with a respectable reputation. Several well to do Cheltenham 'ladies' were in residence, and this large house was situated in a smart part of town.

Lugging the holdalls, I ran panting and sweating all along Overton Road, then down Parabola Road, towards the bus station. The Registry office was a stone's throw away in Royal Crescent, right behind the bus station. Jim and Keith were standing on the corner outside the florist's, probably wondering if I'd make it in time. At least Jim had collected my bouquet of apricot-coloured roses. This was a compromise. I'd wanted orange Montbretias, but by September they'd finished flowering. I was disappointed.

Saying hello to Keith, I dropped the holdalls at Jim's feet and ran back to the grotty bus-station toilets, to comb my hair in the polished-metal 'mirror'. It was difficult to see what my face looked like but as I didn't wear make-up, what you saw was what you got so to speak! Then it was all systems go to get to the Registry Office for our marriage ceremony at 11 am. Neither Jim nor Keith had admired my dress, nor told me I looked nice. Another disappointment.

A few weeks earlier I'd confided in my sister, asking her to find my part-made wedding dress that I had hidden at home, and post it to 'Mrs Adams'. Otherwise what would I have worn to get married in? We were struggling like mad to afford the most basic of things.

I'd phoned my mother recently, to tell her about my forthcoming marriage. "I hope you know what you're doing" was all she'd said. So much for parental blessings!

At 11am the ceremony could not begin. We needed two witnesses, not one. What now? However, by chance, a Mr Smith was sitting in the waiting room, next in line to be married. He agreed to be our second witness. So, at last, after 10 years of parental persecution and my unwavering persistence and prayers, I was marrying the man *I* had chosen at the age of thirteen. But this wasn't how I'd imagined it would begin.

Here, in this gloomy, old-fashioned registry office, furnished throughout in dark mahogany, it seemed more like a morgue than a wedding venue. There were no smiling friends or relatives around us, no music, nothing. And by now, Jim and I had become more of a habit than a romantic liaison, after enduring the hardships of reality for the last few weeks. The dreaming was over. Like two automatons, we went through the motions of getting married; not even very enamoured with each other on that particular morning. We exchanged our silver rings, which were wide, rounded and rather chunky; quite a bargain at £3 apiece. (I had put my pseudo wedding ring on the other hand that morning). Then we signed the paperwork. Jim wrote down his present occupation as 'Lorry Driver' while I put 'Interior Designer', hoping, still with the optimism of youth, that I would become one.

Back in the sunshine, Keith took a couple of photos of us on the steps of the Registry Office. At least we were smiling now and could relax. The pressure was off; we were 'all legal' and wouldn't risk being chucked out of Elmfield. And at last, I could tell my friends and relatives where we were living.

At midday we planned to meet the other drivers for a celebratory drink at the Star in Regent Street, the street behind Cavendish House. So with time to spare, Keith took more photos of us, posing in front of Neptune's fountain on the Promenade, with its rearing horses – an imitation of the Trevi Fountain in Rome but equally nice (I thought) especially with the very impressive Municipal Office buildings in the background.

After celebrating at the pub, where Jim declined many of the drinks offered by the lads while I was photographed being scooped up in the air by some of the more exuberant drivers, it was time to catch our coach to Grantham. There we planned to spend a long weekend with whichever Auntie would put us up.

When we reached St. Margaret's coach station, it was thrumming with engine noise and full of suffocating fumes. All the Black and White coaches made their mass exodus at 2pm. Ours was the Scunthorpe coach, which would take us on a very scenic route through Warwick and Leamington Spa, Oakham in Rutland and on to Grantham. It would then continue up through the Lincolnshire Wolds to Scunthorpe.

Jim, who was somewhat inebriated, was first to climb aboard. Gosh, where were we going to sit? The coach was packed. But Jim found an empty seat near the front and plonked himself down next to a well-dressed lady, while I scanned the rest of the coach behind. There was one space left, right in the middle of the back seat. I had no choice. I squeezed between a row of muscular men who, I soon discovered, were Welsh rugby players. How foolish and embarrassed I felt, sitting amongst them in my cream and lacy white wedding dress, clutching my bouquet of apricot roses – just married, but with no husband in sight. Looking up the aisle I could just make out Jim, leaning over to one side. He'd apparently fallen asleep on that smart lady's shoulder. I wondered what sort of life lay ahead for me.

CHAPTER 16

Variety – the Spice of Life

Moran's Eating House, before and after (by kind permission of Beano Moran)

I was missing Choukee and Twiggy, but felt guilty that I didn't miss my parents. Jim and I soon got into a pattern of work. He enjoyed his job, learning his way around the beautiful Cotswold countryside as he went. My job, selling toys and prams, was less exciting but I worked with a friendly group of women. Cilla, petite with long blonde hair, was married; the eldest of a large family, whose mother was still having babies. She, as yet, had none, but confessed that her house was full of cuddly toys, bought from the shop. The youngest, at nineteen, was Rosina, who was recovering from throat cancer. We all had our fingers crossed for her. She was a bouncy, bubbly girl with (naturally, due to her circumstances) a rather husky voice. Joy, wife of the under-manager, Peter Wakeman, was dark-haired and pretty and also petite. She came in on Saturdays and filled in when necessary. They had two young children.

On the other side of the shop was the bike showroom. Roger, a tall young man, blond, slim and smarmy smart, was the bike salesman. Out the back, in the untidy workshop, worked Len Rutt and Fred, who I supposed to be in their late 50s. Len, who had been in a Japanese prisoner-of-war camp, had circular scars down both arms from cigarette burns. He was heavily built, with a gruff voice. Fred was thinner and milder natured. Together they made a good team – full of humour. Upstairs, across the top of both shops, was the pram showroom. I don't remember where the manager, Mr Wagstaff's office was. Mr Wakeman dealt with the staff.

I was fascinated by the local accent; it sounded a bit American. I'd been used to asking for a 'coop o' coffeh', whereas they'd ask for a posh sounding 'cap of coffeee'; and it was all 'aahs' and 'r's.' When Len and Fred made references to bikes, they would say, "Er's got a puncture," or "Ee be a bit rusty."

I worked from 9 - 5, Monday to Saturday, earning £8 per week; £6 10 shillings after tax. Jim finished at noon on Saturdays, earning £10 per week before tax. I had put my name on the 'professional register' at the Labour Exchange.

They would contact me if a suitable job came up. Meanwhile I made enquiries at Kieler's antique establishment. They offered me a curtain-making job in Broadway (miles away) for £8 per week. How would I even get there? With my qualifications, what were my future prospects, I wondered?

Then a job came up in the Planning Department at the prestigious Municipal Offices on the Promenade. I lugged my portfolio there for an interview. Apparently, they were well impressed with my 'swimming pool' design. At the time, Cheltenham Council was planning a new swimming pool in Pittville Park. Unfortunately, of us two short-listed candidates, the job went to the other woman. She'd worked there before. When the pool was subsequently built, its copper 'cupola' roof blended well with Cheltenham-type architecture, but the inside looked sparse, gloomy and uninviting.

In October, Richard and Bettina paid a quick visit to say farewell before emigrating to Canada. Richard told Jim to take good care of me, thinking that perhaps he might not.

That November, we caught gastric flu. I felt weird as I weaved my way through throngs of people on the promenade with my head spinning, wondering if I'd make it home. Jim was equally affected. It was an awkward situation in the bed-sit. We could be sick in the sink if caught out, but the toilet was halfway along the landing, which made things understandably 'iffy'!

Then, before we'd recovered, Grandma died. Even if we had been well enough, we couldn't have afforded to go to the funeral. I was upset, but Mum told us not to worry.

That Christmas, Rosina's mum made us a Christmas cake. Everyone was so kind. I joined Cilla's Christmas Club, which allowed me to borrow money and pay it back later. That helped us to have a semblance of a Christmas.

January of 1968 was very snowy. The drivers received praise from the customers, who extolled their efforts in getting through snowdrifts and icy conditions to make deliveries to their isolated Cotswold mansions. Some only needed cigarettes and matches! Jim relished the challenge.

William's shop was not so exciting, except on occasion. One day a customer wanted to buy a pram for her five little dogs. She was reputed to be the ex-circus woman on whom the Daily Express cartoon 'Jane' had been based. Although obviously ageing, she was still voluptuously pretty, with long, curly blonde hair and plenty of make-up. Together with her dogs, she brought her pock-faced 'minder', who was half as tall again. She insisted on trying her scrabbling dogs in each pram, while I flipped a protective cover from one pram to another in quick succession. It was such a hoot, trying to suppress the mirth that was trying to explode.

We became acquainted with Mrs Cole, who lived in the adjacent room. Formerly she'd been Emélie Roberts, a harpist in the Hallé orchestra. As Jim had begun making model aeroplanes on the kitchen table, I'd often go next door for a chat. We became close friends.

By February, we had enough money to buy a Standard van, although we never seemed to be able to afford tax and insurance. Mum helped us out on several occasions, for which we were most grateful.

At the end of March, Helen was to marry Carl, whom she'd met on a blind date while at Teacher Training College in Saffron Walden. He was studying horticulture at Writtle Agricultural College in Essex. I was to be Matron of Honour, which was going to prove awkward for Dad and Jim.

We stayed at Auntie Beat's for my dress fitting and again for the wedding. Carl asked Jim if he'd record their wedding on a tape recorder. If he stood behind a pillar in St Anne's church, he'd be hidden from view, which would save him and Dad any embarrassment.

Expecting Dad to be at the Post Office the day before the wedding, we called to see Helen at 142. As we walked through the gate, Dad came unexpectedly out of the front door. He passed us, looking straight ahead. Then Jim called out, "I say Mr Carrington," and Dad spun round. "I'm sorry for all the trouble I've caused you in the past." "Oh that's all right Jim," replied Dad, and they shook hands – and that was it! Such a relief to clear the air before Helen's special day.

It was a beautiful wedding, with five bridesmaids in cerise satin dresses, plus two soldier boys. With the men in top hats and tails, there were 130 guests in the ballroom of the George Hotel, where each table held an elegant vase of roses (Carl worked for a well-known Essex rose-grower at the time). What a contrast to my wedding, six months earlier! I wasn't at all jealous. I couldn't have coped with all the pomp and ceremony.

Aunties and uncles who'd just found out we were married were giving us five-pound notes here and ten-pound notes there, for belated wedding presents, while Grantham relatives had presents waiting for us. When we called on Jim's parents, we were well received. Another hatchet had been buried. They gave us a nice barometer in a wooden case, to hang on the wall.

On Sundays, we drove through all the Cotswold villages that Jim had visited the previous week. We loved the Cotswolds. Later he joined the Glevum Model Club and flew planes on Sunday mornings on Moreton Valence Airfield, trying all types of models, from rubber-band-powered planes to diesel-engine ones. Then, at the end of the 1960s the M5 motorway was built, ploughing right through the middle of the airfield, which put a stop to the club's activities there.

Making models had brought Jim into contact with a large model shop on Bath Road in Cheltenham. The owner, knowing we were living in a bed-sit (for Jim chatted a lot) told us of a vacant flat just two doors up the road, with a front room, kitchen, toilet, bathroom and bedroom – all for £3 per week, the same price we paid for our room at Elmfield. We snapped it up before it went to anyone else. It would be so convenient, with all the shops one could possibly need on Bath Road. Our laundrette was just around the corner on Suffolk Road, so much less distance to lug my two holdalls of washing, like before.

A Miss Edwards, who shopped for Mrs Cole, knew many influential Cheltenham 'ladies', for whom she also shopped. Through one of these, a Mrs Carruthers-Little, we were able to acquire our first mismatch of furniture, left over from an auction at the County Hotel on Parabola Road. We took it gladly: a little wooden kitchen table with a flap, three unmatched kitchen chairs, an old Italian-looking oak sideboard on 'barley-sugar' legs, a sprung double-bed base and an old sofa with a drop-down arm. We also picked up a carved, warped shelf made from driftwood.

Although we liked our flat, it needed much cleaning and decorating. The bedroom, with its corrugated roof, was an add-on and was not well insulated. It was accessed through the 'bathroom' (a bath set on huge, uneven flagstones that oozed dampness). The toilet was next to the back door, a short corridor away from the kitchen.

In the beginning we slept in the front room, with the window looking onto the busy Bath Road. The coin-slot electric meter was underneath in the damp dark cellar, where a central pit prop held up our floor, wedged with layers of slate, to level it off. Every night slugs crawled from under the skirting board, leaving slimy trails over the bedspread and floor. If you trod on one, it was almost impossible to remove the slime. I can't think why lubricants aren't made from it.

Bill, who drove lorries at night, lived in the flat above,

with his tall attractive daughter and her young son. His other daughter lived nearby. She had three children and was not at all tall and pretty. The Border Cleaners, next door, was owned by the same landlord, an elderly man from Kington in Herefordshire, and behind it was a third flat, occupied by another Bill. He was large-framed, square-faced, big and blustery, and had been a pilot in the war.

Our flat had a garden to both the front and back, both needing much attention. I relished improving them. Firstly I laid a front lawn, surrounded by a narrow flower border. It looked quite neat and presentable with its wrought iron fence and gate, which Jim painted. Some time later, big Bill asked if he could take over this garden, seeing that we also had the back one. Now I watched, as every month my lawn grew smaller and smaller as he enlarged the border, until it was postage-stamp-sized in the end.

It's amazing that our grotty flat, together with the laundry next door and more recently, the double-fronted former model shop, have now become Moran's Eating House, a very popular up-market establishment. The plaster has been removed from the whole length of the brick wall, showing where our fireplaces were. If people only knew what it was like then. Blowflies were forever buzzing out from behind the hardboard that covered our kitchen fireplace, as we ate at the table in front of it. When Jim removed the hardboard one day, while I stood squeamishly some distance away, he revealed three dead pigeons. One was a dried-out skeleton, the second, a squirming, grub-ridden carcass, and the third was newly dead, still waiting to be devoured by maggots. There would be more to follow.

While sleeping in that front room we encountered some strange goings-on. We came to recognise the onset of these occasions. A torch would be seen flashing on and off across the road. Then we'd hear the light upstairs being clicked on and off. That was the 'OK' signal. The next thing we knew, a man was clambering up the drainpipe to the window above, to spend time with the pretty woman upstairs. We recognised him later. It was her sister's husband.

We decorated the bedroom at the back and moved in, but that winter the walls were running with damp and the paper peeling off the walls. We complained to the woman in Border Cleaners next door, to whom we paid our rent. She contacted the landlord, who said the dampness was our fault, due to condensation from the bathroom, as we didn't air it properly. This wasn't true because we didn't use the bathroom in winter. We complained to higher authorities and a tribunal was arranged. The old, wealthy landlord offered us £200 to sort things out ourselves. We refused, so he was obliged to get builders in to check the roof – and what a blessing that was. The corrugated roof had slipped down 2 inches from the top, leaving a gap, and the roof timber was rotten; almost ready to collapse. So once again we slept in the front room while the roof was put to rights.

One very windy night, when we were back in the re-roofed bedroom, the howling, whistling wind kept us awake for much of the night. But what we hadn't realised was, that part of the noise was from an electric drill, drilling into the safe at the back of the shop. We felt spooked, realising that the robber must have climbed our high garden wall to accomplish this deed, and had also escaped with his booty, back over the wall – unless it was an inside job!

A heatwave was forecast for the Saturday of Jim's birthday, at the end of July. We wanted to spend the weekend in Weston-super-Mare, so I requested to have the Saturday off work. Mr Wakeman said he couldn't refuse me, but as Cilla was going to a wedding and someone else couldn't come in, he'd like me to be there. Selfishly, I took the time off anyway and we had a lovely time. When I returned the following Monday, all red and glowing from sunburn, Peter Wakeman took me aside to tell me I'd been given a week's notice. Sacked – from my very first job!

However, by the following Monday, I'd secured another job, as an orderly on the accident ward at Cheltenham General Hospital, for £14 per week. The hospital was just down the road and round the corner from our flat, following the perimeter of the prestigious Boys' College. I could run there and clock in in less than 10 minutes – which I usually did, stepping over the low wall, to cut across the grass of the college, to get there in time!

Meanwhile Jim had switched from Cavendish House deliveries to Cavendish House removals. He was now one of two passengers on the front seat, while the foreman, plump Frank, sat in a little 'boxroom' within the body of the lorry, with a small window looking into the cab. Sometimes

Chris, the driver, would go round and round a roundabout to annoy Frank, who'd rage and splutter, spitting out his sandwich but unable to do anything from his position in the back of the lorry. They were forever getting his back up. Every time we met up with Chris and his wife Mags, he and Jim delighted us with all the latest goings-on. Chris could imitate Frank and have us in fits of laughter. There was always an incident to relate, like when they couldn't hold a piano on a flight of stairs and it smashed into the wall of the half-landing. Or when they delivered an extremely heavy slate snooker table to Reginald Bosanquet and couldn't even lift it indoors without dismantling it. They 'moved' a great many eccentric people, and all the incidents they related could have made a TV series.

I began my new job on tenterhooks, not knowing what orderlies were supposed to do, but smart in my newly made-to-measure green uniform. I was glad not to have cleaning to do. Firstly, I'd do the flowers and tidy up. Then it would be time to prepare the trolley for 'elevenses,' which because of their very early breakfasts, the patients had before eleven. Feeling embarrassed, I wheeled the trolley round with hot drinks and biscuits. Similarly at teatime, I took the trolley round with the sandwiches I'd made, together with the large teapot, which was almost too heavy to lift. In between I went home for my dinner.

That first morning I was confronted with three young men in their beds, each with a leg held up in traction. All three had been involved in motorcycle accidents. They formed a trio of merriment as they endured their recovery. "What's your name?" was the first thing they asked me. "Mrs Adams," I replied primly. "No, what's your first name." "Frances," I divulged, then regretted it. "Oh - sweet FA!" they all chorused and I went a deeper, sweatier shade of red. That was a good start, I thought. This was my greeting every time I entered their ward.

Another duty was to check on conditions in the sluice, where the bedpans were emptied. I discovered two bedpans at the far end that hadn't been sluiced properly. They were crawling with maggots. I reported my findings to Sister, who gathered the nurses into her office for a 'telling-off'. I was a whistle-blower! Then three weeks later, I was moved to Casualty, where I had much wider responsibilities. Each morning I went round to the bed-bureau for the list of patients due to be admitted. When they arrived at 2pm, I filled in their admission forms, then took them to their allotted wards.

I was based on the accident side of the main entrance. On the other side was the waiting room, where minor injury patients waited patiently to see the doctor. Our phone would ring to tell of an emergency coming in, then the nurses (on 8-week placements) would hurriedly prepare the trolley with the appropriate equipment. I often gave them some input, as it became second nature to me, for what was required.

There'd be some regulars, possibly in a diabetic coma or having an epileptic fit. One lady, from Stow-on-the-Wold, would swear profusely as she came round. Everyone was ready for it! Children with cuts to be stitched, or those who'd taken poison, were treated in the small theatre next door. I'd hold them firmly on the theatre bed, wrapped in a blanket, while the procedure was carried out. I'd ring Cardiff Poison Centre for advice on treatments. Then I created a 'Poisons Book' for the staff to reference, which often saved valuable time. Minor operations and minor accidents were also treated in here. It was my job to clean and stock up supplies in this theatre.

Once, when the ambulance men were dashing in with a schoolgirl with minor injuries from a cycling accident, they collided with a young Polish boy on his bike. He was brought in, severely injured and crying like a young baby. This, I was told, was a sign of a certain type of brain injury. His parents arrived, shouting and rowing with each other. This, I was also told, was often a reaction to extreme shock. I don't know what sort of recovery poor young Bruno made, but I hope he did recover.

There were four Sisters on Casualty. Sister Thomas was in charge. She was small and fierce and wouldn't stand any nonsense. Formerly, she'd been a nurse in the army and was always the one called upon to free a 'John Thomas' from a zip, or similar. (She liked me, especially after I'd made a detailed sketch of her antique teapot to send to the editor of 'The Connoisseur', to find out its worth. The editor, Rupert, was a personal friend of Mrs Cole.) Next in line, and age, came Sister Hayward. She was tallish, married with grown children, and was fussy; always unnecessarily rushing about looking flustered. Sister Bundy came next. She was a really lovely, tallish, dark-haired woman, who was calm and softly spoken, having a very levelling influence in times of urgency. Then there was fat, freckle-faced Sister Latham, who was outspoken, disgruntled, overweight and lazy, although I got on quite well with her. We often discussed gardening. It was no secret that Sister Hayward and Sister Latham disliked each other.

The lady running the Bed Bureau was fond of cats. This I discovered one day as I entered her office. There were kittens running everywhere. She was trying to find homes for them. They were offspring of the feral cats living under the physiotherapy huts, and if Matron had found out, there would have been hell to pay, so the kitten homing was kept strictly secret.

One bank holiday, when she'd be away for three days, I took a little kitten home in a box for the weekend, to help out. I placed the opened box on the floor of our lounge and went through to the kitchen, without saying anything. It would be a surprise. Soon this fluffy little creature came wobbling down the steps, through the little passage to our kitchen. Jim gasped on seeing this beautiful kitten, with her soft tortoiseshell colours of sandy beige and dark grey, with a creamy white chest. Of course, we kept her, even though we weren't supposed to have pets, naming her Pippy.

That summer of 1969, Jim had a long-awaited operation. He had some congenital defect in the base of his spine, aggravated by a wrestling incident, and also from an injury sustained while laying railway tracks (one of his many occupations that didn't last long). He fairly frequently put his back out, usually when performing some innocuous task like picking up a letter off the floor, whereas he could hump heavy furniture about all day, it seemed.

It was pioneering surgery then, to remove discs and fuse the vertebrae together, and this took place at Standish Orthopaedic Hospital, several miles away. Luckily, the lady from the model shop had a relative in there at the same time and gave me lifts to visit Jim.

Two weeks later, the day before his release, his cousin Lindsay was to visit us. Not having a clue what she looked like, I had to meet her from the Norfolk coach. However, we got on well.

When Jim arrived home the next day, encased in a plaster cast from his chin to his pubic bone, he felt really claustrophobic and lay on the floor panicking. He'd already spent a freezing night in bed in his still-wet plaster cast, in spite of the boiling hot weather we were having at the time.

Having overcome his fears, we took Lindsay by bus up to Cleeve Hill, where Jim, now in his 'nothing will beat me' mode, walked all the way to the top with us. Quite an achievement. Coming down was worse! The plaster cast was to stay on for three months and during that time bits of cotton wool from between the cast and the 'net vest' next to his skin kept falling out at the bottom, until it was virtually non-existent. We had to keep cutting bits of plaster off both ends, as when he sat down the cast would hit him under the chin.

My school friend, Pat Bowser was to remarry towards the end of November, having at last found a caring partner, Dennis. They asked us if we'd be witnesses to their wedding. And so it was that we arrived at no. 142 just after 8pm on the Friday night for their wedding the following morning. Unfortunately, we just missed seeing Mum and Dad, who had gone to a Conservative dinner and dance, held in the ballroom at the Guildhall – where I'd had my first dancing lessons, years ago.

Around 10pm we received a phone call to say that my father had been taken ill and was being taken to hospital, and that Mum would be coming home. Could we make her a cup of tea? Something didn't ring true, but I wasn't sure what it was. Then at 10.30, Uncle Jim and Auntie Nellie rang the doorbell. As I opened it Auntie Nellie blurted out "Isn't it terrible?" "What?" "Didn't you know? Your Dad's dead."

Although I was shaken to the core, my semi-conscious mind already knew, for if an ambulance took away someone who was already dead, the relatives didn't go with them.

My father's death shook us rigid. We were devastated like never before. My active, full-of-life father was dead before his 65th birthday. He'd died doing the 'Gay Gordons' with Mum. Of course, we didn't go to the wedding next morning and phoned to explain.

Richard came straight over from Canada and asked Dad's GP if he'd had any inkling of our father's heart problem. The answer shocked us – two years earlier, Dad had been warned to stop smoking and take things easy. Instead, he'd bought a towing caravan and had taken Mum all over Devon and Cornwall during the last two summers, enjoying life to the full. He had stopped smoking though.

His funeral was the following Thursday after an inquest. It was a raw, penetratingly cold, dark November day and Richard couldn't bear it, having become so used to the dry cold winters of Canada. He realised now why Dad had looked so stricken when they'd said farewell to go to Canada. He probably knew then that he'd never see Richard again. Mum and Dad had planned to visit Richard and family in Canada for the first time the following summer. Now Mum would be going alone, and would continue to do so every year for the rest of her life.

By coincidence, that same year, unqualified teachers were barred from teaching. So Mum, of course, took over the Post Office, and made a great success of it.

I was absolutely convinced that Dad would 'appear' and communicate with me after his sudden death. But this never happened. Weeks went by, then months, so that gradually my faith dwindled, until eventually I stopped believing that there was any God at all. I was on my own!

I returned to Casualty a week later. That week a man was rushed in having a heart attack. I still felt raw from my father's death and watched as this man lay on the floor, his body jumping as electric shocks were administered, even though he might already be dead. While this was going on, Sister Hayward and Sister Latham were arguing about the treatment they were giving. I couldn't take any more. I rushed into the small theatre and sobbed my heart out.

Then, after a year and a half on Casualty, I got word from the Labour Exchange that an interior design job was going. That was exciting, although I'd enjoyed working on Casualty, having learnt far more than I'd learnt as a Student Nurse. Sister Thomas was sorry to see me go, but happy that I'd found work in my chosen field.

So, I began working for Bernard Cleary in his basement studio on Imperial Square – right in the hub of Cheltenham. He was an amenable man, in his fifties I presumed, with black wavy hair combed back from his squarish face, and of fresh rosy complexion. I likened him to an Irish horse-trainer.

My first assignment was to make sketches of a lounge, in the house of the Cheltenham MP – a Mr Charles Irving. Mr Cleary was to give this room a makeover. What a pleasure this job was going to be!

My jobs were varied and individual, although more like interior decoration than design – no plans and elevations or lighting plans to draw; more akin to window dressing, I'd say. My first major job was to mend an ancient leather screen consisting of twelve panels, with an oil painting on each one. Three panels had been broken (as if punched) and I was to mend them then repaint the pictures. Richard, the tall, young, well-spoken upholsterer, gave me his input, suggesting I use Unibond to join the edges together, because it would remain supple. This worked well. I made a good job of the screen, although it took me quite some time.

Mr Cleary also had a contract with Holiday Inns, travelling the country and taking on various jobs. Once I went with him and Richard to a hotel in Sheffield. My task was to hem the wall curtains, already hung around three sides of a hall, working at speed to complete the job in a day. Another assignment was to make velvet-covered mounts for brass 'Cherub' light holders for the Ladies' toilets at Alveston Manor; a prestigious hotel on the outskirts of Stratford upon Avon. We made two visits that time.

However, the business was struggling, so we joined two of his long-standing employees who made soft furnishings in an old building on Knap Road, opposite the RSPCA, somewhere off Lower High Street. One was Madge, a middle-aged blonde with her hair in a French pleat, who was sweet on Mr Cleary (it was reciprocated). Then there was an older German woman, who was forever exclaiming "God luff us, Charlie"! There was also Jean, a recent employee like me, who was divorced with a young child, and living with her parents. Together we learnt to make full-length hand-headed velvet curtains. We sewed the panels together on the huge industrial electric sewing machines (where we had to tug hard on the underneath layer to stop it from ruching up). Then each curtain was spread out and skewered onto a huge wooden table. The lining was spread evenly over this and also tethered down. Everything was done the 'proper' way; the linings and hems being sewn by hand, with the corners all turned up in the correct fashion. I was also shown how to make padded pelmets and lambrequins (which are like pelmets that extend down the sides of the window frame, in fancy curves).

Meanwhile back at Bath Road I'd made friends with the elderly lady in the double-fronted house next door. She was Elsie Marsh, twice widowed, whose first husband had made ceramics for Queen Mary. She was becoming poorer and poorer, as she spent her savings on everyday living, not knowing until it was too late that she was entitled to Social Security benefits. She was great fun to talk to; young at heart and broadminded. Sometimes I cut her hair, and actually snipped her ear once and made it bleed. I felt awful, but she didn't make a fuss. When her money ran out she was moved three-quarters of a mile away and, to my great shame, I only visited her twice after that. Meanwhile Mrs Cole was taken into the Radiotherapy Department in Cheltenham Hospital with ovarian cancer.

Mr Cleary couldn't afford to keep me any more and, after six months, I was given a week's notice. He called me into his basement office with its low curving ceiling, put his arm around my shoulders and told me the sad news. The thing was, only two nights earlier, I'd dreamt of this scenario exactly as it happened. Was I a clairvoyant?

I spent that last week at his house in Leckhampton, where I fabricised the hall, stairs and landing, sharing a nice cooked lunch with him and his wife each day, which we ate with a glass of wine. It was a very pleasant few days.

I think they were sorry to be losing me. I was sorry too. I'd learnt a great deal – the correct way to make hand-headed curtains, how to make loose-covers with piping, a little about upholstery and how to make padded pelmets and lambrequins. I now had many more strings to my bow.

Madge had cleverly machined together all the fabric for the job in hand, so that it went up the wall of the stairs at the correct angle, while Richard had fixed battens along the tops and bottoms of all the walls to be covered. It was just left to me to tack this fabric tautly to the battens on the walls, making sure it was evenly 'stretched'. The result looked marvellous but would have been highly impractical, had there been young children living there.

Towards the end of that week, when I visited Mrs Cole in hospital, I bumped into Sister Thomas in the corridor. She greeted me warmly, asking how my new job was going. "Actually," I said, "I'm being made redundant at the end of the week, because they can't afford to keep me." She grabbed me by the shoulders. "We want you back," she said. And so it was that I returned to my old job, while the person who'd been doing it was moved to another department. However, it wasn't my old job anymore. The Whitley Council had clamped down on the duties of orderlies and I could no longer perform all the tasks I'd once done. Also a hospital manager had taken the place of Matron. But I was happy to find Dr Omar in casualty, the man who'd performed Jim's operation at Standish. We really liked him. He was doing a six-month stint on Casualty.

The bulk of my duties seemed to be cleaning, cleaning, cleaning – mainly the clinics downstairs, which I hadn't known existed before. But I stuck with it, because the pay wasn't bad. That Christmas, soon after my father's death, Sister Thomas invited Jim and me to their Christmas lunch, which was an ordeal for me. There wasn't much of a Christmassy atmosphere to the celebrations. Sitting eight to a table in the canteen, under bright fluorescent, Supermarket-style lights brought back all my former hang-ups. I ate my dinner totally embarrassed throughout. Then I noticed a blonde woman from the office on another table. Like me, she had a bright red face and looked miserable. I wasn't the only one then!

Mrs Cole was moved to a home in Farnham in Surrey. Before she left, she gave me her two screens that she'd used around her washbasin, a bamboo table and also her silver Christening spoon, bearing her initials. I treasure it, but I don't know to whom I should give it before I die. She had a niece in Dorset, who won't be alive now. When Jim and I visited her in Farnham, she confided that she hadn't walked a single step since arriving at the home, being wheeled everywhere. This upset her, but she didn't make a fuss. That was the last time we saw her. She was another elderly friend I'd abandoned as her life was ending!

Meanwhile another job had come up; a really good one, painting plaster-of-Paris animal heads (about the size of a lady's palm), to be sold in Bristol Zoo for half a crown. I worked in part of the basement of a big house near Pittville

Park on the other side of town. Ken Cowling, the owner, was an artist; a man of good stature, probably in his late fifties, who also owned an art gallery in Tewkesbury. In the other half of the basement lived Vera with her young teenage daughter, Helen. I think they also had a room with a view, on the ground floor. Vera was divorced, and covered the cost of her rent by making these plaster-of-Paris heads.

Ken was the most 'Heath Robinson' chap you could ever meet; everything was worked out to a T. In the basement were large hooks attached to the ceiling at regular intervals, on which could be hung home-made wooden racks in fours, one beneath the other. Each rack held twenty-six animal heads, spaced out on small hooks, each hung by a small rubber loop embedded in the back of the head. I'd take one rack at a time, hang it next to my work area and perform one procedure at a time to each head. For instance, if I was painting cheetahs' heads, I'd first paint each nose black on the first rack, then continue until I'd done several racks of noses. The next procedure would be to spray each head yellowy-orange, using a pressure gun, accentuating the colour on the top and down the nose, and also on the cheeks. The third task would be to fit a stencil mask over each head and spray it black, for the markings. I also painted tigers, lions, brown bears, golden eagles and others.

When many heads were finished and completely dry, I'd varnish them. This set-up was ingenious. Taking one rack at a time to the other side of the room, I'd hang it from the ceiling, picking up the bottom end to also hang from the ceiling. The heads hung downwards. Underneath, fitted firmly to a table, were 26 jugs, almost full of shellac varnish. As I carefully lowered the rack by pulley, each head would fit neatly into a jug. I'd submerge them 'up to their ears' so to speak, then raise the rack and exchange it for the next one.

Vera and I became good friends. She was middle-aged and pretty with shoulder-length brown hair, curled up at the bottom like my mother's used to be. Her curvy figure was squashed into a short frame and like me, she could have done with longer legs. Vera had been attached to theatres in her past life, calling everyone 'Darling', to which I soon became accustomed. Sometimes we'd spend long afternoons in conversations while I worked unimpeded; with practice I was able to work faster and faster. I was sub-contracted, buying my own insurance stamp, and could choose what hours I worked – I was able to manage on one day per week in the end, earning £18.

As well as animal heads, Vera made rectangular plaques of Gloucester Cathedral, Lichfield Cathedral, Tewkesbury Abbey, Ludlow Castle and others. I disliked these; they looked naff with no subtle colouring: stark blue sky, mid-grey walls and green, green grass. I should have worn a mask when spraying the skies because, after spraying them all afternoon, I'd find the blue running out of my nose as I ran home, especially in cold weather. It must have been of a finer consistency.

Through Miss Edwards, I learned of a gardening job near Pittville Pump room. It was Chacely Lodge, the last house along the lane before the Pump Room. The garden stretched back towards the main Evesham Road then, although several houses have been built on it since. Colonel Laird and his wife lived there with their eight King Charles Spaniels. I worked for four hours, two afternoons a week, sweeping leaves from the lawn in autumn, weeding, tidying and also trimming the bushes. Halfway through my stint, Mrs Laird would bring out a tray with pieces of two different homemade cakes, and a glass of homemade lemonade that tasted of nectar. This elderly couple were so kind to me. One afternoon, I trimmed the many bushes around their drive, which had grown into odd shapes, due to earlier neglect. According to their shape, I did a topiary job on them. The Lairds could have been annoyed, but they were tickled pink, and I kept them trimmed in their new shapes for as long as I worked for them.

Now I had some great news – I was pregnant. At last! Back in my schooldays, having babies had been my career ambition. Now it had nothing to do with careers – just a longing. Jim was cautiously pleased, but worried that he might not be able to shoulder his responsibilities. He'd had a few outbursts of violent temper while we'd been living in the flat. They came from nowhere, and I tried to work out what triggered them. He would become like someone possessed, thumping walls, doors and furniture but never (to his credit) hitting me, or anything that might break his knuckles, so he wasn't completely irrational. He'd never lost his temper at Elmfield, so I'd hoped they were a thing of the past. Obviously not! Meanwhile I carried on with both jobs for as long as possible; in fact, I was painting animal heads to within three weeks of the baby being born.

We'd made friends with a Chinese family living opposite us. Wai Ling and Tony ran a Chinese take-away. They had four young children and Wai Ling was expecting her fifth. We'd go for walks in the park with her and the children, laughing at our attempts to talk Cantonese, and at the English words that sounded rude to her – like 'Lurpak' (the butter). She always tittered when she mentioned this word, squinting her eyes in mirth, but never telling us what it meant in English.

Jim and I began house hunting. This flat wasn't good enough for a baby. He now had a job driving for Benson's the builders, so fingers crossed we'd be ok for a mortgage. One day he excitedly phoned me at the Lairds'. He'd heard of a little terraced house for sale at Charlton Kings and if we wanted it we had to be quick. I'd only be able to view it from the outside. It was up to me to make a quick decision on it.

I caught a bus and got there as quickly as possible, walking round and peering through the windows. It looked dark inside, but I was sure it had possibilities. I rang the estate agents and said, "Yes!"

CHAPTER 17

Charlton Kings

Peter and Malcolm on Peter's second birthday in our Charlton Kings garden.

Helen and Carl had very kindly lent us a sum of money to help with the down payment on our little cottage which, in 1972, cost us £3,500. It was in a terrace of four; small two-up, two-down cottages, with narrow kitchens joined on at the back. The house was roughly 12 feet wide, so correspondingly, the garden was equally narrow and looked like a ribbon, being so long. Down at the bottom, out of sight from the house, flowed a little brook with towering willow trees on the other side.

Charlton Kings had a rural feel to it, even though it was joined to the west side of Cheltenham. Our cottage was in the older part, on School Road. Opposite us were two pairs of large red brick council houses, still with obsolete gaslights outside. Next to these was the village school. Two doors down on our side was a community hall, also built of red bricks. School Road was fairly narrow, and beyond the school was a left turn into Lyefield Road East. This was wider, and lined with 1930s houses. School Road became a narrow lane past this turning. We didn't discover it at first, so we always thought of it as our secret lane. It led down to the brook, following its course up to the A40 Oxford Road. At the opposite end of our road was the Merryfellow pub on the corner, with a couple of small shops across the junction.

We'd been promised a £1000 grant for a bathroom and damp proofing, but there was deadlock – we couldn't have this until we had secured our mortgage. Conversely, we couldn't have our mortgage until we had the bathroom grant in our hands. Charlton Kings still had its own Rural District Council then. It now comes under the jurisdiction of Cheltenham. I made frequent trips to the RDC to get this sorted. The situation held us up considerably. When, at last, we could move in, I began drawing plans and elevations for a conversion, changing the second bedroom into a bathroom and having a new bedroom over the kitchen. It would entail turning the staircase around.

Because the kitchen footings were 'iffy', the new bedroom above it would need to be as lightweight as possible; timber-framed with a flat roof. This frame would be covered with expanded metal, with a 'Tyrolean' finish sprayed on top, to match the rest of the house. I became acquainted with a young man running a small building firm on our side of town, who helped me with my working drawings regarding the expanded metal covering, with which I wasn't familiar. At least my former training saved us paying architect's fees.

Jim became unemployed once more – suffering back problems. It wasn't a good start to becoming house owners or parents, and we had to go through the degrading Social Security system again. Jim was the only father-to-be not to attend the antenatal session for fathers. I think he felt inferior, being out of work. We'd been advised not to move house late in pregnancy, but after all the hold-ups, what could we do?

It was daunting, buying our own house and being unemployed, with a baby on the way as well. Just buying the house would have been a challenge. But dear Mum turned up trumps, searching the adverts in the Post Office window, and finding us a pram and a cot; even a little navy canvas pram-cum-pushchair (old-fashioned, like a carrycot but with a drop-down end – a bargain too good to be missed). Then Helen who, six months earlier had given birth to a son, Richard, sent us his outgrown clothes. Dena sent a big parcel of baby clothes. I was overcome with gratitude. All I bought were two sets of nappies. I kept a drawer free to use as a cot, during the first few weeks.

Three weeks before the baby was due, we visited Grantham for Richard's christening. Jim had swapped the van for an old Morris Oxford saloon, which was really comfy. We always brought Pippy on our four and a half hour journey up the Fosse Way. The poor thing was usually sick; but once we reached 142 she could settle down, having a litter tray in the lobby near the back door. Both Choukee and Twiggy had died now – Twiggy had been run over.

We walked through the front door of no. 142 to find the hall bedecked with great vases of flowers. They looked beautiful but so over the top, we thought. We were about to take our holdalls up to the front bedroom, where we always stayed, when Mum came down the hall to greet us, looking worried. Zoe and her friend had unexpectedly arrived from New York the day before, and Mum had put them up in the front bedroom. She hadn't known what else to do. "Could you stay at Jim's parents house, instead?" she asked hopefully. I felt really hurt. Here was I, almost ready to pop, and there was no room at the inn.

Leaving Pippy at 142 for the time being, we went along to Jim's house, to see if they could oblige. His mum brought out the old feather mattress from a closet, and I helped her to make up a bed on the front room floor, pushing aside her brand new three-piece-suite in fawn bouclé material – her pride and joy.

After a meal and time spent with everyone at 142,

including acquainting ourselves with baby Richard, we went along to Jim's house for the night, carrying Pippy and the litter tray. We hadn't felt exactly relaxed with our relatives, still feeling miffed at being turned away.

The mattress was quite comfy; we would have slept well, had it not been for Pippy. She went ballistic. She just wouldn't settle down, running up and down the backs of the new three-piece suite all night. We dreaded discovering what damage she had done, in pulling out the loops of the fabric. We hadn't slept a wink. In the morning I said, "Let's go home." I felt wrecked. I couldn't face the day. So early that morning we slipped off back to Gloucestershire, without even calling at 142. We asked Jim's mum to explain the situation to my mum, and apologised profusely for the damage done to the thee-piece suite; mostly the chair backs, which would be against the walls. The following week, Jim's parents were coming to spend their holidays with us. Jim would be returning to fetch them.

As planned, Jim fetched his parents down to Charlton Kings, where they spent the last two weeks of July with us (the factory shutdown). They were thrilled at the prospect of becoming grandparents, although, the fact that the baby was due to arrive during their visit was not altogether ideal. While they were staying, Jim and I moved into the second bedroom, which would soon become our bathroom.

The weather was beautiful, and we went on lovely trips and walks: Symonds Yat, Broadway, Cleeve Hill and tours through the Cotswold countryside. On the second Thursday of their holiday, we planned a picnic on Leckhampton Hill. The evening before this, Jim took his parents to the Merryfellow for a drink, while I stayed home to soak my feet in a bowl of water. Then my waters broke! Blimey, what now? I couldn't remember what I should do. With all the activity and turmoil going on regarding the house, I genuinely couldn't recall what we'd been told. Was I supposed to get in touch with the hospital straight away, or what? I didn't want to be one of those mums who is stuck in hospital for days with nothing happening. Anyway, who could go to the phone box for me? So I did nothing. When the others returned, we all went to bed. It wasn't the best of nights, but not bad enough to cause me great concern. As planned, the next day we packed our picnic and set off in the car. I just had to call in for my routine hospital check-up on the way, while the others waited outside in the car park. But on examination the nurse called out, "This one's in labour. Can you bring a wheelchair?" So that was the end of the picnic!

It was late the following afternoon, on July 28th, that my beautiful baby boy arrived. We were elated and I was extremely grateful that Jim had stayed with me. After not attending the antenatal class for fathers, I'd thought he would adopt a similar stance when it came to the birth. It had been a long haul.

We named our son Peter William. (With so many of my cousins having babies, it was difficult to find names we liked that they hadn't already chosen). Peter was whisked away to intensive care for the night, but we were re-united the following morning and spent the next ten days getting to know each other in hospital. Jim's parents were over the moon, but they had to catch a coach home the following day, after first seeing their grandson.

When Jim fetched me home after ten days, I wasn't quite sure how I would cope. The builder and his son had begun our conversion a few days earlier, and I arrived home to find we no longer had a roof over the kitchen or toilet. It was open to the sky and weather, which fortunately remained clement for a while. The kitchen sink had been temporarily plumbed in, in front of the dining room window, with a waste pipe going into a bucket outside. All the furniture was piled up in the front room, leaving just the settee to sit on. It was fortunate that Jim was at home with me, because I'd be concentrating full-time on Peter, keeping him safe from dust and noise.

On the other side of a joint passageway lived two elderly sisters, Edie and Phyllis. They were a delightful pair and were thrilled at the prospect of having this baby living next door. They allowed me to take a bath in their house each day.

Our house was chaotic, and so were the builders – the cheapest we could find. One day, the builder's son leaned on the kitchen wall and it collapsed. That didn't augur well for building on top of it!

When Peter was three weeks old we took him to Weston in the car, taking the little navy pram. It was a gorgeous day and we spent it simply pushing the pram up and down the promenade with our new baby, proud as Punch. We were keeping out of the way of the builders, because our new stairs were being fitted that day (facing the other way).

When we arrived home we discovered two problems. The first was that we'd left the pram wheels in the car park in Weston (outside the boot). The second problem was that when we eagerly ran up our new stairs, we banged our heads on the ceiling. The builder simply said, "Oh well, you'll just have to duck or grouse!" He was quite prepared to leave it as it was. We weren't. We had to argue with him to get him to agree to alter it. The bottom of our bedroom cupboard would need raising up by about nine inches. He really didn't want the bother of re-doing the staircase ceiling all over again. Meanwhile Jim went to phone Weston Police Station. Luckily our pram base had been handed in. We would fetch it within the next few days.

So two days later we were once more walking up and down the promenade in Weston. This time we were there for two reasons: one to retrieve the pram base and the other to allow the builder to raise the floor height in our bedroom cupboard and re-do the ceiling. We had another marvellous day. When we returned, the builder commented, "It's all right for some. Others have to work for a living," which filled Jim with guilt.

Mum came down on the coach to visit us, staying in a nearby B&B, which was really considerate of her. We had a few days out and about, taking her to lovely beauty spots in the area, before she had to get back to run the Post Office. I think she wondered how on earth we could live with all the mess we were in.

Poor Pippy had a lot to contend with. Having been our 'cosseted baby' for some years, she had now had her nose put well and truly out of joint. She would walk along the back of the settee, looking down at the baby with disdain. And besides having to get used to living in a new house, there was all the building work going on. She must have thought she was in hell.

After several weeks the work was finished, including having electro-osmosis installed. I'm not an expert, but I know that the copper wire that is inlaid around the house walls at damp-proof height repels the damp and stops it rising. Something to do with negatives and positives.

We now had a lovely fitted kitchen with a large window looking down the garden, full of brightness and allowing extra light into the once-dingy dining room. The kitchen units were only basic, but to us they were just the ticket. The downstairs toilet was gone; it had been illegal anyway, as it opened into the kitchen. It was now part of our new, roomy bathroom. Then, at the end of the landing (taken from part of the old bedroom) was our new bedroom. All we had to do was decorate everywhere.

Eventually, we had the house to our liking. Jim had knocked a wide arched opening through from the lounge to the dining room, and we hung some heavy velvet curtains along that wall behind the settee, to draw across at night.

Miss Edwards (whom we now called Nina) had given them to us – they were proper old-fashioned velvet, French navy in colour, which set off the 'terracotta rose' walls nicely. We also had a spare one to hang over the front door, which opened into the living room.

By Christmas the house was sorted. We were content, but almost penniless. For a Christmas tree, Jim cut the conical top off a holly tree that he'd found in the middle of a wood. With six colourful chocolate trinkets hanging from it, it looked rather good, standing on top of our sideboard.

By late spring I discovered I was pregnant again – not planned. It was quite a worry with Jim still being out of work; but nevertheless I was delighted. Mum thought I was copying Helen, who'd just given birth to Michelle, only fifteen months after having Richard. But it was truly unexpected. Mrs Carruthers-Little, Nina's friend, said she hoped I wasn't going to be one of those women who 'keeps having babies.'

We set about sorting the garden, laying it to grass to the halfway mark, then growing salads at the top end of the remainder, to where the ground began plunging towards the stream. I remember the soil being beautifully black, and Jim planted lettuces as if he were planting an orchard – laterally, longitudinally and diagonally, they were in perfect lines. He then set about laying a patio of broken slabs outside the kitchen window. This caved-in before it was finished, revealing a rat's nest, full of pink babies and a network of passages. We were horrified, but neighbours told us that the rats came up from the sewers at the bottom of the garden, so getting in the 'rat-man' would only be a temporary solution.

In June, we planned to have Peter and Michelle christened in a joint ceremony. We took Chris and Mags with us to Grantham (Chris was to be Peter's Godfather). The vicar had once been an actor, and didn't we know it! He orated at length, banging on about "the mother cannot be Godmother to her own baby." But he'd got it all wrong. Peter's Godmother was his brother Richard's new wife, who was also Frances Adams. Oh what confusion! Meanwhile I was one of baby Michelle's Godmothers. It was really amusing to see how Richard and Peter reacted with each other; now seventeen months and eleven months respectively. We were well entertained.

A couple of weeks later, Helen and Carl came down to visit, and to see our 'new' house. They were well impressed. Carl thought we'd 'fallen on our feet'. He'd brought us some lovely 'Circus' petunias and helped us plant them in our front garden. They looked a picture – so did our house with its newly painted 'Buckingham Green' front door.

I was invited to join the Mother and Baby Group in the Community Hall, but only attended twice, not being able to cope with sitting in a circle with all the other mums face to face. I'd be bright red and miserable. Instead I pushed Peter to Wai Ling's – about a mile and a half – or she'd bring Wendy to our house. Somehow I seemed more relaxed with foreigners. Wai Ling's other children called me 'Fatsis,' genuinely thinking that was my proper name, especially because I was getting a fat tummy. Josephine, the eldest, was six, Sheila five, Lokson, their only son, four and Linda with the fat rosy cheeks was three. (Jim cheekily asked Wai Ling what had happened then, as she'd gone two and a half years before having Wendy!) I marvelled at the way the children learned to talk beautiful English, just from watching programmes like 'Playschool'.

When we went for a real Chinese meal (nothing like a take-away), Peter was usually fast asleep by the time it was ready – he just couldn't hold on any longer. On special occasions they'd put the food on a carousel in the middle of the table. There might be three different meat dishes as well as a fish dish, and numerous vegetable options, presented in different ways. The children always wanted the fish's eyes, while Tony liked to have a good chew on the cockerel's claws.

Up until now, Peter had slept in our bedroom. It was time to get him used to the new bedroom before the baby arrived. This however was a big problem, and I often ended up slumped against a spare mattress in the corner of this room. I'd try to sneak out as soon as I thought he was asleep, but as soon as I got to the door, he'd rear up and begin crying. It was exhausting. One afternoon, Nina came to look after him, while Jim and I went to town to buy me sensible shoes. (I'd recently slipped on the stairs in my platform sandals). As we were leaving, Peter began crying, up in his cot. Nina clapped her hands loudly and shouted, "Be quiet!" and he shut up. We felt quite reluctant to leave him in her care. We'd never shouted at him before, but the shock certainly had the desired affect.

On the penultimate day of the baby's birth, we spent half the night choosing a name. Jim had a good school friend called Malcolm, a name he really liked, and we thought Robert went nicely with that; both names having Scottish connotations, after Jim's Scottish heritage. We couldn't think of any girls' names. Anyway, I was hoping for another boy.

The following night I went into labour. I got out the twin-tub late at night, to get all the nappies washed, ready for Jim to look after Peter. I hoped he'd cope. He ran to the village around 11pm to phone for a taxi. It felt so lonely, going into hospital alone on that starry mid-December night. Jim couldn't be with me this time. However, the baby was to be delivered by the same midwife who'd dealt with me throughout my pregnancy. I liked her very much. At least I'd know someone there.

Malcolm Robert arrived at 4 am, on December 15th 1973. It was a much easier birth than last time. Another lovely boy, just as I'd hoped! Girls were too much trouble, as my father had found out. Malcolm was a big baby with reddish fair hair. I thought he looked like my Uncle Jim – quite a Lambley! I was put in a small room with four beds; nicer than the many-bedded ward I'd been in before. I acquainted myself with the other three mums, who were astonished that my husband didn't yet know that I'd been safely delivered of a baby boy. But how could he know? He couldn't leave Peter with Phyllis and Edie in the middle of the night to go half a mile to the phone box.

About 10 am I recognised Jim's tuneless whistle coming down the corridor. He acted nonchalantly, not seeming too enamoured with his new son; probably embarrassed, with the other three mums watching him.

The following day he fetched me home. The first things I noticed on arrival were the two bowls and two spoons, laid neatly together on the draining board. Jim had managed magnificently. I felt like an intruder, bringing another baby on the scene – to perhaps be in competition with Peter. Jim adored Peter and hadn't had the bond created by seeing Malcolm born. I think the truth was, he didn't know how to love more than one child at a time, and was probably worrying about how he would support his enlarged family.

In the spring, I took the babes to Grantham on the Black and White coach. Malcolm was in a 'Baby Relax' seat, a lightweight folding contraption made of strong wire with a fabric body; ideal for the journey. I wore my warm grey coat that Mum and Auntie Kath had treated me to for Dad's funeral. It was easy to feed four-month-old Malcolm on the bus, secreted behind the wide flap of this coat. Peter, who was sitting next to the window, frequently banged his head on the window frame every time the bus made a sharp turn. I had to be really vigilant to anticipate when this might happen.

The grandparents and Auntie Kath were eagerly awaiting us as we stepped off the bus. They hadn't seen my new baby, nor seen Peter since the previous summer. He went down the steps first, carrying his little brown suitcase – it melted their hearts. I bundled off behind him, with arms full of bags and baby. "Oh" Mum and Auntie Kath chorused, "doesn't he look like our Jim?" They were referring to Uncle Jim. Grandma and Granddad were equally delighted to see us. I felt it was worth the effort to have made the trip.

Following that success, I repeated the journey while they were still small. This time we were seated at the back of the bus. I began to feel sick, but was able to move nearer to the front when passengers got off at Leicester. Unfortunately, as I was hanging onto the babes, I couldn't warn the driver of my urgent problem and was sick all over the floor. I felt so ashamed and sorry for the driver, who would have to deal with the problem. I don't think I tackled that coach trip again.

Malcolm's hair had now become very blond and curly. He was broader-framed than Peter and had an independent nature. When I fed him his porridge he'd scream as if being murdered, because *he* wanted to hold the spoon. The first time he had something solid, a sandwich, he was sitting in his low-chair under the staircase, while Peter played with a plastic jiffy lemon, minus the little blue top, which we'd carefully disposed of. Next thing I knew, Malcolm went red in the face. I scooped the sandwich quickly out of his mouth, thinking it might be stuck in his throat. Now he was turning purple. In a panic, I scooped him out of the chair, raced upstairs and, holding him over the bath by his legs, gave him a thump on the back. Out shot the very middle of the jiffy lemon – the bit with the hole in, that appears to be fixed. I don't know how Peter had taken that out and I certainly didn't see him go near Malcolm with it. It was a very near thing. I felt dreadful.

Peter was a really bright toddler, always wanting to use the tools that were lying around the house, but knowing he mustn't. "Nooo," he'd say, pointing to a tool on the floor that he longed to get hold of. However, on Malcolm's first birthday, as we watched him in his low-chair, playing with his giant Lego birthday present, Peter suddenly emptied the vacuum bag all over his head. Poor little Malcolm nearly choked to death again. We hadn't seen or heard Peter open up the vacuum and pull out the bag. What a little devil! We didn't think he knew how to do it.

Malcolm was often sick while crawling on his stomach. Peter would run to tell me "Nah-nah icks" when this happened. He always called his brother "Nah-nah." Jim often played his guitar with one foot on a footrest. Peter mimicked this. He'd sit on his little stool, and with one foot on Jim's footrest, play his ukulele, looking just like a Spanish professional. We nicknamed him 'Pedro Maniero'.

Sometimes 'Uncle' Chris called to see us on his motorbike. Peter was scared to death of Chris's crash helmet, which he always tried to hide discreetly behind the settee.

Nina was a regular visitor. She was Auntie Nina to the boys; almost like a Grandma, seeing as they didn't have one within a hundred miles. Every time she came to our house we had to shut Pippy in the bedroom. Nina, with her steel-grey short hair held back by large grips and wearing her no-nonsense lace-up shoes, was absolutely paranoid about cats. As a nurse, she claimed she'd seen lungs full of cat hairs, and she herself had only one lung. Once, when she arrived before we'd removed Pippy, she almost climbed up the wall in a panic, nearly knocking the mirror off its hook. She'd bring little treats, like nice cakes for our tea, and for the boys' birthdays she always gave them something they could treasure.

Now Jim got a job delivering fridges and cookers for Newey and Eyre. It was not a sensible choice of job, considering that he was on the Disablement Register, but he liked driving jobs, especially because there was no foreman to boss him about. My time was absorbed with looking after these boys, with the endless round of washing and drying nappies and clothes. Wash, dry, wear; wash, dry, wear. Would there ever be a break? But although it was daunting, I just loved having these two lovely boys. There was a day, however, when I felt desperate to be on top of a hill, to see a view, to do it independently. I put the boys in their stout Silver Cross twin pushchair that Mum had bought us second-hand and set off for Leckhampton Hill. I decided to go up the private road, Pilley Lane, past Mr Cleary's house and follow the track beyond. But a heavy twin pushchair doesn't lend itself to rough, bumpy ground, and three-quarters of the way up, I had to concede. In tears, I came back home.

I could kick myself, in hindsight, that I didn't involve Jim more with looking after the boys. By coping all the time, I was inadvertently pushing him out. But I remember the occasion when both boys had a stomach bug and had to be starved for 48 hours. Jim was a real brick and I couldn't have managed without him.

As expected, Jim's job didn't last for many months. He wished he was still that super-fit man who was good at wrestling; but the truth was, he wasn't. He found this hard to accept. Going back on the dole was difficult. It always meant losing money in the process, and when you're not managing anyway, it really hits you. Jim was getting more and more depressed, spending hours in the bedroom, practising classical guitar. He was becoming very talented in the process, but often morbid as well. He hadn't had any bursts of temper since we'd moved into this house, but maybe he was holding all the tension in. Now he talked of leaving us, but he couldn't go until he'd fitted safety catches to the bedroom windows. This he never got round to. It was a 'get-out' clause to help him cope – an escape route, should he really need it.

Mr Cleary called round to see if I was interested in doing some work at home. It was embarrassing to answer the door, because I was crying at the time. Life was getting a bit overwhelming. But Mr Cleary was very understanding, and had a long talk with Jim, telling him how he'd gone through a bad patch with his wife, feeling he didn't want to be with her anymore. Now, he said, he couldn't live without her.

I was glad that he had some work for me. The first job was to paint an ornate iron fire-surround in specific colours, chosen by the client. Then he had several large fancy picture frames to be re-moulded, then gilded. It was good for me to earn a little extra and to be 'hands-on' again. I could work at the bottom end of our bedroom.

Mr Cleary had moved from Leckhampton now, buying the first shop on Suffolk Road, just round the corner from our old flat on Bath Road, with a house and small garden at the back. A few doors further up the road, he set up his divorced daughter in another shop, selling mirrors. Then at the end of that rank was another interior design establishment, owned by a Christopher Galloway. Having got the taste for doing jobs at home, I called in, to see if he had anything for me. He had. There was a client of his in Manchester who was installing a circular bath in the middle of his bathroom. Could I do the working drawings for its supporting framework? This was a real interior design job, which would stretch my brain.

Mr Galloway came round to the house and with a bit of input from him, and a bit from me, we worked out how it could be done. I then made the necessary drawings. Of course, I had absolutely no idea what I should charge him, but what I did was probably way below the going rate. I had nothing and nobody to compare with.

Soon he was back with another assignment; this time to design a shop-front for a new shoe-shop on The Promenade. I don't know if my design had any worth or not – there was nothing outstanding about my design – but the night he was due to collect my work, I'd spotted an article in the local paper. A Mr Christopher Galloway had been in court, charged with killing two women in a car when he'd fallen asleep at the wheel. The report continued that because he was very wealthy, he would be fined accordingly. Whereas I'd planned to charge him £10 for this assignment, I now doubled it to £20. He didn't put any more work my way; either my ideas were not good enough or I had charged too much. I don't think it was the latter because, in London, interior designers would be charging hundreds.

I'd walk to Wai Ling's most weeks. One day I cut her children's hair and made their fringes too short. "Sawl wight. Ownee childen," said Wai. Another time she asked me if I'd take them to town to get their feet measured and buy them new shoes, on her behalf. That was very trusting of her. I pushed Wendy, Peter and Malcolm in the twin pushchair, with Peter and Wendy taking turns to stand on the footrest. From the shoe-shop we went into the store next door, where half the children disappeared up to the first floor, exploring. I didn't know where they'd got to or what they were up to. It was bedlam, gathering those mischievous young children together again. When I got them home their Mum was really cross, telling them they were "Velly laughty childen."

One day, Tony brought a newly killed cockerel round to our house and plucked it in the kitchen sink. It was a thank-you gift for helping them out on occasions. We let him keep the claws to cook and chew on.

Now Jim had heard of a violin-making school in Newark, Nottinghamshire. The idea of making violins really appealed to him. He was so good at working with wood and was a perfectionist. He applied for a place, went for an interview and was accepted. The Violin School took only six pupils from the UK each year and six from abroad. It was a great honour to get a place. It boosted Jim's moral no end. However, he couldn't start until the following September. Even so, we needed to move from this little cottage that had once been our pride and joy.

We put the house on the market and it sold for £9,000. The solicitor said to Jim, "If you can make that much money on a house, you don't need to work any more." That was the most stupid thing he could have said, had he known it.

School Road, as far as we were concerned, had been spoiled by modernisation. The two pairs of council houses across the road had been pulled down and replaced with eight terraced council houses, with large kitchen windows on the front. We were confronted with the sights and sounds of all these families, where once there'd been tranquillity. It wasn't the same as the School Road we'd loved.

Phyllis and Edie were saddened that we were leaving. They adored the two boys, who often wandered in through their back door, to sit beneath the dining-room table and sing them nursery rhymes. These two elderly sisters had become so attached to us. Auntie Nina would miss us too, but at least she had relatives and a network of friends nearby. Phyllis and Edie only had each other. The fact was, I was abandoning three more elderly ladies as they reached their latter years. It felt so mean.

We were going to live with my mum in Grantham, until we found a house nearer to Newark. We were grateful for her offer of this option. We moved on December 19th, four days after Malcolm's second birthday, hiring a van to do our own removal. Two days earlier, we'd taken the boys to stay with Grandma and Granddad, coming home to pack everything up. On arrival back in Grantham, we unloaded everything into a storage unit, where it would remain for a few months. Then Jim took the van back to Charlton Kings and picked up his car. It had been exhausting.

Being at Mum's gave us a bit of breathing space. We could share time between 142 and Grandma and Granddad's. Granddad proved to be much better at being a granddad than he had at being a father. Poor Mum, on the other hand, would come home at lunchtimes to find me doing hand washing in the sink with Lux Flakes. Her face said it all – "Oh no, not washing again." I think she found it quite hard coping with us, but was really sad when we left.

By now, we called the boys Pete and Malc, and the two Grandmas were referred to as Grandma Buttons and Grandma Car (because Jim's mum had two large sweet jars of buttons that the boys played with, and my mum had a car). Poor Grandma Buttons said, "I know my place."

We set about house hunting in earnest, considering all sorts of cottages going cheap in isolated villages around

Newark; one had a concrete bedroom floor that dipped in the middle like a saucer. Imagine the wardrobes toppling over! Another had rotten windows that wouldn't close. We were getting quite carried away with the idea of doing up another property. Thankfully we settled for something more normal in the end. We found a lovely 1930s semi-detached house on Dorothy Avenue, on the west side of Melton Mowbray (the district of my birth). It was sixteen miles from Grantham and about thirty from Newark. As well as three bedrooms and a bathroom, there was a large garden at the back with two apple trees and lots of gooseberry bushes. It had been an advantage moving further north – the houses were cheaper, so we could afford something better. Jim had found employment to tide us over until he went to college, so we secured a mortgage. Things were looking up for us.

MELTONIAN

CHAPTER 18

Melton Mowbray

Malc, Lindsay, Pete and Jim on Mundesley beach, August Bank Holiday 1976

Melton Mowbray is a market town set in the rolling landscape of Leicestershire, surrounded by small villages which have an old fashioned, no-hurry feel to them. The area is blessed with rich, dark red soil, full of iron; veritable farming country. As well as the weekly Tuesday market, which has been going since the 14th century, Melton has a thriving cattle market and abattoir. The main employer in town is (or was) Pet Foods. It seems that the town is very meat orientated.

The famous Melton Mowbray pork pies are produced here and also Stilton cheeses. We often saw cheeses hanging in muslin from the overhanging eaves of village cottages – everywhere, it seemed, cheese was being made. A less common sight, but enough to churn your stomach, was to see a truckload of cattle heads encased in a wire cage, passing through town. Their dead eyes stared dolefully through the mesh as they made their way from the abattoir to nearby Stapleford Park, to be fed to the lions. Quite a horrific sight! If the whole population becomes vegetarian, will we still breed farm animals to feed our 'park' lions and 'captive' endangered species?

Melton used to be the centre of foxhunting country, with both the Quorn and Belvoir Hunts in the vicinity. Quorn was the first hunt to be formed, back in the 18th century, and the town had once prospered from visiting huntsmen lodging in the local hostelries. Now its prosperity rests on meat and cheese!

Many Indian families came to Melton – settling here mainly to work at Pet Foods, having first immigrated to Leicester. Although that city has an enormous population of Hindus and Muslims, they seemed to be well absorbed into the community.

The job Jim had taken on, prior to moving here, was to do with plastic bag production. The work place was an open hangar, on a godforsaken airfield on a hill. He and his work-mates endured a foggy, freezing January, even though there was high pressure throughout that month.

They'd been frozen to the marrow. What's more, the pay was a pittance, but it gave us enough income for the small mortgage we needed. So in March 1976 we moved in. It was difficult to remember what we'd packed in which boxes – for instance, we couldn't find the cutlery, plates and cups and everyone was hungry, thirsty and exhausted. I didn't know where to start! If only we'd written the contents on the boxes.

During those early days, we were spending the money left in the bank. Both grandmothers thought we should be more frugal, but for us it was such a novelty to have spare cash. Firstly Jim sold the Morris Oxford and bought a 1302S Volkswagen in shiny metallic blue, which didn't have nearly as much room as the Morris Oxford but would hopefully, be more economical. On Sundays we took trips to the vast open-air Shoby Market nearby, where Jim and I bought a leather coat each. One Sunday we lost Malc. The red balaclava I had recently knitted him showed up like a beacon. But where was it? We frantically asked for an announcement to be made on the Tannoy and within minutes he was spotted. Oh the dreadful thoughts you have, when your child goes missing!

It wasn't very long before Jim gave in his notice. He'd hated every hour of the job, becoming more and more depressed. Now, hoping to improve the house before beginning his training, he set about making alterations. The front door, middle door to the kitchen and the back door were all in a line. It was so draughty, with doors constantly slamming in the wind. Jim planned to block off the middle door and put a small window in its place, then make an opening from the dining room to the kitchen. The first job was this wide opening.

However, it was during this time that Mum decided to sell 142 and move house. She'd rattled around in all that space since Dad had died. Jim and I set about the formidable task of sorting and packing for her, while Grandma and Granddad enjoyed entertaining the boys.

There were so many memories in the souvenirs Dad had collected, so many treasured pieces of furniture that Mum couldn't bring herself to part with, so she took many antiques with her when she moved further down Harrowby Road. The large mahogany sideboard looked so out of place in her modern lounge, but she couldn't bring herself to part with it.

Mum moved house five times during the rest of her life, each time letting go of a few more antiques. On her final move, when she decided to rent rather than buy, she acquired a houseful of modern furniture, with not an antique in sight.

That summer of 1976 was the hottest we'd known and it lasted for ages. We found slight relief by sitting on the hallway floor, waiting for a draught of air to come through. The kitchen door hadn't yet been blocked off. Outside, Jim had levelled a large area for a lawn. Now the new turf was cracked into squares, brown and curled up at the edges. When would it all end?

Lindsey, the cousin who'd stayed with us when Jim was in his plaster cast, invited us to Norfolk for the August Bank Holiday. The thought of swimming in the sea was most alluring, and we eagerly looked forward to staying with her, but that weekend the weather broke. We found ourselves on a stormy Mundesley beach, wearing winter coats and hats, and the boys in their red balaclavas once more. But in spite of this dramatic weather change, we enjoyed staying there. We visited Uncle Victor in Worstead. He looked very similar to Jim, even down to the muscular physique. Needless to say, Malc managed to fall into the garden pond.

That September, Jim began his new career in violin making. What should have been a joyous time was marred by the fact that he couldn't get a grant. Also, the house was unfinished. The labour exchange said that if he gave up the college course he could have dole money, but how could he possibly give up such a prestigious training offer? I was prepared to go through thick and thin for him to remain on this course.

Now we *were* struggling, with no money coming in except my family allowance, and hardly anything left in the bank. Why hadn't we listened to the grandmas? I went to the rates office to explain why we couldn't pay, but burst into tears instead. We couldn't afford to use hot water in the bathroom as the meter under the stairs gobbled two-shilling coins at an alarming rate. Gas seemed cheaper. So we boiled the kettle and washed in a bowl in front of the gas fire in the dining room – the only room with instant heat.

There was a six-foot wide opening into the kitchen, and the middle door, although blocked up, was still waiting for a window to be fitted. We were so cold that winter.

Mum had just bought herself a new lounge carpet and a leather three-piece suite. She gave us her old ones, which were not old at all. I think this was partly as a thank you for helping her to move. The three-piece suite had loose covers in floral patterns on a beige background, set off nicely by the red sculptured carpet. Then my piano was brought over. Now the front room looked really grand, but we only went in there in wintertime to wave goodbye to Jim as he set off for college each day.

The following February, when Richard was over from Canada for a brief visit, Mum brought him over to Melton. I made a fire in the front room grate, trying my hardest to get it blazing. Maybe it was cheap coal, but it wouldn't flare up. When Mum and Richard arrived, we sat in our lovely, newly furnished front room, shivering. I went to poke some life into the fire, and Richard said, "Pass the poker round, Fraan. Let's all have a bit of heat."

Sometimes Jim took us to Grantham on a Saturday morning, then came home to pursue violin repairing or any other woodwork projects. The spare bedroom was now his workshop.

I often walked into Grantham market with Grandma Buttons on Saturday mornings. I remember her telling me that nobody was looking at me when I was getting embarrassed. Grandma Car would collect us in the early afternoon, after closing the Post Office. Then Jim picked us up in the evening, and with Pete and Malc already in their pyjamas, all we needed to do was carry them up to bed when we reached home. They'd be fast asleep by then.

Most Sundays, Mum came over for lunch, bringing a cardboard box of delights with her – vegetables and tins of food to help us through the week, plus little treats for the boys. We'd go for an afternoon walk along the disused railway embankment just up the road from where we lived. And so we kept going until, after six months, Jim was awarded a TOPS grant. We were saved.

Pete had just started going to a playgroup before we left Charlton Kings and was now attending one in Melton for two mornings a week. While he was there, I'd push Malc around town. When Malc joined too a while later, I felt absolutely lost. Pete and Malc had always been with me and had, unknowingly, been my props. Now my old hang-ups came back. I was reluctant to walk home alone, all along that long Asfordby Road. I soon became friendly with another mum, Anita, and used to walk back to her house in town for a cup of tea while our children were in playschool.

Anita was a vivacious, auburn-haired, very alternative sort of woman; she was divorced with three children, the middle one of whom had Down's Syndrome. He was a beautiful boy with dark red hair. Anita's ex-husband was Italian and owned a hair salon in town, but Anita was feisty and independent, and was saving up to emigrate to Australia with her children. Although she was on the dole, she put by whatever she could. The family's staple diet was homemade wholemeal bread, spread with peanut butter and honey. Anita stole telephone directories from telephone boxes to use for toilet paper and she thought of all the cost-cutting things imaginable, legal or illegal, to save up for their fares. I lost touch with her when she left to fulfil her dream. I heard that she 'got off' with the captain of the ship! With her gone, I now stayed on at playschool, to help out.

It took a long time for Jim to complete the alterations to the house. When the kitchen opening was all plastered, I painted the room and hung our lovely velvet curtains on either side in the dining room. They looked really good and made such a difference to keeping the dining room warm.

Jim was really enjoying college life, but being the only student to be married and with children made him feel somewhat 'hemmed in'. Coming home tired, he found he couldn't cope with the boys' exuberant energy and noise in the evenings. (We called the half-hour before bedtime "Hancock's half-hour," because the boys always seemed to have a rush of energy then). So now he'd want them to be in bed before he got home. This meant putting them to bed before 6.30pm. Consequently, Pete was always awake at 5am. It was a long day for me.

Then Jim told me he wanted a divorce. He couldn't afford to keep a family if he was going to be a violin maker, he told me. What's more, he asked me to go to the solicitor on his behalf. The solicitor laughed down his nose and said, "If he thinks he's going to be better off divorced, he's got another think coming." I went home to report on what I'd been told. Nothing more was spoken of the matter. However I began seeing a marriage guidance counsellor, taking the boys with me, because I never liked leaving them with Jim now, since he'd begun having bouts of violent tempers again.

Expecting some sympathy from the counsellor, I was rather taken aback when she said that Jim sounded a very interesting man; she'd quite like to meet him. Then a couple of weeks later, I saw this same woman visiting a near neighbour of mine, with whom I was quite friendly. They were obviously close friends and I felt inhibited telling the counsellor my private business, with this friend living so close by. So I stopped going.

Now, with Jim at college, I enrolled on a 'playgroup leadership' course in the local college. Melton Mowbray had a marvellous technical college at the town end of Asfordby Road, catering for students of all ages and from all walks of life. They also had a lively theatre, which we went to once, to see Punjabi dancing.

Each Friday morning I left the boys in the crèche, where they became acquainted with two more brothers of similar ages. Soon their mum Cait and I were firm friends, and her two sons, Leo and Gideon, became great pals with Pete and Malc. Then, when this two-term course was completed, Cait and I joined a WEA (Workers' Educational Association) discussion group. Most of the participants were university graduate mums, and the intellectual stimulation was good for both of us.

This group prided itself on being the only WEA discussion group in the country then. By avidly absorbing myself in the discussions around a huge table, I found I could cope. Our topics were wide and varied – anything from Palestine to philosophy, or the causes of the Irish 'problem', with speakers coming in from elsewhere, plus being led by several well-qualified tutors, one of whom gave art lessons to the Black Panther, the notorious murderer, in prison!

The children from the Dorothy Avenue area went to school at Asfordby Hill, a small village three miles west of Melton. Pete began his schooling there in 1977. How those first five years of his life had flown by. How I'd dreamed of having young children around me for an eternity, only to find that, in the blink of an eye, they were off to school.

Asfordby Hill School was a lively little school which encouraged much parental involvement. The classes performed frequent plays for the parents to see, and this built the children's confidence no end. Every morning the mums and pupils gathered at the bus stop on Asfordby Road, which was almost opposite the end of Dorothy Avenue. This main road was quite dangerous, with heavy lorries tearing to and fro from the gravel extraction works at Frisby-on-the-Wreake, so road safety was paramount. On the mornings when a school play was to be performed, the mums, and sometimes dads, would travel on the coach with their children.

Barton's Coach Company provided the public transport

around town and the surrounding villages. These red coaches served Melton well. As well as the comfort of the high-backed seats, the fares were very reasonable. Conversely, sitting on a Lincolnshire Road Car bus to Grantham was much less comfortable; just like the stagecoach buses of today, with their hard, low-backed seats with a metal grab-rail along the top, at the height of a child's face. What's more, the fares were not reasonable.

Not long after Pete started school, I began childminding. It would be company for Malc and I could, at last, earn myself a bit of cash. Meg, the childminder assessor, came round to assess me. With the carrot and turnip tops growing untidily in saucers on the mantelpiece, and with the dust on the sideboard, she assessed that I had got my priorities right, and put more store in the children's interests than in keeping the house spick and span. She enthused over the 'stick people' that Malc was busy drawing and asked if she could replicate them in the next 'Childminder' magazine. We were delighted. A big perk for me was that I would be given a large all-encompassing fireguard for safety reasons. I could now air clothes on the large flat top.

My first children were Andrew and Laura, a brother and sister. Their mother was an architect, going back to work for two days each week. This would be a gradual introduction to my new undertaking. Andrew and Malc were the same age and got on well with each other. Laura was a one-year-old – a very contented baby who slept for quite a lot of the time. One day, while I was taking the two boys upstairs,

Andrew remarked, "These stairs are filthy." I was taken aback and felt rather ashamed that a four-year-old should be making such judgements. But then I remembered why Meg had thought me suitable for childminding – I wasn't obsessed with cleaning!

CHAPTER 19

Laxmi et al

Kavita and Sumita.

There were two Indian ladies in saris that we often passed as we went to the little shop on Asfordby Road, both wearing a red friendship spot in the middle of their foreheads. They'd smile and nod as they passed. Before long we got chatting with them and were soon invited into their house up the road. They were Laxmi and her daughter-in-law Angela (Manjula), who worked at 'Thorn Lighting' (or 'Torn Lighting' as they called it) in Leicester, going by bus.

In the Patel household with Laxmi lived her elderly husband, their son Ken (Kirit) and wife Angela, who was pregnant. When their daughter Mumpta was born, Angela soon returned to work, leaving Mumpta in Laxmi's care.

Lovely Laxmi had lived a life of servitude. At thirteen she'd been married to a man of thirty-five and as tradition dictated, had gone to live in his household, looking after his elderly parents as well as her husband. Kirit was born when she was fifteen and was their only child. The family then moved to Uganda, to begin a new life together. However, under the dictatorship of Idi Amin, the Ugandan Asians were expelled in 1972, and Laxmi's family came to England. Her in-laws had died and now she cared for her elderly husband, who was overweight and diabetic. Although only a few years my senior, she seemed a generation older, having already cared for her in-laws, now her husband and before long, she'd have four grandchildren in her care. I admired her greatly. She wasn't in perfect health herself, having a permanent pain in her leg – "caused by the devil," she said. In spite of this she also grew vegetables in the garden. Ken told us that, in India, it was easy to grow two sets of crops a year.

Ken was a bit of a bragger, but justifiably so; his job at Pet Foods was very repetitive and a certain amount of bragging enhanced his status. He'd allowed his little fingernail to grow long, so that it twisted; a sort of status symbol – implying that he didn't have to work hard! Ken referred to nearly all the Hindu men in town as his cousin-brothers. They had an altar in an alcove in their house, where a candle burned constantly. Candles seemed to play a big part in their religion. Angela took the boys and me to their Diwali celebrations once, where women carried lighted candles on flower-adorned trays. We joined in with their dances as best we could, our favourite being the 'Clap Dance'.

Laxmi and Angela did an enormous amount of cooking preparation, and loved showing us how it was done. They'd grind dried peas to a paste, mix it with something spreadable, then spread it onto spinach leaves, to be rolled up and cut into slices; just like a Swiss roll. Yoghurt was made on their worktop and spices kept carefully in tightly sealed containers, in the dark.

I was invited to Mumpta's first birthday celebrations, where naturally, much cooking was done beforehand. I arrived to find the men seated on settees in the lounge area of the living room, while the women sat gracefully on the floor in the dining area. Mumpta was sitting in her pram nearby, her eyes lined thickly in black, and with a black 'bracelet' around her wrist. This, I was told, was to keep out evil spirits. I seated myself self-consciously on the floor, trying to cover my knees with my short wrap-over skirt. The Indian ladies sat elegantly, with not a bit of leg showing. I felt distinctly inelegant, but they smiled politely!

Only two at a time could dine at the small table. so, in order of seniority, the men went first, with Laxmi and Angela hovering on the kitchen step, to address their every need. After we'd all partaken of the feast, Laxmi and Angela sat down to eat the remains.

Jim and I once watched them making a chicken curry

in their kitchen (for the men-folk who didn't stick to vegetarianism). Then they helped us to make one at our house. Firstly, we were taught how to dissect the chicken into sizable portions. Then the spices were sizzled in the pan in a certain order. We learned the spices by their Indian names first, before learning their English equivalents. Another time they showed us how to make dhal curry, then chutneys and jams. They were patient tutors, giving us lots of tips.

Once we went to an Indian wedding in town, held in the Polish Community Centre, which was a large hall in a Nissen hut. We sat amongst rows of chanting women, between Laxmi and Angela on folding chairs, facing the stage. There was much activity behind us, where food was being prepared noisily, with much crashing of pans. Meanwhile, the bride was seated on one side of the stage with her husband-to-be on the opposite side, while the chanting priest sat centrally at the back of the stage. They sat cross-legged on low cushions. The groom had recently arrived from India (the couple had never previously met) and a long, thick rope, adorned with flowers, was looped across the stage around both their necks. Was this a portent of a life of servitude?

Eventually there was a pause in proceedings. The disruptive young men from the back of the room handed out trays with hollows in (like you get on aeroplanes). Then, from large pans, steaming spicy concoctions were dished out into the various hollows of our trays.

We'd arrived at 9.30 am. Now Pete and Malc were becoming restless, wanting to run about. By 2.30pm we made our excuses and left, relieved to get into the fresh air after five hours. We might have felt obliged to stay to the very end if the boys hadn't been with us.

Ken often brought Mumpta round to play during the day. He worked shifts. Little Mumpta had a habit of putting things in her pocket. She was innocently taking things she liked, like bits of Lego or a dinky car. Ken always returned them next time he came round. The boys used to chant (out of their earshot) "Mumpta, Mumpta, stick it up your jumper."

After Andrew and Laura, I began looking after Sumita, a two-and-a-half-year-old Indian girl. Her father, Saga, was a Professor of Engineering and his wife also had a good job in town. Sumi, a chunkily built little girl with a thick crop of short hair, came to me at 8 am and was collected at 6 pm, five days a week – a long day for a youngster to endure. Twice a week, her best friend Sabina joined us, which helped Sumi settle in. Sabina was a vivacious, pony-tailed, half-Indian little girl; her father, Wolf, being German.

When Malc went to playschool twice a week, I wheeled them to town in the twin pushchair. That faithful pushchair was great for carrying shopping home along the tediously long Asfordby Road, with the lorries hurtling by. Malc was really kind to Sumi and included her in his games. I was proud of the way he treated her.

In the holidays I had five children to look after with

Sumi's elder sister, Kavita, and then Sabina twice a week. Kavita was Pete's age, but went to a school in town. We'd have a 'school' session for the first half-hour, to calm them down when they first arrived – each tackling a project appropriate to their age. This settled them really well and Sumi progressed in leaps and bounds. Cait often joined us later in the morning, bringing her boys and their sister Caroline, who was nine. There was plenty of garden to play in when it was fine, and two apple trees to climb – one was now Pete's and the other Malc's. However, we'd take them to all the holiday events going. Cait and I made lots of pirate outfits for them all, one holiday. When Jim was working upstairs, we'd try to go out somewhere, to give him a bit of peace and quiet.

Like any normal children, Pete and Malc enjoyed having stories read to them, but Malc had no respect for books at all when he was young. I'd catch him dropping them out of his bedroom window, trying to get them into the large square water butt below. The wooden cover didn't quite fit, leaving a narrow gap at the back – big enough to swallow a 'Ladybird' book, if you got it just right. It wasn't until Pete started school that Malc actually began to look inside books with interest. So absorbed did he then become that he taught himself to read words from an alphabet book without my help. The first word he worked out was 'hill'!

Ken and Angela now had another daughter, Maneesha – a very pretty curly-haired baby. It seemed that Ken was forever coming round with Mumpta and I began to wonder if he had ulterior motives. I got into the habit of quickly getting out the vacuum cleaner when I heard his knock on the door, to appear too busy for visitors. That seemed to do the trick eventually. I was quite happy to see Laxmi and Angela, but too much Ken was too much for me.

When Ken's father died, some time later, his body was taken to India for cremation. Ken accompanied his father's body, as it was his duty to set fire to the funeral pyre on which his dead father was laid. After walking around the pyre three times, as was tradition, he lit the fire. What a brave task for these Hindu sons to perform, to then watch their beloved being burnt to cinders. I'd seen my father's photos of funeral pyres and had thought it a cruel way to dispose of dead people. But in retrospect, it was a sensible way of preventing the spread of diseases in such a hot country.

Not long after this event the family moved into a new house the other side of Melton, and sadly we hardly saw them after that. I felt guilty that we lost contact. I could have written to them.

CHAPTER 20

Indian Cultural Society

Students at Newark School of Violin Making (Jim sitting cross-legged in the centre)

The students at the Violin School had been taken to see Joan Baez in concert at The Crucible in Sheffield, and on another occasion, to see the marvellous South Korean violinist Kyung Wha Chung, in the same venue. Jim's musical interests were broadening greatly. He could now play many types of music on his guitar – classical Spanish, Venezuelan, Flamenco, American 'finger-picking' and early English lute and harpsichord music as well. Now he was going one step further – he joined the Indian Cultural Society in Leicester, to learn to play the sitar.

Once a week he would dash over to Leicester after college, to this fascinating set-up run by an Indian lady named Nilam. In the large space, everything would be going on at the same time. In one area, girls were learning dances, in another, a group of men sat on the floor playing tablas (a type of drum) and yet another group of men, also seated on the floor, were playing their shruti boxes (like a melodeon in sound, but in an actual box, where one side is pushed in and out to pump air through). Finally, a small group would be learning the sitar. Whether playing the shruti box or the sitar, every note the player played had to be sung as well. There are more notes to an Indian scale of music than our octave of eight, and these had to be thoroughly learnt, in order to sing them at the same time as playing them. Therefore, from these large interconnected rooms, there emanated many conflicting noises, although it was vital to concentrate on your own noise and your own particular notes.

Jim became friendly with a Muslim girl called Zehra. Sometimes after the session he would go to her cousin Kanese's house for some food. Zehra was training to be a pharmacist – her cousin was a married woman whose husband knocked her about a lot and had even pushed her down the stairs while she was pregnant. But in spite of this she was a cheerful woman, always willing to welcome visitors to her house. The guests would sit cross-legged around a tablecloth on the floor, waiting for the chapattis that Kanese was cooking on the kitchen stove. As these became ready, she would fling them through the open door to land on the tablecloth – waitress service! Jim thought this was hilarious.

As I've mentioned before, Jim talked a lot. He would tell me all about Zehra; how much he liked her looks. He was always very open and honest, but it hurt. He'd been through a spell when he'd been infatuated with Wai Ling, and we'd got through that. Now it was Zehra's oriental looks that he was extolling. For the first time in my life, I began wearing eye make-up. I was a novice, but felt I needed to compete. I think Mum suspected that things weren't quite right in our household – not that Jim had an affair; he would have told me – he wouldn't have been able to help himself.

Then one dark rainy night, on his dash to Leicester, he had a crash. It was entirely his fault – he was overtaking a lorry on a long left-hand bend. He'd seen the road ahead clearly beforehand; there was not a vehicle in sight, but he didn't realise that there was a little lane halfway round the bend, and a car came out from it. He'd have pulled back in behind the lorry, had the lorry driver not slammed on his brakes, but there was nowhere to go. With the weight of the Volkswagen engine in the back, the car swung manically from side to side, eventually colliding with the oncoming car on the passenger side, then rolling over several times before coming to rest on the driver's side. What a lucky escape Jim had had – the passenger seat was folded in two, the rear seat was bent up double and the only space uncrushed was the driver's seat.

Jim, who'd been very knocked about, managed to climb out of the broken passenger window to go to the aid of the other driver, whose feet were trapped. When the police arrived, Jim heard them say, on seeing the Volkswagen, "He's a goner." They didn't realise that Jim was already out of the car. Anyway, that brought an end to sitar lessons for a while, and I stopped wearing make-up.

Jim was concussed but luckily, wasn't kept in hospital. He spent a very quiet week resting in the armchair, nursing his bruises. Now he had to find public transport to get to Newark, which meant setting off very early in the morning. Then we had to pay for the amount of time the crashed car had been kept in a compound, and also for its removal to a scrapyard, which stripped us of all cash, adding insult to injury. However, someone in the college knew of a Morris Traveller going cheap and Jim scraped up enough money to buy it. The engine was fine, but the gearbox not so good. Jim purchased another one from a local scrap dealer, and together, out on the road, we installed the new gearbox into the old Traveller. My input was not mechanical!

Now the Morris Traveller went fine, but a few days later, two policemen came to the door, making enquiries. There had been some falsifying of licensing details. It had nothing to do with us. So now, a subdued Jim continued with his sitar lessons until the end of his second year at college. Zehra was off to join her parents in Sweden, having finished her studies in Leicester, Nilam was going to live in America and Jim would need to find a job in his new chosen career.

During that summer, he found a job repairing violins at Haken and Bell in Abingdon. There were two other young men already working there; one, Michael Kearns, made and repaired violins, and the other, Mark Yakoushkin, made and repaired bows. They listened to Radio 3 all day long, which drove Jim nuts, but he'd had the training and now he had to use it. Michael and Mark now have a prestigious establishment in Oxford.

Jim found himself a first floor flat in Oxford. Above were three West Indians and below him, in the ground floor flat, was Denise, a woman of about thirty. Most nights the West Indians held parties until about 3 am, while Denise, downstairs, befriended him; indeed she tried to seduce him – enticing him into her flat on one pretext after another. I know, because he told me all about her. She didn't wear knickers (told him, not showed him, apparently) and she stole bicycles whenever she needed to get anywhere.

On Friday nights Jim came home on the train, with his holdall full of washing. I can't remember why he didn't drive. Maybe there was nowhere to park. First thing on Saturday mornings I'd wash his clothes in the twin-tub. They had to be dry enough to iron by Sunday mornings, because he had to leave by afternoon. The weekends weren't at all pleasurable; the main occupation was getting washing dry and ironed. We were lucky to have the big fireguard to help them on their way.

Mum still came over for Sunday dinner, and Jim still jumped up to make the custard, which was about his only input at weekends, knowing it impressed Mum. He did make good custard though, so I shouldn't be bitchy. If we had enough time and it was fine, we'd fit in a walk along the embankment before Jim had to leave. He wasn't at all happy in his job or flat, but continued to stick with it, trying to find other interests to occupy his evenings in Oxford.

He heard of Indian cookery lessons in the Summertown area of Oxford, and went along to join. Now, on cookery nights, he'd carefully bring his hot, newly cooked meal back on the double-decker bus - usually in a Pyrex dish with a lid that leaked. At weekends he'd carefully copy out the recipe into my cookery book. So now we were augmenting our Indian culinary delights. Jim stuck with this job for several months, but in the end he cracked and gave up.

CHAPTER 21

Normalising

Mischief-makers in the back garden at Melton Mowbray

Now we were back on the dole – 'same old, same old', couldn't seem to break the mould. The boys had qualified for free school meals while Jim was a student, and now they were entitled to them again.

With my child-minding money of £16 per week (the amount I could earn before tax in 1980) I took the boys to Grantham on Saturdays, which cost £5. It was a treat to sit upstairs at the front of the double-decker to enjoy the sixteen miles to Grantham. It was a rural, winding route where, as we turned a sharp bend on a rise in the road, we could glimpse Belvoir Castle in the distance, amongst the rolling hills. In those first years, beautiful elm trees had graced the landscape. But this was the dawning of Dutch elm disease, and before long, these lovely big wide trees became skeletons, silhouetted against the sky-line, their former glory gone forever.

After the bend came the 'dip dippers' as the boys called them – three humps in a row towards the village of Croxton Kerrial where, in the car, Jim always drove at speed to make the car 'take off' to give the boys a thrill. The road would then rise up to Waltham-on-the-Wolds, where, in May, the majestic chestnut trees lining the road were covered in pink 'candles.' Before we reached Grantham we'd pass historic Harlaxton Manor on our right, with a long drive that swooped from the gatehouse all the way down to the grand stone mansion, set in a green vale with a backdrop of dark trees. From the top of the bus, the views were splendid

Once we'd reached Grantham, Granddad would often take the boys on long walks, sometimes along the top of the railway embankment towards Ponton, where we'd found that wooden bogie years earlier. They would come clomping back with their shoes inches deep in clay, having had a wonderful time. In inclement weather, their Uncle Richard, now divorced and living at home and training to be a teacher, would allow them to use his typewriter. They wrote endless letters to each and everyone. Richard observed (with his teacher training eye) that they both possessed great levels of concentration. Jim would fetch us in the evenings, from whichever house my Mum had moved to at the time!

I was glad to get the boys out of the house for a break. On the occasions when Jim lost his temper, we'd race upstairs to the boys' bedroom to 'ride out the storm,' standing shaking in the middle of the room, trying to blot out the manic screaming and punching that was going on downstairs. I'm sure it gave Malc a nervous disposition. Pete seemed to cope, but it must have affected him inwardly.

After the storm we'd tentatively creep downstairs to find Jim calmly carrying on with whatever he'd been doing beforehand, or cleaning out his sideboard drawer or his side of the cupboard. This seemed to cleanse his mind.

I confess that I resorted to hitting the boys for wrongdoing. I even think I was getting rid of my own inner frustrations. I could use the excuse that I was brought up with a certain amount of violence myself (most people were, then) but I'm aware now that two wrongs don't make a right. I kept a wooden spoon in the drawer as a threat, but sometimes used it, when I was at breaking point. One day I broke the spoon on Pete's shoulder - an incident he hasn't forgotten. But I have to say in my defence (if indeed I'm allowed any defence) that it was a cheap wooden spoon, with the grain of the wood going diagonally across the handle, so it readily broke.

Jim never laid a finger on me, or the boys. He knew he had a temper and didn't want to risk hurting us. That was a very good thing, but meant I was the one who had to reprimand the boys, or stop them doing something dangerous. I remember Jim saying, from the comfort of his chair, "Go out and stop those boys from playing with that stick. They'll poke their eyes out." I always did the dirty work.

One early Saturday morning, the postman delivered a package. It was a Weetabix lorry that we'd sent off for with Weetabix coupons. Nipping back for an extra half-hour in bed, I left the boys to play with their new toy. When I came down, there was fluff all over the dining room from the packaging. I saw it clinging to the walls and hanging along the picture rails – it was everywhere. I was furious and chased Pete down the hall to smack him (poor Pete, being the eldest, was the first to be blamed). As he turned to run upstairs, he skidded on his too-long pyjama trousers and fell on his face onto the stairs. The poor child had put his top teeth through his lip and it was hanging.

Now Jim came downstairs ranting and raving as I tried to dress the boys at speed, to take them to the surgery in town. It was dreadful; I felt dreadful; I was dreadful. I was ashamed of myself. But I didn't need Jim shouting at me as I tried to get them ready (perhaps he was reacting as young Bruno's parents had reacted in Cheltenham Casualty). It wasn't helping at all. The boys and I went down to wait for the bus into town, poor Pete with his lip hanging. I can't imagine what he thought of me.

It was good for me to be friends with Cait. She never

smacked her children. This was a new approach for me – smacking was the only form of 'last resort' that I seemed to resort to, but I'd never do it to anyone else's child. I tried to follow her example. Then one day, when Cait and family were round at our house, her daughter Caroline, now ten, was being as obnoxious as was ever possible, and could not be brought into line. Suddenly Cait gave her a resounding smack on the bottom. Caroline was SO surprised, having never been smacked in her life, that it did the trick immediately.

★ ★ ★

Our garden was a lovely playground for the boys, with an apple tree each that they loved climbing. There was a big lawn and a yard with a shed. Pippy had settled in well, but she wasn't the same cat as she'd been before the children came along. She just kept quietly in the background.

Then one hot Sunday, when we could hear everyone outside enjoying the sunshine, something strange started happening. One household after another was disappearing inside and shutting their doors. Everywhere had gone quiet. Then a cat appeared over our fence and jumped onto the water butt. It was a grey and white kitten – a large kitten; a teenage one! The side of its mouth had a wound filled with pus, and from its backside came a continuous stream of diarrhoea. Ugh! No wonder everyone had gone indoors. They didn't want anything to do with this messy cat. We felt sorry for it and put it in our shed, giving it some of Pippy's cat food and a saucer of milk. It wouldn't be able to get into our house, with its homemade cat flap that Pippy cleverly lifted with one paw, to get in

For a day or two we housed this kitten in our shed until, on the third day we found it shitting on our best red carpet in the front room. Not that it could help itself. It had learnt how to open the cat-flap of course. We didn't know what to do, so we took it to the vet. The advice we got was not to give it milk, just water, and to feed it on cod's flaps. So now, from the fishmonger, we bought 'flippin' flaps' as we called them, and boiled them for 'Smokey', as the boys had named him. His abscess healed and he was now another member of our family, becoming an absolutely wonderful cat.

There was a plump, rosy-cheeked Irish woman living up our road, who also had two boys, now tall spotty teenagers. The previous Christmas she'd given us some of their toys: table football, 'Buckaroo' and several other games, which gave the boys hours of fun. The following spring, she found a hedgehog squashed on the road outside her house, leaving five orphaned babies in her garden. She asked if I could try to save them. When they arrived, one was already dead. The following day, another died, suffocated by the others. Fleas ran out of their spines and down their noses. We hoped Pippy and Smokey wouldn't pick them up from this blanket-lined box in the kitchen. The following day I drowned one while trying to feed it, so I went to the vet for advice. He suggested feeding the remaining two with an eyedropper. One had deformed hips; his back legs were behind him rather than underneath. However, he was the only one to survive. We called him 'Spike' (we didn't know his gender). When he seemed big enough to fend for himself, we let him go in the garden.

A year later, Spike arrived at our back door. He'd grown considerably but had an engorged tick on his back. If I'd known what to do I'd have burned it off, but I didn't. I wondered if Spike had come for help at removing it, not just to say hello! He ate a saucer of cat food, then toddled back up the garden. We never saw him again.

That summer I took the boys to Gloucestershire for a week, to stay at a caravan site at Bishops Cleeve, near Cheltenham, where Chris and Mags lived in a residential caravan. We'd be able to visit our old friends in Cheltenham. The first day we arranged to meet Auntie Nina for lunch in a fish and chip restaurant in town. We caught an early bus to Cheltenham, giving us time to spare. So when the boys saw rowing boats on Pittville Lake, we alighted: they wanted to have a go. After all, we were on holiday.

After a good half hour on the lake, I had to drag them away to catch a bus into town. But we waited and waited. No bus came. Now we had to walk into town, as fast as possible. It was further than anticipated and we were twenty minutes late. As we met up with Auntie Nina on the Promenade, she came up and slapped me hard across the face. Then we all went for fish and chips, with my cheek smarting!

Another day we planned to visit several people, calling first at Auntie Nina's flat in Russell Square. She wasn't home, but a lady living downstairs said she'd let Nina know that we'd be back later. We didn't give a time. Meanwhile we visited Vera in her flat, enjoying a lovely afternoon with her. When we returned to Russell Square at 6 pm Auntie Nina didn't respond to our knocking, although we could hear her inside. We knocked again; still no answer. The third time, the door opened a crack, and a deep gruff, grating voice said, "Go away." The boys stepped back, horrified. Had Auntie Nina become an ogre? Perhaps the neighbour had told her we'd be back for tea, so she'd assumed we were late again. The boys didn't want to see her any more. It was a very sad ending to a lovely friendship!

The day we walked to Charlton Kings to see Phyllis and Edie was not easy either. Taking Wendy with us, we walked from Wai Ling's house, a long way for the three of them to walk on a hot day. The two elderly sisters were full of delight to see Pete and Malc again, but I'm not sure if the boys really remembered them. It was the last time we were to see them. Perhaps 'visiting old friends' was not a good idea for a holiday.

Jim and I had always intended to move back to Gloucestershire after his training; we hadn't ever intended staying in Melton Mowbray. But with the boys at school and the grandparents enjoying having us around, we'd done nothing about moving. We both longed to live on a hillside near Stroud, having witnessed the wonderful views from the top of the commons around that town. Jim had enjoyed hours of flying model aeroplanes in the area. Now, back in the doldrums of the dole, it seemed like a good idea to put this dream into practice.

I stopped looking after Sumi in anticipation of us moving, but it was almost a year before we actually did so. During that time, Jim practised various stages of violin making and set up a few violins for schools. He also made toys for the boys, including a lovely crane for Pete's birthday and a Spanish-looking puppet for Malc's, which reminded us of how Pete had looked as a toddler, so we named it 'Pedro Maniero'. Jim also spent hours practising his guitar. Meanwhile I helped run a playgroup in town. The fact that most of the team members were *so* confident made me feel inadequate, and I found myself blushing frequently in all that I did, even though I was equally capable and loved being amongst children.

Then Wai Ling and Tony offered us the use of the flat above their new vegetable shop on Bath Road, while we looked for a house in Stroud. We hadn't known where to start in finding a house down there while still living in Leicestershire. We two families had always helped each other, but this was the most generous help we could have wished for.

CHELTONIAN II

CHAPTER 22

Coming Back

Fran with Wai Ling on Leckhampton Hill

Bringing all our belongings in a hired van was harder than ever, because we'd acquired so much more. We left the piano and three-piece suite in Mum's garage for the time being, and also left the boys with Grandma and Granddad and the cats with Grandma Car.

It was good to see Tony and Wai Ling, and their new shop on the corner of Kew Place, adjacent to the 'Boy's College.' The family now had a house in Hatherley, so they didn't need the flat above their shop.

The two men took the essentials upstairs to our living quarters above the shop, then stacked the remainder in a back room. Our kitchen was on the first floor at the front, with our shared bedroom above. After a night in the flat, we took the van back to Grantham.

So, in the spring of 1981, with the boys and cats installed, we began our new lifestyle in this temporary home, where we'd spend the next three months. The boys joined Wendy at St James' Primary School, which was somewhere behind the opposite side of Bath Road. They soon settled in.

Jim found a job in Andoversford, several miles away, making garden statues. There were no wages for a fortnight, which was a real struggle, especially with only two hot plates to cook on, but we got by. I couldn't afford the vegetables in Tony's shop, which would soon be serving many affluent tutors from the prestigious Boys' College. I hated going into brightly-lit supermarkets to look for reduced items, but needs must. We didn't dare touch our money in the bank; we'd need every penny to buy a house.

Jim became unwell after a fortnight, feeling dizzy and seeing zigzags in front of his eyes. The doctor gave him a fortnight's sick leave, saying if he didn't rest he'd collapse. On his return to work he was told he'd been sacked – as from the week before! This was really out of order and Jim sought help through a tribunal. But the boss, a wily scoundrel (with the 'gift of the gab') won the case. Jim said he'd never work for anyone again.

Another week's money gone! We were back on the dole.

Meanwhile the boys had hours of fun making elaborate 'houses' for Pippy and Smokey out of cardboard boxes and Sellotape. I think the cats enjoyed all the attention they got, which made up for not having a garden.

On Sundays we'd walk up Leckhampton Hill, feeling awkward walking out through the shop while the entire Chung family worked all day. We needed to get out for our sanity. Wai Ling and Tony deserved every penny they made, working seven days a week.

Our nights on Bath Road were eventful. One week a terrific thunderstorm set off the fire alarm at Fine Fare opposite, and other shops up the road. Then there were roadworks outside our bedroom window, with temporary traffic-light motors chugging all night. One night a motorcyclist, ignoring the lights, drove straight over the dugout pile of gravel, ending up down the hole. But even worse was when we were woken by a terrific crash somewhere up the road. We strained our necks out of the window to look. It appeared that a van had crashed into a shop window. It had; it had been deliberately driven into Robb's Electrical Shop. The perpetrators stole televisions etc. before making off in their van. Next morning we told Tony what had happened. With eyebrows raised in astonishment and eyes popping, he said, "Wha'? Lobb's lobbed?" We all thought that was so funny.

Jim and I visited Stroud, looking for a suitable house, preferably a stone cottage. One Saturday, we took the boys to see two houses in Rodborough (a district of Stroud), one a stone semi-detached cottage on Rodborough Lane and the other, just on the market, a red brick semi. Both were on the side of Rodborough Common and priced at £18,000. We had £11,000 from our Melton house.

On the brochure, we didn't like the look of the red brick semi, so we visited the stone house first. But the thick walls restricted the room sizes, particularly the bedrooms. There just wasn't enough room. So, slightly disappointed, we crossed Butterrow Hill into Butterrow Lane to see the brick house. We turned our noses up at the central gate into the shared concrete forecourt, remembering our sizeable front garden at Melton Mowbray. However, when we knocked on the door, we had a surprise! On entering the living room (two rooms knocked into one), we were drawn to the view through the back window – a magnificent view over the 'Golden Valley.' Whatever the house was like, we already wanted to live there. The kitchen, built into the hill, had a 'well' window. No good for washing up, but you'd only have to turn round to see the view. The dining room had its original fireplace, complete with oven.

There was plenty of room in the front bedroom for the boys to share, while the back bedroom, with the view, was just right for us.

The present owners were repairing a car engine on the dining room floor. They were laid back and quite happy for Pete and Malc to run up and down the stairs; you had to walk through the lounge to get to either level.

Beyond the sloping garden, the fields sloped steeply to the valley bottom, where the canal, the river Frome, the railway line and the road to London ran side by side through the valley. These we had yet to discover. The hilltops across the valley were wooded, with a row of houses below, following the contour of the hill. This was the village of Thrupp. To the right, the railway line snaked through the Golden Valley towards Chalford, and on our extreme right was another wooded hill, with buzzards flying high. Beyond the front of this three-storey house rose the grassy top of Rodborough Common. This was the place we wanted to be.

Back in Cheltenham, Jim was helping Tony to finish the shelving in the shop, a work in progress, with plenty more to be done. Tony, appreciating Jim's excellent workmanship, played his trump card. He wrote a letter for the Halifax to say that Jim was working for him for £60 per week. Thus we were able to get our mortgage.

Before we moved, I took the boys by bus to Stroud, to suss out their new school and find out how far it was from Butterrow. We found Rodborough Hill on the outskirts of town and walked up the steep gradient to find the school. Then, timing ourselves, we continued uphill as far as some crossroads, with the Prince Albert on the opposite corner. We turned left into Rodborough Lane, a narrow lane halfway between the valley bottom and the top of Rodborough Common.

Then a fierce storm blew up from nowhere, forcing us to flatten ourselves against some garage doors, being lashed by rain and hail. Foolishly we'd left our macs behind. When the sun reappeared we continued on our way, soaked to the skin and with squelching shoes. As we passed the stone house we'd almost bought, the lane began sloping down towards Butterrow. Now we knew where we were. As we crossed into Butterrow Lane a cool breeze hit us. We carried on, checking our watches and remembering to deduct our 'sheltering' time. We were shivering now and didn't know what to do.

On seeing a woman in the window of a nearby cottage, we walked over on impulse and knocked on her door. This was the beginning of a long friendship. She assessed our situation immediately and invited us indoors, finding towels to wrap round ourselves, as she dried our clothes on her radiators. This was Sylvia, a woman about my age, slim with long dark hair, and with a calming voice akin to Sister Bebb's from Cheltenham Hospital. Drinking cups of tea, we acquainted ourselves with her children, Charlotte and Joanna, aged about five and three, and Sophie, nine months, who was crawling around the kitchen floor. Without Sylvia's kind assistance we'd probably have caught our 'death of cold.'

STROUDIE

CHAPTER 23

Settling In

Pete and Malc, November 1981

I learned an amazing fact after moving to Stroud; when I stood on Rodborough Common, overlooking the Severn Valley across to Wales, I was standing on the same ridge of oolitic limestone that I'd stood on as a child while surveying the Vale of Trent from Belvoir Castle. This rock formation stretches diagonally across England from Lyme Regis on the south coast to Scunthorpe near the east coast, passing through the Cotswolds and continuing through Belvoir and the Lincolnshire Wolds. This revelation made me feel that Stroud must be as much my home as Belvoir had been.

The day we moved in, in mid July, was chaotic. The boys weathered the muddles, although Malc was disturbed by the lack of order and routine. However, downstairs in the dining room, Jim and I embraced. We'd come through some bad times, but from now on, everything would be fine. We were genuinely where we wanted to be.

Mid-week, with the boys in school, we left the cats in the garden to go shopping in town. On our return we found clumps of white fur all over the top lawn, but no Pippy. Then we discovered her cowering behind a clump of mint in the garden. I picked her up but was horrified to see her stomach was slit from top to bottom, with some of her innards hanging out and her leg exposed. We rushed her to the vets at the bottom of the hill, where she needed 34 stitches – some of them internal. Thankfully she recovered well. We discovered the culprit, a big nasty black cat living behind our bottom hedge. Next time it entered our garden Smokey went for it, and clamping it in a bitter and savage embrace, they rolled to the bottom of the garden, yowling like beings possessed, but Smokey had established her territory.

The Halifax had given us six months to complete certain jobs. All the electric cables from downstairs went up the hall wall in one big clump, not encased in anything. The former owners had rewired the house themselves. Then the surveyor had picked up damp in the middle wall downstairs. Jim made a narrow trench right across the floor inside the middle wall, from kitchen to bathroom, lining it with a membrane before filling it with waterproof concrete. Then he inserted a damp-proof layer along the whole wall, sawing between the bricks, bit by bit, to stop the wall collapsing.

We noticed that when we stepped down from either the kitchen or bathroom, the dining room floor bounced. Jim took up the whole floor to discover that the joist ends were rotten and also the wall plates that they rested on. His remedy was to saw them off and make a feature. He built wooden seating out from the wall abutting the kitchen, taking it round the fireplace alcove as well. It looked lovely with diagonally slatted pine on top. He then moved the bathroom door out into the dining room, level with the seating, to enable the door to be opened inwards instead of outwards. Finally, we took the plaster off the downstairs walls for Jim to re-plaster them. We then stained the floor ebony because of the big black oil stain near the window where the car engine had been renovated!

Don't imagine that this happened quickly or smoothly. I remember answering the front door saying, "I'm sorry for the mess we're in. We've just moved in," then realising we'd been in this mess for over a year; stepping over floor joists for all that time. We'd coped with builder's mess in each house we'd lived in, then moved out when everything was finished. Would it be different this time, I wondered? Jim received much praise for his workmanship while I, who'd spent hours clearing up after him, received none!

I began tackling the garden, which was shaped like a

banana, with a sunken path and a washing line down the middle, cutting the garden in two. Jim and I dug out the huge concrete block holding the washing-line post, heaved it to the side and buried it there. Now the pathway needed filling in, and the garden terraced to make it useable. Les and Sylvia next door gave us a pile of unwanted bricks, which I buried, using bucket after bucket of soil from the bottom of the garden, in front of the brick shed. Anything discarded was buried: broken plates, outgrown shoes – anything we could find. Then we sowed grass seed.

I sent off for a couple of Club Books and ordered four trees – an apple, called 'Howgate Wonder,' a Victoria plum, a cherry and a flowering cherry. After planting them, Malc asked, "Mum, when can we climb them?" The boys were missing their Melton apple trees. Meanwhile Jim made a patio at the bottom, using broken slabs. Now we could play swing-ball down there.

Living on the other side of our semi was Daisy, a sprightly white-haired lady of about 70 years. She was tiny and kindly, but when she climbed out onto her top windowsill to clean the windows, three storeys up, we felt so nervous that we couldn't watch.

After planting the fruit trees I ordered rose bushes for a hedge between us. However these didn't work, so Granddad had them to put round his allotment. Next I ordered privet bushes. Daisy had been quite happy to be separated from the house by a wire fence for years, but I liked privacy. She never complained, even though the hedge restricted her view and shaded her vegetable plot. I cut her side of the hedge whenever necessary. We could always chat through the trellis up by the house, and I often went round for a cup of tea in the afternoon.

In the next pair of houses lived Molly, who'd moved in to be housekeeper to Bill, bringing her five offspring with her. Bill had been widowed, leaving him with two teenage sons who'd gone off the rails, becoming drug addicts. One of them, Chalkie, went missing and was found months later at the bottom of a lake at South Cerney Water Park.

There were several elderly women living in our rank of houses: two ladies called Kath on one side, and on the other side of Bill and Molly's pair of semis lived old Mrs Sollers. Kath Pratt had lived in the house all her life. We only saw her when she went shopping each week with Daisy and the other Kath. Then when she was in her 70s, the landlord's son had wanted to repossess the property. Having to move out was traumatic for Kath. But when I visited her a few months later, in her 'old person's' flat in Minchinhampton, she told me she'd never been happier in her life.

Something was always happening in the Bill and Molly household. Bill would sit impatiently in his car, waiting to take Molly to town. We'd hear him hollering "Molly!" in great exasperation until, half an hour later, she'd appear, bringing her large, pull-along shopping trolley, which was already half full. In cold weather, she'd tie hot-water bottles around her waist, making her look even more rotund. One hot summer day, she walked up the pavement for a chat, wearing a long pinafore. When she turned to go, I was gob-smacked to see her near-bare body bulging over her bra and pants.

Lined up along the front wall of their house was a succession of discarded cookers, fridges and washing machines. Later these were replaced with carrier bags full of plants, hanging on nails. More bags were hung on each spike of the iron railings bordering the roadside. It looked so untidy.

After Bill's death, Molly took in Alf, a lodger. He disliked Molly's daughter's husband, who lived in the adjacent semi. One night there was an explosion – Alf had blown up the husband's car.

Talking of explosions, we used to watch Molly's family firework display from our back bedroom window. It was always better than ours. One year, the son, who generally organised this event, went to check a rocket that hadn't ignited, jumping over the newly lit bonfire to reach it while carrying a plastic bag of fireworks in each hand. Of course, the inevitable happened, and the ensuing firework display was the best we were to see for years, although it was soon over!

Still talking of explosions, there was the night the paint factory in Thrupp valley caught fire. Jim and I sat in bed watching one explosion after another. Better than any movie!

Those first few years at Butterrow seemed so exciting. There were two consecutive snowy winters. So violent was the first storm we encountered that the snow blew in a huge vertical vortex right round the valley, amazing to see. No traffic could venture up the hills and even London Road was inches deep in snow. I made my own bread and we intercepted the milkman at the valley bottom, scrunching our way down the hill. The boys and I had a fabulous time sledging down from the fort – as did countless other people.

In summertime we'd walk to the top of the common, to watch Jim and his mates flying their radio-controlled aeroplanes, if the wind was on *our* hill. Mostly it blew onto southwest facing slopes, like Selsley Common, when we'd go there by car instead. We soon got bored though and wandered down to explore the woods at the bottom.

When Molly's daughter moved out, a motorbike enthusiast, called Dick, moved in. His Hell's Angel mates were forever roaring up the road. One bike had a sidecar – a tin bath – which we called a motorbike and side-bath. They'd park up outside, causing a rumpus. Meanwhile, Jim was making alterations on the top landing, resulting in us sleeping in the front end of the lounge while the work was in progress. He wanted to move both bedroom doors, allowing space for a toilet on the landing. It took him a year.

During this time, my sleep pattern went to pot. Dick's roaring bike would wake us up at midnight. Then around 2am he'd return, waking us once more. It was beyond annoying.

The boys and I usually left our bikes leaning against the front railings in daytime, but one evening we forgot to bring them in. When we remembered, they'd gone missing. I reported the theft to the police. Around 11pm, two policemen arrived to investigate. They'd just returned from Derbyshire, where they'd been breaking up picket lines during the miners' strikes of those Thatcher days. It took very little time to take down descriptions of the missing bikes, but I foolishly offered them a cup of tea, as they seemed tired. Idiot! I couldn't get rid of them afterwards, as they ranted on about their miner's strike experiences.

We discovered the bikes ourselves next morning, slung down on the roadside, a quarter of a mile away. Only one group of people around here were capable of such things – Dick and his mates.

CHAPTER 24

UFOs

UFO? The U-shaped object we saw in the sky

It was exciting living on this hillside, with footpaths leading up, down and all along the sides. From our lane there were several routes to the common. The first thing the boys did on moving there was to dash down the lane to drink the spring water that spurted from the hillside nearby. Such a novelty! When the nettles were cut back later, a sign was revealed: "Do Not Drink This Water"!

Our narrow lane followed the side of the hill through the hamlets of Montserrat, Bagpath and Swells Hill to

Brimscombe Hill, where a steep road ran from the top of the common to the valley bottom at Brimscombe Port – a village where there had once been an inland port on the canal. We loved the names of the places and the history we learnt. We loved picking hazelnuts and apples growing freely on the hillsides, if you knew where to look. We found mushrooms and puffballs on the tops of Rodborough and Minchinhampton commons – two commons which were almost joined, with the Bear Hotel between them. From this hotel, known as 'The Bear of Rodborough', were panoramic views across the Woodchester valley towards Wales. Bear fighting once took place here (a stuffed bear stands in the main entrance of the inn). Also, there's a legend of phantom sightings of a coach and horses running out of control down Bear Hill to Woodchester – seen only at midnight, on a full moon.

A rocky track leads up from Montserrat to Winston's ice cream factory, a small shed-like building on our side of Rodborough Common, not far from the Bear Hotel. It became our Sunday treat to walk there for an ice cream. We always took our visitors to this award-winning outlet, less than a mile from our house, where cows roamed freely on the hillsides.

Rodborough Fort stood on the top edge of Rodborough Common, overlooking Stroud. It was a folly with a campsite, enclosed by a three-foot dry-stone wall. In summertime, cars pulling caravans struggled up Rodborough Hill to stay there. The common was criss-crossed by trails with visitors enjoying the views; dog walkers, hikers, kite-flyers, searchers for orchids and butterflies, and with cattle dropping 'pancakes' everywhere. That first July, an almighty thunderstorm caused purple lightning to zig-zag all along the electric wires in the valley, from Thrupp to Stroud. What more exciting place could we have hoped to live?

Then early one morning (October 29th 1981) Jim shouted excitedly, "Come and look at this." We jumped out of bed and dashed down to the middle floor to see what was happening. At first, all we could see was a black-outlined loop high up in the sky, which Jim had initially thought to be the trail of a B52 bomber, but it definitely wasn't. The B52s flew over around 6.30am each day, returning from bombing missions in Iraq, heading for Fairford Air Base (taken over by Americans at that time). Jim loved to watch them.

While we quickly searched for our binoculars, this 'thing' had moved to directly opposite us, above the woods at Thrupp. It was a distinct, black silhouette of a U-shaped object – like a tuning fork without a handle. As we gazed in awe, it descended slowly behind the trees. Was it a large object far away, or a small object nearby? How could we know?

Then, as we continued to gaze entranced, a bright crinkly orange light came across the sky from behind a small cloud to the right, and descended in exactly the same place. Jim, still in a stunned state of excitement, phoned several airports: Fairford, Brize Norton and others, even one on the south coast. None had seen corresponding objects on their radar.

We felt excited yet scared, honoured yet stupid. Who would believe us – that the four of us had witnessed an unidentifiable object in the sky? We contacted the Stroud News and Journal. The resulting report, a week later, described how we'd seen a 'V' shaped object!

Neighbours began telling us of their experiences in the area; all sorts of different sightings that couldn't be explained. Now, walking in lonely places on the common, we felt nervous. Were aliens watching us? Might we be abducted? Or was this object some deadly MOD secret? Eventually, as the ups and downs of daily life took over, this happening featured less and less in our minds.

Then early the following February, we witnessed another strange 'thing' in the sky. The day had dawned blue, with white puffy clouds breezing gently over the woods from our right. Then, within a hole in a cloud, we noticed a distinct black line moving at the same gentle speed. This object, with rounded ends, kept exactly within the confines of the cloud until it was lost from view near Stroud. We knew it wasn't a plane. We frequently saw planes, glimpsing a wingtip peeping above the fuselage, or the tip of a tail plane, or sometimes a trail from behind. But this was a distinct, very black silhouette, which I estimated to be similar in length to the height of the first object we'd seen. Was it the same sort of thing on its side, perhaps?

Suddenly a group of UFO enthusiasts from Bristol got in touch, wishing to visit us. Then the Western Daily Press wanted a picture of what we'd seen. I spent a whole morning doing a sketch of Thrupp: the woods behind, the houses halfway up the hill and the 'object' in the sky above. When the reporter arrived, he only wanted a drawing of the actual shape! He made us pull out the heavy cupboard from in front of the window to take a photo of me up against the glass and pointing to a position on an Ordnance Survey map, bearing no relevance to the spot where the sighting had taken place. So much for reporters!

The following Sunday, six excited (and jealous) members of a 'Probe Society' from Bristol (UFO enthusiasts), descended on our house. They were five young men and a young woman, none of whom had yet witnessed anything UFOish. They were really interested in the first 'U' shaped object, seen back in October, and wanted to take Jim to the woods behind Thrupp, to look for evidence of something landing there!! How stupid. *We* didn't know where it might have landed - probably at Brize Norton, for all we knew – and it was several months ago. Nevertheless Jim, now caught up in their excitement, was driven over to Thrupp Woods, below Lypiatt Manor (residence of Prince and Princess Michael of Kent at the time) to search for – what? However, Jim told us afterwards how nervous he'd felt.

Over cups of tea and biscuits in our living room later, they talked about 'men in black', some secret governmental organisation whose members might come and 'shut us up' if we made a song and dance about what we'd seen. It was all very scary and exciting.

Then we received an A4 printed pamphlet from interested members of the Aetherius Society – some society whose members believe in UFOs and 'cosmic intervention.' Still more intrigue! Inside it were accounts of people from all over the world who had witnessed sightings, from pilots to people in Brazil. There was an account of our experience as 'whole family' sightings, and also mention of a similar 'U' shaped object witnessed from Winter Hill near Wigan, in the 1950s. It was all very intriguing stuff. But in the end, it all fizzled out and left us still none the wiser as to what we'd witnessed. I suppose we'll be speculating for the rest of our lives.

CHAPTER 25

Popmobility

After our first sponsored event in 1984. Fran on right, back row.

One springtime while still at Melton Mowbray, I heard about weekly 'Popmobility' classes taking place at a school on the far side of town. They sounded fun – doing exercises to pop music. So, the boys and I went to try them out. There were about twenty women in the class, some of whom I knew. The instructor welcomed Pete and Malc to join in. The routines, often to some of my favourite records, were lively and energetic. We loved it.

Once we were established in Stroud, I looked for similar classes, but could find none. There was only one thing for it – I'd have to start my own. I heard of a building in Rodborough called the Endowed School, where rooms could be rented on an hourly basis; allegedly the oldest building in Rodborough (apart from the nearby church). I'd need to contact a Mrs Townley, who lived not far from the Prince Albert. So after taking the boys to school one day, I knocked on her door to make enquiries. She let me have the keys to take a look for myself and assess its suitability.

The Endowed School was down Walkley Hill, straight across the crossroads at the Prince Albert. I felt excited yet nervous about the prospect of taking my own classes as I hurried to find this building in Church Place, off Walkley Hill. I fumbled nervously for the correct key to unlock the door. Inside it was gloomily dark. I crept tentatively into the first room, which was equally dark and gloomy and not very large. The adjoining room was just as small and dingy. Neither room was large enough or light enough for keep fit classes. What did I expect from such an old building? I made my way up the bare wooden staircase, without much enthusiasm. But surprise, surprise! At the top was a large, well-lit room right across the top, with windows on both sides. It felt nice and airy. There was a kitchen at one end and a toilet on the half landing. It would be perfect.

I now had to find interested mums to join my classes, which could take place on Wednesday afternoons, when the room was free. If I held them from 2pm to 3pm, we'd have time to pick up our children from school. Sorted! But no it wasn't, not yet. I'd need to advertise my forthcoming classes. I set about making posters, putting one in Rodborough School playground, one in the Prince Albert and others on lampposts. Now I had to buy a cassette player on which to play my one and only tape, recorded from an LP that I'd purchased from Ken Woolcott (the man in London who started the 'Popmobility' movement in 1967 to help athletes in their training – later to be awarded an MBE for his services).

I spent an evening trawling through my newly acquired club books to find a suitable 'Ghetto Blaster' and posted off my order, hoping to make enough money to cover the weekly payments and also the rent of the room.

Mums were now expressing an interest in my classes, so I booked the room for an hour and a half on Wednesday afternoons, giving myself time to vacuum the room beforehand and to set up my cassette player. How would I cope, I wondered? Would I blush a lot, or could I pretend to be hot and sweaty from the exercises? Fingers crossed.

At 1pm on that first afternoon I set off with our two holdalls, one containing the cassette player and the other the speakers. These were bulky but luckily just fitted inside the holdalls. I also had an exercise book to record the women's names and the monies received. I was wearing black exercise tights under my wrap-over skirt as I hurried along Rodborough Lane, my arms stretched by the weight I was carrying. I was suitably warmed up by the time I arrived!

Putting on an oversized T-shirt, I was ready to roll. I found the vacuum and ran it over the floor. We didn't want fluff on our bottoms. Then the mums began to arrive. Gosh! It felt quite overwhelming but I busied myself with taking names and money. There was a tall, smart and very well-spoken lady called Gail, who'd brought along her four-year-old twins – that was fine by me. Then a smiley lady with dark curly hair arrived, carrying her new baby daughter. She was Katie.

Two of Pete's schoolfriends' mothers arrived – Dan's mother Rosemary and Lauren's mother Lyn, both of whom lived on Rodborough Lane. There were also two from Butterrow Lane – my new friend Sylvia and her friend Diana. Rosemary brought her sister Shirley and Katie brought her friend Polly, whose children went to a different school. There were some whose whereabouts I didn't yet know; even, apparently, Mike Oldfield's sister-in-law.

The time had come – I had to set 'Popmobility' in motion. Showing everyone a simple routine, I started the music, and David Dundas's voice filled the room: "When I wake up in the morning light, I pull my jeans and I feel alright. I put my blue jeans on; I put my old blue jeans on..." and with hands on hips, we were moving – flexing our knees, twisting our waists, then swinging our arms.

I wasn't taking this class in the conventional manner, however; I had my back to the class, so-say that they could follow my movements, but really, so that I wouldn't have to face them, because of blushing. When I glanced round, everyone seemed happy. I was happy; I was coping and doing Popmobility again. We continued through the tape with a variety of exercises, some dynamic, some slow and some seated on the floor. All in all, it seemed a great success, and the participants seemed keen to come the following week.

That same term, I'd been assisting in Malc's cookery classes on Thursday mornings. One week his teacher, Mrs Hansford, had forgotten to bring her music and movement tapes for the class's afternoon session. "You take keep fit classes at the Endowed School don't you?" she asked. "Would you come back this afternoon and try it with the children?" I did so and it went down very well – the children loved it. So I began regular classes with them.

We'd form a large circle in the school hall to do our exercises. One particular one was done on hands and knees to a song called "Angelo". This involved a double arching and flexing of the spine, like a double ripple. It was in the days when Angela Ripon was often on television, and Malc always referred to this exercise as 'Angela Ripple Ripple'. He confided in me that the boys could see down the neck of my over-large T-shirt and always positioned themselves opposite me in the circle. When we did 'Angelo' and I said, "ripple ripple," these eight-year-olds were saying "nipple nipple!"

Mr Leyland, the headmaster, pleased with my voluntary input for teaching Popmobility, offered me the use of the school hall on Monday nights for free. So now, with winter approaching, I began another class for mums. But walking with my equipment in holdalls was a big effort to keep up, and I disliked walking along Rodborough Lane in the dark, so when Wai Ling offered me a folding 'town' bike that nobody else wanted (it was very heavy), I gladly accepted it. I bought some cheap panniers from my club book to carry the ghetto blaster and speakers. Now I could cope.

One particular Monday night in winter, when a blizzard was blowing, I pedalled along Rodborough Lane with my eyes screwed up to see the way, thinking that nobody would turn up on such a night. I was wasting my time. However, that night, I had one of my biggest classes – 19 in total!

The following summer term, I was asked if Mrs Hansford's class would do a Popmobility performance at the school concert. I went down to school for extra hours each week to hone the pupils' abilities, being allowed to take them out of lessons for this. Since Malc's revelation about the boys looking down my baggy-necked T-shirt, I'd bought a black leotard to wear with my black tights. All the women were buying leotards now, as exercise classes gained popularity. Rosemary's had press-studs at the bottom, so she didn't have to strip off to go to the toilet. Her sister Shirley was very entertaining – always coming out with local colloquialisms that 'tickled us pink.'

I was becoming acquainted with the members of my class by now. Katie, the one with the young baby, would sit quietly feeding little Briony in the corner of the room without causing an ounce of disruption. She'd impressed me with her flexibility; she'd been a bit of a ballet dancer in her youth. She lived nearby and spent her spare time, if she had any (for she had two young boys as well), writing romantic novels and trying to get published by Mills and Boon. She is now the very successful Katie Fforde, of great acclaim.

Gail's twins Elly and Edward posed no trouble and joined in, in their endearing way. I missed them when they started school. Gail came from Amberley, a few miles away. I felt honoured that mums other than locals were coming to my classes.

Polly lived at the bottom of Walkley Hill, on Bath Road, always bringing her little rough-coated black dog 'Bear' with her. He was as good as gold. I was becoming friends with a small group comprising Katie, Lyn and Polly.

The children's display at the concert went down well. We formed a circle facing the middle, with the whole class taking part. I was embarrassed, in retrospect, that the parents had been seated in such close proximity, so that every time I'd bent down, as part of the routine, their faces were barely three feet from my backside! But just as when I'd performed at Miss Selby's in my childhood, I wasn't embarrassed while showing off.

When I began taking Mrs Hansford's next class the following September, most of the former girls wished to continue with Popmobility. Therefore, with Mr Leyland's permission, I began an after school Popmobility club on a Wednesday. I could come straight down from the Endowed School, already dressed for action.

The following spring, Rodborough Fete Committee asked if I'd consider doing a display at the fete, which was held each summer in the Rectory Gardens, halfway down Walkley Hill. My girls were delighted at this prospect.

A dinner lady's husband was a DJ with records going back to the 50s. He was very willing to record any numbers I liked, a great asset to our repertoire. We Popmobility ladies also planned to participate in the fete display. Both the children and the adults would do two numbers each, with both groups combining for the last number. I had five routines to work out, but I loved it, prancing around the lounge to practise different moves.

The children still had the school concert to train for, which was a week after the fete. That meant even more practising for them. In those last few weeks of term I'd be forever at school practising. I'd decided not to take part with them in the school concert. They were capable of doing it themselves.

Both these events went down well, with the girls now dressed in black leotards. I hadn't requested that they wear leotards; it was the mums who'd decided.

The following autumn, I was invited onto the Rodborough Fete Committee. I felt really chuffed. At our meetings in the Prince Albert, it was suggested that we have cheerleaders parading down to the Rectory Gardens to 'advertise' the fete. One of the members, Nifa Hinds, offered me the loan of some royal blue pleated skirts for the girls to wear – sportswear from Bownham Park school, opposite the Bear, where she taught. (Nifa was the mother of the tall modelling twins Nifa and Nishan, who were often featured running athletically up a flight of steps in deodorant adverts on ITV. They had delayed taking up university places for a short spell in modelling).

My girls would now be identical, wearing their white PE Aertex shirts and blue skirts. I wanted them all to be in white daps, so Mr Leyland allowed me to take those girls who didn't have a pair to the Shambles second-hand market, to be kitted out with them.

We planned to begin our parade from the cattle grid below Rodborough Fort and proceed down Rodborough Hill, turning left at the Prince Albert, and on down to Rectory Gardens. More new routines needed to be learnt and more preparations made. Katie came over to help me make pompoms for the cheerleaders to shake; more than twenty pairs in all, using sawn-off lengths of bamboo. We attached a bundle of red, white and blue crepe-paper strips to the end of each. While we sat working away at the dining room table, we heard scuffling under the stairs. Then a head popped up briefly through the floorboards, making a quick assessment of the place. We thought it was a sweet little mole, but it must have been a rat!

On the day of the fete, my 'crocodile' of girls waited excitedly below the Fort, eager to begin. I turned on the tape and we set off downhill - with me walking alongside with my ghetto blaster at full blast. The girls looked so good, doing their thing.

Later that year I joined a yoga class at the Endowed School with Lyn, Katy and Polly. Then Malc joined Stroud Athletic Club. Together with the relaxation techniques I learned from yoga, and the advice that Malc gleaned concerning warm-ups and exercises, I was able to incorporate these into my sessions. I was on a learning curve, adapting to any good practices.

Then Katie, Lyn and I joined Jill Wood's Jazz Dance Classes on Wednesday nights at Minchinhampton Youth Club, which were fabulous. Initially, I'd hoped to pick up ideas for my own classes, but we really got into it – gaining our Bronze and Silver medals. Lyn and Katie got top marks, while I was Highly Commended. I felt rather miffed, but considering that I had thought my sporting days were over after Harlow Wood, I was still going strong. The fact that I hadn't fully straightened or fully bent my knee since 1962 went almost un-noticed, I believe. I tried to hide the fact.

There was no doubt that I was gaining confidence from doing Popmobility, although I still associated many situations with my former fears. I found I could now look people in the eye when talking to them, instead of focusing on their mouths, but I still felt trapped when sitting round a table.

In 1984, when there was great drought and famine in Ethiopia, we wanted to hold a sponsored keep fit session, to raise money for Save the Children Fund, specifically for Ethiopia. One of the Monday night mums, Carol, was au fait with how to address a letter to Princess Anne, the

Patron. She helped me draft a letter. Carol and her sister Jane, like many of the Monday night mums, were in full-time employment. Some Wednesday mums had also switched to Monday nights when they'd found jobs. But new faces kept turning up on Wednesdays.

Jane Wells was one of my first Monday night participants. She'd instigated the Meningitis Trust after her young son contracted meningitis. Stroud had more than the average number of incidents of this disease at that time, which was a great worry to the town.

Now we had more practising to do for our sponsored event. It would be held in the school playground on a Saturday, if fine; otherwise, in the school hall. We planned to keep going for four hours. This was before Band Aid's mammoth event.

Mr Leyland agreed to buy 30 rush mats for us, for our floor exercises. They would become part of the gym equipment for the remainder of the year. The date was fixed and luckily it was a fine summer day. Everyone did marvellously, with many of the parents spurring us on. We raised around £250, which was worth much more then, although it wouldn't make much difference to the lives of Ethiopians. But we'd made a gesture. We repeated our sponsorship the following summer, raising a similar amount, and still Ethiopians were in dire need of help, being blighted as much by war as by drought.

Alan Hogg took over when Mr Leyland retired. He proved to be equally accommodating. I rediscovered him years later, on the Bristol jazz scene, as 'Oggie' in the Panama Jazz Band, playing guitar and banjo!

In the 18th century a Roman pavement was discovered under the churchyard of North Woodchester Church, a few miles south of Stroud. This discovery had come about when small coloured square tiles turned up in the soil while graves were being dug. Bodies were being buried through this ancient work of art. It was considered to be the largest Roman pavement in northern Europe – the 'Orpheus Pavement'. A man named Samuel Lysons recorded it in meticulous detail that same century and documented his findings in a huge, leather-bound tome. There are in fact more copies – one in French. Stroud Museum is proud to have a copy.

In 1973, it was uncovered for public viewing. However, the interest was so overwhelming, and the traffic so chaotic, that public viewing has ceased since then. So two brothers from nearby Wotton-under Edge, John and Robert Woodward, began producing an exact replica, making the tesserae as the Romans would have done. It took ten years to complete and was a tremendous work of art in its own right, but where could it be displayed?

For a whole month in 1987, it was installed in the ballroom of Stroud Subscription Rooms (Stroud's equivalent of a Town Hall). It looked magnificent in its entirety, viewed from the stalls above the ballroom.

Elizabeth Sargent, a trustee of Stroud Museum, was instrumental in getting this work of art displayed. When

I went to see it, I got into conversation with her at the entrance. She confided that they weren't sure where it would be going next, but were desperate to keep it in the locality. So I decided to hold a third sponsored event – this time to help keep the replica in the Stroud area. There was much interest shown in having it elsewhere, including the Getty Museum in America!

Again we were blessed with dry sunny weather. I felt honoured that Robert Woodward came to support us, but I doubt if our efforts made much difference to the outcome of the search for the pavement's final home. After being displayed at Prinknash Abbey near Painswick for a while, it was sold at auction for £75,000. I have since heard that it might be sold back to Great Britain, although I haven't heard the outcome. How wonderful for the Woodward family to see it again. Robert Woodward, who lost a child to leukaemia, began the CLIC organisation in 1986.

During the following winter, Carol and Jane asked if I'd help out with their mother's housework for a few weeks. Mrs Foote, the mother, suffered from bronchiectasis, on top of which she'd caught flu. So I agreed to help out for two mornings a week, for three weeks. A near neighbour covered the other three days. Mr and Mrs Foot lived in 'The Old Farmhouse' on Rodborough Lane, almost opposite the stone cottage we'd nearly bought. Those three weeks ended up being thirteen years!

During that time, our neighbour Molly became an Avon Lady, that glamorous job selling cosmetics from door to door. My cousin Dena had been one for a while. You needed to be well turned-out, with immaculate fingernails, etc. Well Molly astonished us when she knocked on the Old Farmhouse door announcing that she was the Avon Lady and dragging her large shopping trolley into the house. She plonked herself on the settee, then after giving us her brochure to browse through, began guzzling lemonade from a large bottle, and ate a packet of crisps. After she'd gone, we roared with laughter, so much so that Mrs Foote couldn't stop coughing. I don't think Molly's Avon days lasted long.

By now, the upstairs floor in the Endowed School was becoming more and more splintery. I needed to do something about it. So during the summer holidays I hired a heavy sander from Ermine Plant Hire and, with quite a bit of effort, sanded the whole floor. Mrs Townley had agreed to reimburse me for all monies spent. This sander was too big to get close to the skirting boards, so Katie's husband, Desmond, kindly helped me go over the edges using small, hand-held sanders. It took us three afternoons, leaving loads of dust to get rid of. I then varnished the floor, planning to give it four coats in all. Mrs Townley had allowed me time for this.

After two coats, I left it for a week to harden. Imagine my horror then, when I returned to paint the third coat, to find tramlines all over the floor. The 'Friendly Circle' had dragged heavy stacks of chairs across the room. I was gutted. With Desmond's help, we went over all the ridges with his little sanders, before I could continue varnishing. The finished floor looked good and felt good – my keep-fitters reckoned I'd made a grand job of it. But then, just a few weeks later, this highly desirable space was taken over by the downstairs nursery school, which was moved upstairs. We were delegated to a dark room downstairs. That was the death knell, and my now diminished Wednesday afternoon class gradually diminished to extinction. All that effort!

Monday nights continued enthusiastically however; so did the after-school club, which lasted until 1991. I'd enjoyed a harmonious class of enthusiastic girls up until then. But that year I had two distinct groups of girls from the top class, who kept bickering and falling out. They were spoiling things for the others. As I was volunteering, I felt that enough was enough and wound up the club. As other keep fit classes were starting up all over the place, my numbers gradually diminished, until I was left with four staunch members from Amberley. These were Gail and her neighbours, Cecile, Pauline and Sue, who came together in one car.

When Pauline dropped out, a year later in 1996, they picked me up from home. Now I no longer needed to cycle in the dark. We'd spend three-quarters of an hour exercising enthusiastically before going up to the Prince Albert for a drink. It was great. Then one night they picked me up and said, "We're not going down to school tonight. We've booked into Griffin Mill gym." So off we went down to the old mill at Thrupp, for a very different set of exercises.

However, after four sessions, these fizzled out – and that was the end of my local classes. I'd never made much money out of Popmobility, just managing to pay the rent, the club book and new equipment. I'd enjoyed doing it so much though that it hadn't mattered.

CHAPTER 26
Dining-Room Table

Jim's first viola

Jim had insulated the shed and set it up as his workshop, installing the heavy workbench he'd made at Melton. So two years after we'd moved in, he set about making violins for real. He was a perfectionist, but not only that, he'd tell us in minute detail every aspect of the procedure. We already knew that the most desirable wood for making the 'bellies' came from pine trees that grew halfway up a south-facing mountain somewhere like Bavaria, where the rise and fall

317

of the sap would be about equal, giving the wood an even grain.

Now he began his first violin, based on his favoured 'Messi' style of Stradivari. The initial task was to split in half the seasoned wedge that had come from the trunk of a spruce tree, glueing the two wider edges together by means of a rub joint. This would become the belly of the violin. The back would also be made from two sides of a wedge, generally maple, similarly glued down the middle. The two sides would have almost identical markings to both left and right.

Although Jim ran an electric cable to the shed to give himself good light, there was no heater to keep him warm in winter, so many procedures were done on the dining-room table. Thus, we were able to watch the violin grow, from the formation of the ribs, the gauging-out of the belly, and eventually to the carving of the neck and scroll from lovely maple. With no table available, we'd frequently eat in front of the television upstairs. I can't say that it worried us much.

Jim did beautiful purfling – the narrow decorative strip following the contours around the edge of the plates. He took great pride in emulating the long points into the corners, like Stradivari had done, called 'stings.' Then when the top and bottom plates were almost complete, they had to be 'tap-tuned' until they resonated at a certain note. More wood would need to be carefully scraped from the insides of each until the correct note was reached. It was all so technical. With the neck, peg box and scroll firmly glued into place, his finished violin looked perfect.

Then came the varnishing, which was a craft in itself. At college they'd had constant discussions about the merits of oil varnish versus spirit varnish. Nobody was absolutely sure which was put on the violins of Stradivari or Guarnieri. Kyung Wah Chung, the famous South Korean violinist, had owned both. She found her Stradivari had a strong, bright sound (spirit varnish?) while her Guarnieri had a deeper tone, but carried well (oil varnish?) But who am I to make these assumptions? It wasn't by any means that straightforward, because other things were put on before the varnish – like isinglass.

In all, Jim made five instruments, three violins and two violas. He was a slow and methodical worker and, considering the quality of his finished articles, his returns were small. One violin went to Chethams college in Manchester and another to a pupil from Goldsmiths in London. His first viola went to Laura, who was the lead voila player in the Gloucestershire Youth Orchestra, and another to Maritza, a gifted pupil from the nearby Steiner School. The final one was sold to Adam, who lived opposite us at Butterrow. This almost giving away of Jim's beautiful instruments reminded me of when I'd sold my craftwork so cheaply, after that Christmas stall. Not that my stuff bore any comparison, but it's hard to become wealthy from crafts.

Jim's instruments were made over a few years. Meanwhile the boys were growing up. In Stroud there was much objection to the existence of grammar schools. The thinking was that all children should have equal opportunities at comprehensive schools. So when Pete failed his 11-plus, that was fine by us. Jim hadn't involved himself in matters of schooling, never coming to school events or parent's evenings. Initially he'd attended concerts at Asfordby Hill, but nothing since. Perhaps he felt inferior, being unemployed; or was it my constant involvement with Rodborough School making him step back? Was I dominating the scene? Jim didn't like to feel outdone or challenged.

Manor School at Eastcombe was where Pete would be going, on top of the opposite side of the valley, beyond Brimscombe, and being more than three miles away, he would get free bus fares. It was a small comprehensive school without a sixth form, which wasn't a problem. Pupils could transfer to the sixth form at Archway School in Stroud if they wanted to.

There were such good reports about Manor School – the way the pupils were caring and considerate. The teachers knew all their pupils; there was a homogenous feel to the place. I felt happy that Pete would be going there.

Two years later, Malc passed the 11-plus. I didn't want him to go to Marling Grammar School and acted on my principles, sending him to Manor School. Astounded mothers thought I should at least send him to Archway, the big comprehensive in town. But for Malc, who was sensitive like his father, I thought he'd feel swamped at Archway.

I felt Manor School would be ideal. Also, remembering Auntie Kath's school situation was another reason why I wanted both boys to have equal chances in life.

Malc's teacher, at a parent's evening soon after, thought I was wrong to take him away from his peer group and friends. I told Malc what he'd said. His reply was, "Oh, I'm not bothered about them." Whether that was what he really felt or if he was saying it to please me, or even that he didn't fully take on board what I'd decided for him, I don't know. But I found out that only three of the boys, including Malc, had actually passed; others were going to the grammar school because they had siblings there, or because their parents had written pleading letters. I didn't like the system and felt so strongly about it that I wrote to Margaret Thatcher.

There were only fifteen pupils per class at Manor, which I knew would be absolutely ideal for Malc. But this dwindling of numbers, I discovered, was due to the fact that either Manor School or Highfield School in nearby Nailsworth would soon have to close. So I got involved in the 'Save Manor School' campaign, drawing a series of cartoons to go into the school magazine, depicting the likely scenarios should Manor pupils have to get to Sir William Romney's school in Tetbury each day. The decision was that Highfield, which was closer to Tetbury, would close and Manor School remain open. Manor School was enlarged and improved, becoming Thomas Keble school, but still retaining its reputation for turning out caring and considerate young people, as well as all their achievements.

While all this was going on, Jim had begun making a cello. This was a big undertaking on the dining-room table, the rub joint being the very major starting point, or 'sticking point', you might say! Nevertheless, Jim made a wonderful job of this cello, and it was all completed, except for glueing the belly on top. He went straight on to make a second cello, which was equally perfect – except for the fact that he couldn't 'tap-tune' the plates. How could you hold the big belly of a cello up to your ear, to tune it to a certain musical 'note'? So the cellos couldn't be finished until the plates were ready. What was the solution going to be? Jim decided he needed an oscilloscope to 'tap-tune' these plates, as the notes would be shown on the screen as waveforms. He sent off for a correspondence course in building an oscilloscope. And that was the beginning of the 'electronics era'!

Soon he was constructing an oscilloscope on the dining-room table. When would we get it back? Upstairs we watched all the children's programmes as we ate our tea, keeping away from the dining room. Every time we went downstairs, Jim would engage us in electronic jargon. Not that we had a space to say anything, for when he got to the end of a sentence he would say "but" or "and," so that you knew he hadn't finished and there was more to come.

It was ok to see violins and the like, progressing – but diodes and potentiometers were not something that we were so keen on. The boys developed a fine art of getting from their bedroom, where they spent much of their time, to the bathroom. Whenever they needed the toilet they'd descend the bottom flight of stairs at speed and leap across to land on the bathroom step with a thud; quickly nipping inside. That didn't give Jim time to engage them in conversation, because it was difficult to get away, once he had you captive.

Then, as a result of watching all this kid's stuff on telly, Malc entered a competition. It was to send in a photo of your cat, to see which one looked most like 'James the Cat.' He wrote a babyish letter, sending in a photo of Smokey, stretched on his back on the lawn, with his lovely white tummy and dark grey sides that looked just like a butler's garb. The next week we watched the result: "and the winner is – Smokey from Stroud." We couldn't believe it! We knew Smokey was a very handsome cat, but he wasn't black and white like James the Cat. Next thing we knew, Smokey received a cup, a rosette and a book voucher for £5. They hadn't even checked to see if he was able to read! Ha! Anyway, I have Smokey's cup and rosette in my glass cabinet to this day, a reminder of a wonderful cat from dubious beginnings.

The boys spent much of the time in their bedroom. Pete made a beautiful large picture of a Lamborghini car, which he put on the wall – a car he hoped to have, one day. Unfortunately it was slightly marred by the fact that he had neatly painted 'Laborghini' on the bottom. It reminded me of when Jim's friend, Jack Tracey, had leaned over the back of his motorbike seat to paint a painstakingly neat 'L' on the plate at the back. When he'd finished, it was back to front!

Malc was always drawing cartoons, to the extent that by the time he was in the fourth form, he was making all the posters for school. Pete still liked constructing things from cardboard boxes. At ten, he'd won the model-making competition at school with a car made from a cardboard box, complete with a moveable gear lever and lights that worked. Now he'd moved on. From a shoebox he made a printing machine. This really was a work of art – it fed miniature sheets of paper into the printer, causing a light to come on every time. Then as each piece was printed, a bell rang. His skills didn't go unnoticed at school. In his fourth year at Manor, he was one of only two boys from Gloucestershire to be chosen to spend a week at Warwick University, with a project run by the Smallpiece Trust. It was based on the TV series presented by Professor Heinz Wolf called 'The Great Egg Race'. At Warwick the teams of four worked on projects in a big hall. The team that Pete was in won overall, and Pete recalls that they received many prizes.

That same year Malc was invited onto a mathematics masterclass held at Stroud College each Saturday morning for a term. Being at Manor School hadn't sidelined them.

Talking of masterclasses, Jim once attended a guitar masterclass in the Subscription Rooms in Stroud, from beginners to more advanced players. Jim had been practising and practising the 'Variations on a theme by Mozart,' which had about five movements, each one being a little faster than the one before. He'd mastered it well. Being considered the most advanced player amongst these amateurs, he was last to go on stage. He began beautifully, but when he reached the end of the first movement, he froze. Three times he tried and the same thing happened. In the audience, the boys and I were curled-up with embarrassment for him. Then the lady in front of us, sympathising, turned round to tell us that the same thing had happened to her, when she was playing the piano in a concert.

Now the tutor was going to play alongside Jim; but we knew he'd started the first movement too fast, and just as we expected, Jim floundered by the time he'd reached the third movement. It wasn't a concert, it was a masterclass – but we felt *so* sorry for Jim.

Back at KGGS, the year that Josephine Bailey and I had won the piano duet, I'd also entered a solo piano competition, playing the Albeniz Tango. In the audition, I'd frozen at the bottom of the first page, and after three attempts, conceded.

Meanwhile, the oscilloscope was completed, but instead of using it for the purpose it had been built for, Jim embarked on another oscilloscope, then other electronic devices, so the two unfinished cellos remained on Jim's lovely alcove seating with their bellies loosely laid on top, waiting for the time when they would be completed.

The dining room was becoming a bit of a storeroom. There were two oscilloscopes on a table in one fireplace alcove, and the two cellos on the pine seating on the other side; then in the alcove at the bottom of the stairs were seven cardboard boxes full of hazelnuts. Jim had picked 400 pounds of them one autumn. Each hoard had been poured into a sink full of water, and any that floated were chucked out. We had 200 pounds left to keep in boxes and were still eating them almost seven years later, although the flavour changed somewhat and many became bitter.

At the weekends Jim joined the 'lads' flying their radio-controlled aeroplanes on the hills. Now he was mending faulty escapement mechanisms for his mates. More taking over of the dining-room table! But by now the modellers were moving on from making plane wings in the old-fashioned way, with wooden ribs spaced out along a spar; to then be covered in fabric and 'doped.' Now they were constructed from polystyrene. Again Jim stepped in and began cutting out wings for them, using a hot wire. Thankfully, he did this in the shed as it created a lot of mess on the floor. So at last, we had our dining-room table back, but the poor cellos have remained belly-less for thirty or more years.

CHAPTER 27

Breaking the Promise

Invitation ride with Stroud Cyclists' Touring club. Fran 6th from right
in dark V neck top; Malc and Brian Marks in foreground.

Looking back, I can see how important it was for Jim to spend his weekends flying planes on the hillsides with his mates. Much of his week was spent on his own, while I'd be out and about – doing Popmobility, helping Mrs Foot or working on the allotment we'd acquired at Butterrow West

Jim always let me deal with the finances because I was strict with money. The mortgage and utility bills were paid before anything else then Jim had £17 per fortnight to run the car, with a little over for modelling. I took great pride in managing money, but it was a permanent headache. Then I discovered a perk – all the bills were paid monthly, twelve times a year, whereas we were paid for thirteen 4-week periods. I kept meticulous accounts in a little book in the kitchen drawer, and realised I could save the utility money from two of our fortnightly dole allowances each year. This was my secret, although I often had to dip into this to pay the milkman, who also provided potatoes and eggs; and the baker, from whom we also bought apples and oranges.

We shopped in Stroud every fortnight. It was disheartening to see other shoppers piling their trolleys with giant packets of this and that while we paid through the nose for piddling little jars, tins and boxes. Whatever ran out before payday, we'd mostly go without. I'd hide things from the boys, because on shopping days they'd rifle through the kitchen cupboards as soon as they came in, looking for goodies to eat – treats that were supposed to last a fortnight. They never thought to look inside the potato sack.

When my twin-tub packed up, I did the washing in the bath for a whole year without much complaint, except that I couldn't wring out the sheets and towels like my spinner had done. But exercise kept me trim. However, when the next second-hand washing machine packed up, I spent another six months doing washing in the bath, becoming rather disgruntled with my lot.

If I'd had a proper job, my earnings would have been

deducted from Jim's dole money, so there was no incentive for me to work. In actual fact, Jim didn't think mothers should go out to work. It made him feel threatened, because women were now taking men's jobs from them. Not that he was actively looking for one! However, I enjoyed being a stay-at-home Mum while the boys were growing up, in spite of the deprivations. I felt it was important to be there for them. Truth be known though, it was also an escape. I couldn't have coped with working in a public place – like being a cashier on a supermarket till, with all the people in the queue looking at me. Just *being* in the queue was embarrassing for me.

I'd spend hours in the kitchen on Sundays, although the boys and I often walked to Brimscombe alongside the canal beforehand, for extra flour and margarine from a shop there. Jim would pop back for Sunday lunch but was soon out again for an afternoon of flying. I'd make cakes, tarts and biscuits to last the week. But when my predators were around there was no chance – so much disappeared as soon as it came out of the oven! I felt fettered, being stuck indoors with the sun beckoning me. I wanted to be out there.

At every opportunity, the boys and I went cycling round the local villages. Then I heard about an 'Invitation Ride' with Stroud Cyclists' Touring Club, taking place the following Saturday afternoon. Malc and his friend Brian, both aged ten, joined me on the ride. It was a fairly flat ride of about twenty-five miles, going down towards the

River Severn. With me wearing my short wrap-over skirt and riding Wai Ling's 'town' bike, and Brian on a small-wheeled bike, we didn't do badly at all. Only I, from the whole group, needed to walk up a short steep hill, pushing my heavy 'shopper.' I swallowed my pride. It was a pleasant afternoon, full of camaraderie.

I hoped that by taking the boys out with the club, they'd get used to cycling on main roads. Pete, was growing as fast as a beanstalk, becoming too tall for his bike. So I took over his bike and we found him a larger one. Now he was keen to cycle on an all-day Sunday ride with the club. The previous Saturday, I'd ventured out for their afternoon ride, where the members considered I'd easily cope with the following week's 75-mile ride to the Forest of Dean.

So the following Sunday, Pete and I sallied forth. Most club members ate a pub lunch while Pete and I could only afford a coffee each and a shared portion of chips, plus the buttered slices of malt loaf we'd brought with us. But it wasn't enough. Before we reached home I 'bonked-out,' having to sit on the curb to recover. I felt like a legless, limp, good-for-nothing. Pete, on the other hand, with youth on his side, waited patiently until I had the energy to get going again. It was a good lesson to learn. You need plenty of 'fuel' to keep you going.

I enjoyed cycling with the club; it felt like being back amongst my carefree cousins again. I was gaining confidence. Popmobility had helped, but now I was becoming more and more at ease about entering cafés without a feeling of dread and was able to sit face to face at a table. I'd often 'flush up' as soon as I sat down, but I could pretend to be hot and sweaty from cycling. Eventually, I looked forward to our café and pub stops. What a release – such a sense of freedom. I was gaining enough confidence now to find a job, except that I was trapped on the dole, so there was no point.

Someone new was moving into the semi, two doors up from us – a woman, with a son, a daughter and many cats. She made a stir in our community the minute she moved in. To begin with, her removal van was enormous; much too big for Butterrow. Then her house was too small for all her possessions. So she gave her spare fridge to the driver, and something else to the driver's mate. When the van was empty (almost) it needed to turn round. A passing neighbour said they'd be able to turn just down the lane, past the spring. But, they couldn't. So at snail's pace they crept up the slope to Montserrat and down the other side, winding their way to Bagpath, with brambles catching and scratching the lorry's sides. Still they couldn't turn. Finally, having become jammed under the roof of a house at Swells Hill (which was lifted up by two inches) they were well and truly stuck. The dilemma was featured on TV news that night.

Back in our dining room, while having coffee with our new neighbour Pat, we had no idea about the plight of the removal men. To be neighbourly, we'd welcomed her in; now we were discovering more about her. We found her very entertaining and outspoken. She shocked us with some of the outrageous things she came out with – or made us laugh outright. In her twenties, she'd come to England from South African with her brother Brian. He was, by now, a well-known teacher in Stroud. (His pupils called him 'Ooster-booster' behind his back, because they couldn't pronounce his surname, which started with double 'O'. Pat told us it was pronounced 'Whisthazen'.) Amazingly, she and Brian had shared a flat in London with Desmond Tutu back then. Brian and he remained good friends.

Pat and I had an easy friendship, feeling free to pop into each other's house at any time. We'd have discussions on any subject imaginable, although I was often on the receiving end of much teasing. But I soon learnt to stick up for myself. I thank Pat for making me more assertive.

Many of the neighbours in our rank of semis were soon amalgamated into a friendly bubble. We'd sit on her front forecourt drinking wine, something we'd never have dreamt of doing before. There were times when Trevor, from the first house of the row, set up his telescope after dark, for us all to observe a comet or something of interest in the night sky. When Pat's 'Uncle Bob' stayed, Pat organised hilarious parties with all the crazy games that Bob taught us. It was so refreshing for me.

Hearing about all the foreign holidays that my cyclist friends were going on made me feel frustrated. We could never afford holidays – just the odd day-out to Weston-super-Mare. I felt that my boys and I were missing out.

At thirteen, Pete had taken on a local paper round while, when he was twelve, Malc began washing the baker's van on Saturdays. So they had a little money of their own. They joined Stroud Canoe Club, and I'd cycle down into town with them to watch. The winter sessions were held in the indoor swimming pool in Stratford Park. As I watched from the sidelines, I'd pick out their faults as they zig-zagged down the pool. Then one night when few members had turned up, Colin, the organiser, invited me to have a go. Now *I* was zig-zagging all over the place. It wasn't as plain sailing as it looked. I never achieved an Eskimo roll, but my 'pièce de résistance' in the outdoor pool was to dive off the high-dive platform. This was thrilling. Two willing assistants pushed the canoe off the top, to hit the water at about 45 degrees. As soon as the boat re-surfaced, it would need urgent, lateral stabilizing with the paddle.

Occasionally, Colin took us for day trips to the River Wye. From Lower Lydbrook we'd canoe to the 'rapids' at Symond's Yat. The first time we went the river was in flood, which made the rapids rather insignificant. The third time the river was low, making the rapids quite bubbly. We were loaned other people's canoes and on my third trip I borrowed a smart canoe with a very tight spray-deck, so tight that I could only pull it off with both hands. After negotiating the rapids I turned towards the bank and capsized, managing to hold my mouth above water by pressing my fingertips on a large underwater stone. I couldn't pull the spray-deck off; I was stuck. In deeper water, I might have rolled upside down to fall out of the boat with my weight.

Seeing me struggling, a young man waded in to assist me, and after gratefully thanking him, I carried my canoe up the riverside for another go. Again I capsized – idiot! I became stuck in the same way, and the same young man came to assist me. I wonder what he thought of me?

We were always borrowing equipment, so nothing was ever the right size. Once Malc went down the rapids upside-down with his too-large helmet pushed back off his forehead, bumping over the pebbles. Another time, while canoeing in the sea at Rhossili, in a canoe too large for him to reach the footrests, Malc hit the shore with a thud and disappeared inside. We never had suitable clothes for cycling either, always making do with second-hand items from the Shambles market in Stroud.

★ ★ ★

Back in Grantham, Mum's post-office business was thriving. Uncle Tom often helped out and the premises had been made safer with a substantial sliding front window and a lockable side-door. One afternoon, two bandits in balaclavas burst through the door, brandishing baseball bats. Uncle Tom immediately slammed the front window down, trapping the first fellow's baseball bat, while Mum quickly locked the side door. Realising their attack was thwarted the men ran out and jumped into their car, only to be stuck at Bridge End Road traffic lights. They ended up in Lincoln Crown Court.

Rosemary Turnor, now Mrs McCorquodale, got re-acquainted with Mum at the post office. Sometimes she'd bring in cases of clothes for Mum to buy, if she thought Helen or I might like some of them (as Mrs Catlin had done years before). Many were cast-offs from Rosemary's daughter-in-law, Lady Sarah, who was Princess Diana's sister, and who, with husband Neil McCorquodale, farmed at Stoke Rochford, near Great Ponton. On occasion, I'd be wearing her clothes, some from well-known high street shops. One I fondly remember was a beautiful long, pleated grey woollen skirt, a quite heavy wrap-over, like a narrow kilt. I hung onto it for years, wondering if I'd ever wear it. Eventually my chance came. One winter I attended Carlo Curley's organ recital in Stroud's St Laurence's church. It was memorable, especially because my friend and I were seated in the choir stalls. My long thick skirt served me well on that freezing night. We were directly opposite the organ and Carlo frequently looked up from his playing to give us a broad smile. What a lovely memory of wearing that skirt!

Mum ran her post office until she was 83 years old. Years earlier she'd promised Uncle Ralph first refusal to buy the property when she sold it, which I think she later regretted. That's why she'd hung on for so long perhaps.

When she sold up (in 1995), Uncle Ralph razed the building to the ground, concreted over the plot and parked his car on top. It was so disheartening. The thriving business went to the VG shop down the road – for nothing. For all Mum's efforts she never received a penny for the business. Regrettably, she died at the end of that same year, after a long holiday in Canada with Richard and Bettina.

★ ★ ★

After reading a book by Dervla Murphy, who'd cycled from Ireland to India, I was all fired up for an adventure. Perhaps the boys and I could go cycling abroad, taking tents with us – that's all we could afford to do. I had my secret savings in the kitchen drawer but they wouldn't get us far. However, from my club books I began ordering things we might need, a little at a time. It would take two years.

A cyclist called Neville Chanin lived just down the lane. He was well known in cycling circles, having cycled all over the world and given slide shows of his travels. He clocked up almost a million miles in his lifetime. We went down to see him and find out what tips he could offer us for a cycling holiday. We planned to go to Brittany – the nearest 'abroad' we could afford. He was enthusiastic and helpful.

That holiday was a life changer. Once in Brittany, I felt as if a pressure had been lifted off my head – a pressure I hadn't even known was there until it had gone. I felt rejuvenated. We enjoyed ourselves so much that we returned the following year, and by that time I had a strong desire to be rid of my life on the dole. I wanted to be free.

Jim continued to spend most of his weekends out with the modellers, while I became more and more fed up with my Sunday ritual. I began going out on all the Sunday rides with the club, every fortnight. So alternate Saturday afternoons were spent baking nice nibbles, making a meat pie and perhaps an apple pie for the family to eat the next day, because I felt guilty to be abandoning them on Sundays. I'd be out of the house by 8.45am to join the start of the ride. I revelled in it, learning all the country lanes to everywhere – just like when Jim and I had first moved to Gloucestershire and he'd taken me out in the van.

Jim still had violent outbursts of temper from time to time. When this happened, I'd put another brick in my wall of defence, continuing with whatever I was doing, perhaps peeling potatoes at the sink, while Jim ranted and raved behind me, calling me Margaret Thatcher, because I seemed so aloof and unfeeling. Every temper tantrum left me caring a little less for him, although as soon as he simmered down, I'd run upstairs to have a good cry. I wasn't as brave as I appeared.

We seemed to do less and less together now, but he still needed people to talk to. There was no doubt he could talk – he never stopped. It was a necessary outlet, but we three found it tedious to cope with. What about when the boys left home? What then? I'd have to face life with just him. I talked to Pat about my feelings. She said that if I really wanted to, I could change things. So, I plucked up courage eventually and told Jim I wanted a divorce.

The news knocked him sideways. "It's that bloody Pat the Cat that's put you up to this, isn't it?" he accused. Well, she hadn't actually recommended my divorcing Jim; she'd just opened my eyes. For so long Jim had been living in his bubble, doing as he wished, with hardly any commitment to anyone else, thinking it could continue forever. Now, with a change of tack, he was offering to take me out to somewhere nice for tea, or to some beauty spot that we hadn't visited for years. He was almost begging me; digging his heels in and desperately trying to woo me back; clutching at straws. This sudden niceness threw me. It made me feel more guilty than I already was; for wasn't it I who had chosen him; who had vowed to stick by him, to make him happy? Now I was casting him aside.

It was 1991, and Pete would soon be leaving for university, while Jim was asked to move out. It would be just Malc and me now, and I'd have to provide a home for him until his schooling finished. That gave me breathing space. After that I'd have to sell up and pay Jim his half-share, or remain, and somehow pay him. We'd cross that bridge when the time came.

Although I was divorcing Jim, I felt hugely sad for him. After all that I'd gone through, I was now abandoning him. I knew he needed my emotional support and I was pulling the rug from under his feet. But I needed to live *my* life too. Now that I was overcoming my blushing, I could face the big wide world, and I didn't want to be held back by the dole. I worked out that we'd spent eighteen of our twenty-four years of marriage on the dole. Enough was enough!

Mr and Mrs Foote happened to be wardens of a large house on Rodborough Lane for homeless ex-military men. They offered Jim the whole attic to live in, until he could find somewhere more suitable. What a kind offer! I was so grateful for their kindness.

Now I had to take my own life in hand. Firstly, I had to sign on the dole in my own right. I hoped it wouldn't be for long, so I signed up for a 'Women Returners' course in Stroud. I hadn't been employed since 1972, painting animal heads for Bristol Zoo. I was amazed to find my staunch Popmobility friend, Gail, was running this course. She was ideal for the job, being very encouraging, getting us women to aim high. But jobs were scarce at that time, and I left there without one. Then I joined a Business Study course at Stroud College, taking Levels 1 and 2. After ten weeks' work experience with a solicitor's firm in Stroud, I thought of moving up to Level 3 with French, for which it was recommended to have A level French. This I didn't have, but Gail, who was also embarking on the course, reckoned I'd be ok. Relishing the challenge, I signed up. However, I soon fell behind and joined A level French instead.

When I bumped into Elizabeth Sargent in town, she had some sage advice for me, recommending that I offer my voluntary services to Stroud Museum. Big changes were afoot. The long-standing and much respected Curator,

Lionel Walrond, had retired and a young woman had taken his place. Soon I was spending Friday afternoons volunteering; totting up the takings from the Museum shop. After six months I was offered employment there. Fantastic news! But it was a hard choice. The job was for only 20 hours per week, and the pay identical to what I received on the dole. However, I bit the bullet.

I was almost forty-eight and at last I was independent. I was not being kept by anyone, but standing on my own two feet and making my own choices. As far as finances were concerned, I could barely keep my head above water, but I was free, free, free. Frances means 'free' – and I was finally living up to my name.

That evening I stepped out of the front door and took the nearest footpath up to the common. Breathless, I reached the top, in time to watch the sun slowly setting behind the purple-hued hills of Wales. Just like the sun, my past life was slipping away. Tomorrow would be a new dawning – a new beginning for me. I took in a long, deep breath and shivered. What would I do with my new life? Would I cope? My emotions were mixed – I felt scared, but at the same time excited; worried, yet relieved. One thing was for sure; I would do all I could to care for my beloved sons for as long as I lived, but I would never give up my freedom again.

BV - #0057 - 271022 - C12 - 229/152/20 - PB - 9781861516534 - Gloss Lamination